Strategic Planning for Nonprofit Organizations

A Practical Guide and Workbook

SECOND EDITION

MICHAEL ALLISON

JUDE KAYE

CompassPoint Nonprofit Services

D0017191

WILEY

John Wiley & Sons, Inc.

Published by John Wiley & Sons, Inc., Hoboken, New Jersey.
Published simultaneously in Canada.

For general information on our other products and services, or technical support, please contact our Customer Care Department within the United States at 800-762-2974, outside the United States at 317-572-3993 or fax 317-572-4002.

Wiley also publishes its books in a variety of electronic formats. Some content that appears in print may not be available in electronic books.

For more information about Wiley products, visit our Web site at *www.wiley.com*.

Library of Congress Cataloging-in-Publication Data:

Allison, Michael (Michael J.)
    Strategic planning for nonprofit organizations : a practical guide and workbook / Michael Allison, Jude Kaye.—2nd ed.
      p.   cm.
  Includes bibliographical references and index.
    ISBN-10: 0-471-44581-9 (paper/CD)
    ISBN-13: 978-0-4714-4581-4 (paper/CD)
    1. Nonprofit organizations—Management. 2. Strategic planning. I. Kaye, Jude. II. Title.
  HD62.6.A45   2005
  658.4'012—dc22   2004016486

Printed in the United States of America

For my parents Lee and Margot Allison,
my wife Jennifer Chapman,
and
my daughters Sarah and Madeline Allison
—Mike Allison

In memory of Gregor E. McGinnis,
a man of great vision who understood that the
process is as important as the end product.
—Jude Kaye

We dedicate the second edition of this book to the
employees, volunteers, board members, and
financial supporters of nonprofit organizations.
Your commitment to the nonprofit sector is
helping make the world a better place.
Your gift of now promises a brighter tomorrow.

About the Authors

Mike Allison served as Director of Consulting and Research at Compass-Point Nonprofit Services for 15 years and is now an independent consultant. He actively consults in the areas of strategic planning, governance, and organizational development. He has written many articles and manuals and is a frequent speaker at nonprofit sector conferences. Mike is the former executive director of a community-based organization and received his MBA from the Yale School of Management.

Jude Kaye is a Senior Fellow with CompassPoint Nonprofit Services and a nationally respected author, trainer, facilitator, and consultant. She specializes in strategic planning and organization development. Over the past three decades, Jude has worked with hundreds of large and small nonprofit organizations and has served on many nonprofit boards. She teaches consultants how to have a greater impact through CompassPoint's three-day Institute for Nonprofit Consulting and provides executive coaching services through her company, Intentions to Action.

Founded in 1975, **CompassPoint Nonprofit Services** is one of the nation's premier consulting, training, and research firms focused exclusively on the nonprofit sector. With offices in San Francisco and Silicon Valley, CompassPoint's mission is to increase the effectiveness and impact of people working and volunteering in the nonprofit sector. We are guided in our belief that nonprofits serve as the agents of democratic involvement, innovation, and positive social change.

A nonprofit ourselves, CompassPoint works with organizations in areas including nonprofit finance, boards of directors, fundraising, technology, strategic planning, organizational change, and executive leadership. Every year, over 10,000 nonprofit staff and volunteers attend our workshops and conferences, and nearly 300 nonprofits choose us as their consultants. CompassPoint's programs support the growth of an effective nonprofit sector. We are a center of learning for nonprofit staff, an affordable consulting partner to the sector, and a research institution for innovation in nonprofit organizational effectiveness.

For more information, see our Web site at *www.compasspoint.org*.

Contents

What You Will Find in This Book

Strategic Planning for Nonprofit Organizations: A Practical Guide and Workbook, Second Edition, offers a conceptual framework and detailed process suggestions for strategic planning in nonprofit organizations. This book is the product of the authors' experiences as planning and organization development consultants. The concepts, process design, and language presented here have been shaped by our work over the years with hundreds of nonprofit organizations on strategic planning. Many of the worksheets and approaches to formulating strategy were developed while working with individual clients in response to particular situations. In addition, the book builds on the work of many authors before us and incorporates the wisdom and experience of CompassPoint's strategic planning practice group members.

We hope that this book provides you with a practical approach that is comprehensive without being either overly complex or unduly simplistic. The user-friendly tools and techniques should help you put the framework into action. Those who have experience with strategic planning will find the book a useful refresher and "one-stop source book" of fundamental concepts and techniques; those without such experience will find it a valuable introduction to what strategic planning is—and is not—and how to make the best use of the process.

When done well, strategic planning is both a creative and a participatory process that engenders new insights and helps an organization focus its efforts in pursuit of its mission. It is an important tool that can help nonprofit organizations achieve their goals. A tool's effectiveness, though, ultimately depends on how well it is wielded: a hammer is a good tool for nailing together bookshelves, but just swinging a hammer doesn't mean the bookshelves will get built, nor does failure to build bookshelves reflect poorly on the hammer. With this workbook, the authors hope to help others understand enough about the potential and the requirements of this particular management tool to create sound strategic plans that contribute to the viability and success of their organizations' work.

Intended Audiences

This workbook is written to help the board and staff of nonprofit organizations, and other planning practioners, perform effective strategic planning. The book is written with small to medium-size organizations (those with no budgets to those with budgets of several million dollars) particularly in mind. However, the general nature of much of the discussion will also serve larger organizations, consultants working with nonprofit organizations, teachers and students of nonprofit management, and others interested in this area.

Structure of the Workbook

The workbook is organized so that it can be easily followed and referenced during the course of strategic planning. After the introduction, each of the seven phases of strategic planning is discussed. "Cautions to Facilitators" are included at the end of each chapter. An extensive resource section is included to provide various types of suggestions and instruments to assist with strategic planning.

The introductory chapter provides a brief introduction to the strategic planning process by defining the process and its components and by differentiating strategic planning in nonprofit organizations from other related topics. This chapter will give readers a good overview of the subject and provide more detail about the following phases:

- *Phase 1 raises several questions.* What do we want to accomplish through strategic planning? Is this the right time for strategic planning and, if so, what do we need to do to get ready? If the time is right for strategic planning, the chapter covers several steps that can greatly increase the chances for a successful planning process.

- *Phase 2 involves articulating mission and vision.* This is an opportunity for planners to reflect on the fundamental reasons for their work, the nature of the contribution they are trying to make through the work of the organization, and the challenge of finding language that communicates such important and lofty ideas.

- *Phase 3 provides guidance for gathering the information necessary to make informed plans.* How is the environment changing? What do our board, staff, and perhaps others think about what we do well and where we can improve? Who else do we need to consult? In what ways do we need to build our organization's capacity to deliver our programs and services? Identifying key questions and the methods for answering them is the topic of this chapter.

- *Phase 4 is where the process turns from exploration to decision making.* After reconsidering mission and vision and gathering new information, it is time to set priorities. This chapter provides a structured approach to choosing strategic directions and agreeing on goals.

- *Phase 5 covers the steps involved in writing a plan.* Most of the big-picture thinking has been completed by this stage, and the task of developing a clear format and understandable language is at hand.

- *Phase 6 reviews the first key to successful implementation:* incorporating the strategic plan—which likely covers several years—into an organization's annual operating plans and thereby making clear what is to be completed in the coming year.

- *Phase 7, the final phase, covers the other key to successful implementation:* approaches to monitoring and adapting the plan in a structured way. Clarifying an organization's overall planning cycle is a focus of this chapter.

- Finally, the appendices provide key process aides, survey instruments, and suggestions for various ways to accomplish the tasks involved in each of the seven phases of the planning process.

The workbook contains several features—worksheets, sidebars, and case studies—to help explain concepts and to help readers work through the various planning phases. These features are described in the following sections.

Worksheets

An integral feature of this workbook is the series of worksheets that complement the text. The worksheets will help planners structure and focus the thought process involved with each planning step. Each worksheet is discussed in the text and includes process notes, which provide brief instructions for using the worksheet. Blank worksheets are included in Appendix A and on the CD included with this book.

Please note: We have heard from people who used the first edition of this book that using the worksheets provided the necessary structure for their planning committees to write a strategic plan. We also know that not all of the worksheets are necessary in every situation: They are meant to provide guidance for a comprehensive planning process.

Sidebars

Throughout the workbook, short case studies and commentaries drawn from real-life experience with nonprofit organizations are included as boxed sidebars to illustrate particular situations that may arise during a planning process. In some cases, the name of the organization is used, but in others, the name has been disguised for reasons of confidentiality.

ASO/USA Case Study

The AIDS Service Organization/United States of America (ASO/USA) is a fictional organization. To illustrate the kinds of questions and issues raised in the planning process, a strategic plan for this organization has been completed, in a step-by-step process, throughout the book. Worksheets that have been completed for the ASO/USA case study are included as examples at the end of the chapters. A complete strategic plan for ASO/USA is included at the end of Chapter 6. Following is an introductory profile.

AIDS Service Organization/United States of America (ASO/USA) is an organization in a midsize Eastern city founded in 1988 to meet the needs of the growing number of people infected with and affected by HIV/AIDS. Ken Brown, the founding executive director, led the organization for 12 years and was succeeded by Joseph Chin in 2000. The organization started out operating a hotline and doing prevention work and won a federal grant to continue its work in the second year of operation. Since its inception, ASO/USA has gained a reputation as a reliable community agency serving low-income men and women of all racial/ethnic backgrounds.

In 1993, the agency received its first federal grant to provide health care services in addition to prevention services. Under the direction of program manager Delores Molina, the Support Services Division was established. This division provides case management services, support groups for people living with HIV/AIDS (PLWHA) and their care-givers, transportation vouchers, benefits counseling, and employment referral. The agency also continues its prevention work through community outreach, a program under the Public Education Division. ASO/USA also continues to operate the hotline (currently housed in the Support Services Division), which provides information on prevention and transmission, as well as information on treatment and care. ASO/USA also has a Public Policy and Communications Division, which does a limited amount of policy work and media advocacy, supported by local foundations.

The organization's expense budget in 2003 was $1.6 million, with 25 FTE staff (20 FTE program staff and 5 FTE administrative staff) and a core team of 80 volunteers. In 2003 their revenue was generated from four principal sources: $900,000 came from federal sources, $400,000 came from the city health department and general fund, $200,000 came from foundations, and another $85,000 was raised from special events, individual donors, and other fundraising. Revenue fell short of expenses by $15,000.

Four years ago, ASO/USA collaborated with the largest independent health clinic in the city, City Clinic, to conduct more aggressive outreach to people who are at high risk for acquiring HIV (e.g., injection drug users, homeless persons, and sex workers), but who were not receiving ongoing medical care or social services, due to various barriers to access. ASO/USA conducts the outreach component of the program, and City Clinic provides the HIV testing and referral component. This project is funded by the city's department of public health for $400,000 per year for three years, which is split between the two organizations. The collaboration has presented significant challenges in terms of clarifying roles, responsibilities, and accountability.

Five years ago the organization completed a strategic plan. The process was somewhat unsatisfactory, characterized by key board members as too staff-driven. The board recognizes the need for planning, but tends not to be active in this process. Sam Green, the board president, is supportive of the organization and of the staff, but he has put little time into energizing the rest of the board.

The executive director and the board president have decided that, given the changes happening in the external environment, increasing demands for services, and other challenges facing the organization, it is time to revisit strategic planning.

ADDITIONAL RESOURCES

Additional resources to support strategic planning are included in the appendices. Some of these resources can also be found on the CD that accompanies this book.

- Blank worksheets (Appendix A)
- Sample workplans for a strategic planning processes (Appendix B)
- Self-assessment survey for boards and staff (Appendices C and D)
- Tools and techniques for program evaluation (Appendix E)
- Group process tools (Appendices F, G, and H)
- Templates for strategic and operational plans (Appendix I)
- Process recommendations and suggested questions for gathering information from external stakeholders (Appendix J)
- Selected references (Appendix K)

HOW TO USE THIS WORKBOOK

For anyone who is looking for an overview of the strategic planning process, the introductory chapter should suffice. Many resources, including worksheets and the description of various phases (e.g., data collection), can be referenced to support a process guided by an experienced planner. However, for anyone considering leading a strategic planning process for the first time, we suggest that you read the book all the way through before beginning. We believe you will find that the benefits of familiarizing yourself with the full process upfront far outweigh the cost of time in additional preparation. There are many points in the process where, depending on one's specific goals and the circumstances the organization faces, different choices are possible. In order to make the best choices in navigating through the full process, being familiar with the flow of the overall process is invaluable.

A WORD ABOUT WORDS

Every person in the world benefits from the work of nonprofit organizations every day. Both in the United States and abroad, our water and air are cleaner, civil rights have been advanced on many

A WORD ABOUT WORDS *(Continued)*

fronts, culture continues to be renewed and celebrated, people are cared for, and the policies and practices of both government and business are shaped and monitored—all through the work of non-profit organizations.

The beneficiaries or consumers of the goods and services nonprofit organizations produce are called by many names: Legal service and human service organizations serve clients, health care organizations serve patients, arts organizations serve patrons, advocacy organizations serve constituents, and other organizations serve customers, members, and so on. We have chosen the term "client" to serve as a representative name for the primary beneficiaries or consumers of the goods and services produced by nonprofit organizations. We recognize that it is not a wholly satisfactory solution, but it seems less distracting than using different names and more appropriate than using a more generic name such as customers.

Nonprofit organizations are not owned as are private corporations, nor are they subject to the electoral process as are government organizations. Nonetheless, nonprofit organizations are accountable to many parties for their work, in addition to their clients. And, as with clients, the individuals and groups of people to whom nonprofit organizations are accountable are called by many names. We have chosen to call funders, clients, the general public, other organizations, regulators, and so on "external stakeholders," and to call board members, staff, and volunteers "internal stakeholders." Simply stated, a "stake-holder" is anyone who cares, or should care, about the organizations—anyone who has a stake in the success of its mission.

Finally, many titles are in use for the top staff person who is selected by the board of directors and to whom all staff ultimately report. These titles include executive director, CEO, president, director, and others. In this book we use the term "executive director" for this person, because it is the most commonly used term.

Introduction to the Second Edition

Over the past seven years since the first edition of this book was published, the two of us have been astounded and delighted by the reception the book has received. We have received letters and e-mail from people all over the country and from abroad who have let us know that the book was helpful to them in various ways—leading their own organizations through planning, as consultants to nonprofit organizations, and as university instructors at both the undergraduate and graduate levels. In the past seven years we have also learned more about strategic planning ourselves.

Changes have taken place in the nonprofit sector at large and in the field of strategic planning. The nonprofit sector has matured in many ways, with more influence, a higher public profile, and more attention to issues of accountability and organization performance. Capacity building is now a major topic for nonprofits. Venture philanthropy came into vogue, and the stock market soared and crashed, greatly affecting foundation and individual giving patterns for nonprofits. Strategic planning is more widely practiced—valued by nonprofits and funders alike—and increasingly attends to business issues, including revenue generation, risk management, and cost control.

In this new edition, we undertake two tasks: (1) we add new material particularly about business planning and the inherent challenges in implementing your plan, and (2) we draw on our experience over the past several years and that of our colleagues at CompassPoint to refine and enrich the text, examples, and worksheets. However, readers familiar with the first edition will find the fundamental approach to strategic planning unchanged. We have found that our basic principles and insights about group process have withstood the review of thousands of readers and the test of time. We remain dedicated to the principle that the best results come from sustained, intentional efforts, and we believe that the practices associated with strategic planning that we describe in this book can contribute to just such efforts.

One last change worth noting is that, for this edition, we have added some cartoons created by CompassPoint's resident cartoonist, Miriam Engelberg. These cartoons are to remind us that amidst the hard work and seriousness of the issues that face the nonprofit sector, there is also humor and joy.

We welcome comments from readers and colleagues and are always looking for opportunities to improve our tools, add new ones, and share our passion for supporting the world-changing work of nonprofit organizations.

We are proud to be colleagues with you in working for a better world!

MIKE ALLISON
JUDE KAYE

San Francisco, California 2004

Acknowledgments

The origins of this book lie in the strategic planning worksheets that were created by Jude Kaye for training she conducted on strategic planning. This training inspired Paul Kawata and the National Minority AIDS Council (NMAC), located in Washington, D.C., to produce a handbook that we published jointly with NMAC in 1994. This book is much expanded from that first work, but we owe its existence to the impetus created from these important beginnings.

Although the ideas and presentation of the strategic planning process have been put to paper by the two of us, we gratefully acknowledge our debt to the many other consultants, writers, and friends who have kept us sane and contributed to our learning and to the field of planning over the past many years:

- Many of the individuals who made significant contributions to both the first and second editions of the book include: consultants Lee Allison, Jane Arsenault, Tom Battin, Christina Chan, Dara Coan, Jan Cohen, Ann Danner, Miriam Engelberg, Lane Erwin, Anushka Fernandopulle, Doug Ford, Richard Fowler, Diana Gray, Peter Ginsberg, Denis Greene, Jennifer Hamilton, Grace Hammond, Marla Handy, Steve Hartranft, Gary Levinson, Steve Lew, Jan Masaoka, Barbara Miller, Antoine Moore, Pat Murphy, Jeanne Peters, Nancy Ragey, Rick Smith, Sabrina Smith, Alfredo Vergara-Lobo, Tim Wolfred, and Robin Wu. Thank you all.

- We owe a great of gratitude to all of our clients who have helped us to develop and refine much of our thinking over the past several years and continually inspire us to make our written materials as user-friendly as possible.

- We have benefited greatly from all of the authors whose work we reference.

- Finally, in the list of people to whom we are intellectual heirs, we would like to acknowledge a special debt to the late Jon Cook, founder of the Support Centers of America and a pioneer in bringing the practice of strategic planning to the nonprofit sector. Jon was an important teacher to both of us, and many of our best ideas originally came from him.

In writing this book, we had the good fortune of working with two delightful editors at John Wiley & Sons. We want to thank and acknowledge Maria Bobowick and Martha Cooley who worked on the first edition, and Susan McDermott and Jennifer Hanley on the second edition. All were a joy to work with. We wish that all authors could receive as much patience, support, and understanding in bringing a book to fruition.

CHAPTER 1

Introduction to Strategic Planning

WHAT IS STRATEGIC PLANNING?

Strategic planning is making choices. It is a process designed to support leaders in being intentional about their goals and methods. Simply stated, strategic planning is a management tool, and like any management tool, it is used for one purpose only—to help an organization do a better job. Strategic planning can help an organization focus its vision and priorities in response to a changing environment and ensure that members of the organization are working toward the same goals.

In short we define strategic planning as follows:

> Strategic planning is a systematic process through which an organization agrees on—and builds commitment among key stakeholders to—priorities that are essential to its mission and are responsive to the environment. Strategic planning guides the acquisition and allocation of resources to achieve these priorities.

Several key concepts in this definition are worth expanding on to better articulate the authors' approach to planning and our values and beliefs regarding a successful planning process:

- *The process is strategic because it involves choosing how best to respond to the circumstances of a dynamic and sometimes hostile environment.* All living plants respond to their environment, but as far as we know, they do not choose how to respond. Nonprofit organizations have many choices in the face of changing client or customer needs, funding availability, competition, and other factors. Being strategic requires recognizing these choices and committing to one set of responses instead of another.

- *Strategic planning is systematic in that it calls for following a process that is both structured and data based.* The process raises a sequence of questions that helps planners examine past experiences, test old assumptions, gather and incorporate new information about the present, and anticipate the environment in which the organization will be working in the future. The process also guides planners in continually looking at how the component programs and strategies fit with the vision and vice versa.

- *Strategic planning involves choosing specific priorities.* The collection of data should (1) surface a variety of choices about what the organization will and will not do, (2) analyze the implications of those choices, and (3) result in making choices, some of which have significant trade-offs. Hard choices are often not overly complex, but are those that require making agonizing or unpopular decisions. Planners must strive for consensus on priorities at many levels, from the philosophical to the operational.

- *The process is about building commitment.* Systematically engaging key stakeholders, including clients and the community, in the process of identifying priorities allows disagreements to be engaged constructively and supports better communication and coordination. An inclusive process allows a broad consensus to be built, resulting in enhanced accountability throughout the organization. This commitment ensures that a strategic plan will actively be used for guidance and inspiration.

- *Finally, strategic planning guides the acquisition and allocation of resources.* Too often, decisions are made quickly about new funding opportunities or spending for program and administrative needs in response to situations as they arise without a thorough assessment of the implications. An approved strategic plan helps leaders make proactive and realistic choices between competing funding strategies and between spending for various program and administration needs. Balancing the resource acquisition and spending plans is the essence of the business side of strategic planning.

WHY PLAN?

Why should an organization embark on a strategic planning effort? After all, planning consumes resources of time and money—precious commodities for any nonprofit—and defining the direction and activities of an organization, in an ever-changing environment, is daunting and can almost seem futile. The answer is that strategic planning helps organizations do a better job by helping leaders to be intentional about priorities and pro-active in motivating others to achieve them.

Leadership guru Warren Bennis writes in his book, *On Becoming a Leader:* "Managers are people who do things right, and leaders are people who do the right thing."[1] Strategic planning is both a leadership tool and a management tool. As a leadership tool, a successful planning process encourages the organization to look at the question: "Are we doing the right thing?" As a management tool, an effective planning process focuses on whether the organization is "doing things right."

Planning alone does not produce results; it is a means, not an end. The plans have to be implemented to produce results. However, well developed plans increase the chances that the day-to-day activities of the organization will lead to desired results. Planning does this in two ways: It helps the members of an organization bring into focus its priorities, and it improves the process of people working together as they pursue these priorities.

Successful strategic planning improves the focus of an organization in that it generates:

- An explicit understanding of the organization's mission and organizational values among staff, board, and external constituencies
- A blueprint for action based on current information
- Broad milestones with which to monitor achievements and assess results
- Information that can be used to market the organization to the public and to potential funders

Successful strategic planning improves the process of people working together in that it

- Creates a forum for discussing why the organization exists and the shared values that should influence decisions
- Fosters successful communication and teamwork among the board of directors and staff
- Lays the groundwork for meaningful change by stimulating strategic thinking and focusing on what's really important to the organization's long-term success

- Brings everyone's attention back to what is most important: seeking opportunities to better accomplish your mission

WHAT STRATEGIC PLANNING IS NOT

Everything said previously to describe what strategic planning is informs an understanding of what it is not.

- *Strategic planning does not predict the future.* Although strategic planning involves making assumptions about the future environment, the decisions are made in the present. "Planning deals with the futurity of current decisions. Forward planning requires that choices be made among possible events in the future, but decisions made in their light can be made only in the present."[2] Over time, an organization must monitor changes in its environment and assess whether its assumptions remain essentially valid. If an unexpected shift occurs, major strategic decisions may have to be revisited sooner than they would in a typical three- to five-year planning cycle.

- *Strategic planning is not a substitute for the judgment of leadership.* Strategic planning is a tool; it is not a substitute for the exercise of judgment by leadership. Ultimately, the leaders of any enterprise need to ask themselves: "What are the most important issues to respond to?" and "How shall we respond?" Just as a tool such as a hammer doesn't create a bookshelf, so the data analysis and decision-making tools of strategic planning do not make the decisions. There is no right answer. Strategic planning merely supports the intuition, reasoning skills, and judgment that people bring to the work of their organization.

- *Strategic planning is rarely a smooth, predictable, linear process.* Strategic planning, although structured in many respects, typically does not flow smoothly from one phase to the next. It is a creative process, requiring flexibility. The fresh insight arrived at today might very well alter the decisions made yesterday. Inevitably, the process moves forward and backward several times before the group arrives at the final set of decisions. No one should be surprised if the process feels less like a comfortable trip on a commuter train and more like a ride on a roller coaster, but remember that even roller coaster cars arrive at their destination, as long as they stay on track!

KEYS TO EFFECTIVE STRATEGIC PLANNING

The elements highlighted previously in our definition and approach speak to the characteristics of strategic planning that we believe are most necessary for success. In addition, a few other thoughts about our approach are suggested here as advice to prospective planners:

- *Focus on the most important issues during your strategic planning process.* It may take a while to become clear, but inevitably there are only a few critical choices that the planning process must answer. (If you don't have any really important choices to make about your organization's future, you don't need strategic planning.) Resist the temptation to pursue all of the interesting questions. You simply won't have the time, energy, or resources to do it all.

- *Be willing to question both the status quo and sacred cows.* In order to understand what is most important in the current atmosphere and in the expected future, old assumptions about what is important must be challenged. It is possible to honor the past and still make new decisions. Don't allow new ideas to be characterized as inherent criticisms of the past.

- *Produce a document.* Whether an organization engages in an abbreviated process or an extensive strategic planning process, a planning document should be created. A useful strategic plan can be only a few pages long. The document is a symbol of accomplishment, a guide for internal operations, and a marketing tool for current and future supporters.

- *Make sure the strategic plan is translated into an annual operating plan for at least the first year.* A critical test of a good strategic plan is that the operational implications are clear. Without a practical operating plan that articulates short-term priorities—and clearly identifies who is responsible for implementation—a strategic plan will rarely be implemented. Writing the first year's annual operating plan and supporting budget with the strategic plan in mind makes sure your strategic plan passes this test.

We like the following cartoon about strategic planning because it pokes gentle fun at the too-common tendency for strategic plans to be filed but not used.

SUMMARY OF KEY CONCEPTS

Strategic planning:

- *Is strategic.* Intentionally responds to the current environment, including competition
- *Is systematic and data based.* Gathers new information to make decisions
- *Sets priorities.* Makes decisions about direction and goals
- *Builds commitment.* Engages appropriate stakeholders
- *Guides resource acquisition and allocation.* Takes into account the business of nonprofits

Strategic planning is not:

- *A prediction of the future.* Instead, it is a plan based on current information.
- *A substitute for judgment.* Instead, it is a vehicle for informed decision making.
- *A smooth, linear process.* Instead, it is iterative; insights at one stage may change earlier conclusions.

Keys for effective planning:

- Focus on the most important issues.

- Be willing to question the status quo and sacred cows.
- Produce a document.
- Make sure the strategic plan is translated into annual operating plans.

DIFFERENT TYPES OF PLANNING

What Is the Difference Between Strategic Planning, Long-Range Planning, Business Planning, and Operational Planning?

Although many people use these terms interchangeably, strategic planning and long-range planning differ in their emphasis on the assumed environment. *Long-range planning* is generally considered to assume that current knowledge about future conditions is sufficiently reliable to ensure the plan's reliability over the duration of its implementation. In the 1950s and 1960s, for example, the U.S. economy was relatively stable and somewhat predictable; therefore, long-range planning was both fashionable and useful. It was not uncommon for U.S. corporations to have large planning staffs developing long-range plans with highly detailed goals, strategies, and operational objectives identified over a 20-year time period or even longer.

Strategic planning, however, assumes that an organization must respond to an environment that is dynamic and hard to predict. *Strategic planning* stresses the importance of making decisions that position an organization to successfully respond to changes in the environment, including changes by competitors and collaborators. The emphasis is on overall direction rather than predicting specific, year-by-year, concrete objectives. The focus of strategic planning is on strategic management (i.e., the application of strategic thinking to the job of leading an organization to achieving its purpose). As a result, although some organizations may develop visions that stretch many years into the future, most strategic plans discuss priority goals no further than five years out, with operational objectives identified for only the first year.

Strategic planning and *operational planning* involve two different types of thinking. Strategic decisions are fundamental, directional, and overarching. Operational decisions primarily affect the day-to-day implementation of strategic decisions. Whereas strategic decisions usually have longer-term implications, operational decisions usually have immediate (less than one year) implications.

Business planning typically attends to not only strategies and goals, but also detailed (at least three years' worth) projections for revenues and expenses. The audience for a traditional business plan includes potential investors and lenders; a business owner uses the plan to convince investors and lenders that the business activity will generate enough money to pay a return or to pay back a loan. Thus, a business plan relies on decisions made in a strategic plan but is likely to be much more focused on the implementation and financial elements of a plan. Increasingly, nonprofits are developing business plans not only for investors and lenders but to help make explicit the relationship between money and mission in their enterprise.

These various levels of planning often overlap. Strategic plans should outline core strategies (the primary focus of the organization's resources to best achieve its mission) and usually contain a description of longer-term program and administrative priorities (long-term goals and objectives). Both long-term and operational (short-term) goals and objectives are needed to support core strategies. All of these goals are important and need to be done well. However, it is important not to confuse the four concepts: strategic planning, long-term planning, operational planning, and business planning. These concepts can be summarized as follows.

Long-Range Planning

- Views future as predictable—assumes current trends will continue
- Focuses on setting long-range objectives
- Assumes a most likely future and emphasizes working backward to map out a year-by-year sequence of events
- Asks the question: "What should we be doing each year for the next three to five years?

Strategic Planning

- Views future as unpredictable
- Views planning as a continuous process
- Considers a range of possible futures and emphasizes strategy development based on assessment of the organization's internal (strength and weaknesses) and external (opportunities and threats) environment
- Asks the questions: "Based on our current understanding of the environment, are we doing the right thing? How can we best use our resources to achieve our mission?"

Operational Planning

- Focuses on setting short-term (less than one year) objectives

- Assumes much more detailed planning regarding by whom and how activities will be accomplished

- Asks the question: "What do we need to be doing for the upcoming year and/or immediately to best accomplish our mission?"

Business Planning

- Is typically expected to include not only strategies and goals but also detailed (at least three years' worth) projections for revenues and expenses

- Is used by a business owner to convince existing and potential investors and lenders (the audience for a traditional business plan) that the business activity will generate enough money to pay a return or to pay back a loan.

Incorporating a Business Planning Approach into Your Strategic Plan

Traditionally, few nonprofits have been able to borrow money to fund operations—largely because their operations did not generate new revenue. Nonprofits did not spend money they did not have; rather, they raised money from grants and contributions and spent it. However, as more nonprofits have begun to manage revenue-generating activities, often called social enterprises, the use of business plans has increased. When a museum runs a store, or a community development corporation collects rent from apartments they developed, these activities generate revenue as opposed to being funded with grants or other contributed revenue.

More recently, nonprofits are coming to value the discipline of business planning even for activities that are not generating revenue in the aforementioned sense. The business strategy of an organization with 100 percent government funding is to be fully grant funded. If the outlook for continued government funding dims, then the desirability of this business strategy decreases.

Most nonprofits are unable to provide the kind of detail anticipated in business plans because of unpredictability of revenue flows (e.g., it is difficult to forecast what grant funding will be received three years hence).

Still, business planning is becoming an increasingly useful concept (i.e., to think of operations in business terms), and such thinking should be incorporated into a strategic plan. Do we have a sustainable business strategy? What are the assumptions on which our strategy is based? Do the current and future political, economic, social, technological, and demographic trends support the sustainability of our current business strategy? A business planning approach informs the model of this book in that we attend to where money and other resources come from and how resources are used.

Should Strategic Plans Always Have a Longer-Term Focus?

Typically, yes: a strategic plan articulates both core future strategies and specific longer-term goals and objectives. A strategic plan may also—or sometimes only—be current focused and articulate shorter-term goals and objectives.

Strategic Decisions	Operational Decisions
Fundamental, directional	Focused on current operations
Longer-term impact	Shorter-term impact

Is Strategic Planning Capacity Building?

Yes. In fact, strategic planning is one of the most frequent activities nonprofits undertake among various types of capacity building. In the last decade, we have seen an enormous growth in attention to capacity building for nonprofit organizations. Paul Light, noted researcher and author, identifies strategic planning as one of a handful of capacity-building activities that are most frequently undertaken.[3] Others include strengthening internal management (e.g., through new information technology), reorganization, team building, leadership development, and hiring consultants in a variety of roles. Moreover, recent studies show that nonprofits use these various capacity-building activities nearly as often as private-sector companies. According to Light, a 2002 study by the Bain management consulting firm found that 89 percent of their private clients had conducted strategic planning within the previous year or two. Light's own research suggests that 69 percent of nonprofits conducted strategic planning in a similar time frame.[4]

How Is Strategic Planning with Nonprofit Organizations Different from Planning in For-Profit Businesses or Government Entities?

Strategic planning is interdisciplinary and incorporates concepts from competitive strategy, history, business practices, and organizational theory. It came to prominence as a distinct discipline in the 1950s and 1960s because of its popularity among many corporations headquartered in the United States. Still, the essential concepts are applicable to any organizational setting.

What is similar about strategic planning in nonprofits, for-profit businesses, and government entities is the essence of strategic planning—in an organizational setting, deciding what to accomplish and how to go about it in response to a dynamic operating environment. What is different is the nature of the internal and external forces that bear on the essential task.

The governance of organizations in the three sectors is quite different and has significant implications for strategic planning. A board of directors governs both nonprofits and for-profit businesses, whereas government organizations are governed by a wide variety of publicly elected bodies. The boards of for-profit businesses represent—or are—the literal owners of the business. Nonprofit boards represent the public interest.

For-profit businesses, especially in the past 20 years, have emphasized customer satisfaction to a greater degree than either nonprofits or government. For-profit businesses have invested heavily in market research and in attempts to improve quality as they compete for customer business. Because the direct consumers of the products and services of nonprofits and government organizations typically pay only a small portion of the cost, the funders—whether foundations or taxpayers—have had a much greater influence than customer satisfaction on the strategies of organizations in these two not-for-profit sectors. This situation is beginning to change, however; witness the popularity of *Reinventing Government*,[5] a book that emphasizes increased responsiveness of the government to the public and increased focus on accountability in the nonprofit sector.

Finally, values and orientation to a mission have typically been the hallmark of nonprofits and less influential in for-profit business and government. This attitude is also changing. In the past decade, much of the for-profit business sector literature, starting with *In Search of Excellence*,[6] has emphasized the importance of values and mission statements in well-run companies. Similarly, it is not uncommon now to find government offices with mission statements that articulate the unique contribution the office aspires to make to the public welfare. Despite these differences, with minor translation to different contexts, much of the conceptual framework in this book is equally applicable to organizational settings in either the for-profit business or government sectors.[7]

What Does a Strategy Look Like?

Contained within a strategic plan should be the articulation of an organization's three to five core future strategies. These strategies help the reader understand where the organization will be primarily focusing its resources for the time frame of the strategic plan. Strategies communicate what priorities are most important for the organization to be focusing on—priorities that will help an organization make substantive progress toward the achievement of its mission and assist the organization get from where it is now to where it needs to go in the longer term.

> Strategy is not a response to short-term fluctuations in operations or the environment. . . . Strategy deals with the predetermined direction toward which these quick responses are pointed. It is concerned with the longer-term course that the ship is steering, not with the waves.[8]

Following are some sample strategies.

Sample Program Strategy   After many years spent caring for neglected animals, one local Society for the Prevention of Cruelty to Animals (SPCA) shifted its overall program strategy toward prevention. This shift required keeping the care programs at current levels, but increasing the education and advocacy programs. To implement the strategy, all programs were instructed to develop and implement an education component to their service, and the staff increased their efforts to pass legislation designed to prevent unwanted pets and animal abuse.

A possible long-term objective to support this strategy would be:

- Within the next five years, reduce by at least 50 percent the number of animals that have to be put to sleep.

Sample short-term objectives to support this strategy include:

- Within the next year, have each department develop and implement a plan for adding an education component to its scope of work.

- Hire an education director to coordinate education efforts.
- Develop and implement a "Spay and Neuter" campaign.

Sample Resource Development Strategy   In pursuit of their mission to "increase opportunities to experience world-class art in our community," a relatively new museum chose an innovative acquisition strategy: They chose to rent much of their collection, rather than primarily raise money to increase their art collection. Although this strategy did not directly affect all departments, it did have a major impact on the use of resources.

Sample long-term objectives to support this strategy include:

- Acquire at least 50 percent of exhibitions from other museums' collections.
- Focus art collecting on twentieth-century California artists.

Sample short-term objective to support this strategy includes:

- Within the next year, collaborate with other museums to put on one exhibition that highlights nineteenth-century Japanese drawings and one exhibition that highlights French impressionists.

Sample Administrative Capacity Strategy   During its planning process, an organization received feedback that while clients valued their services, most people—referral agencies, potential donors, etc.—knew little about the organization's work. One of their core future strategies was "greater emphasis on visibility." Each department was asked to add a visibility component to its long-term objectives and annual workplan.

A sample long-term objective to support this strategy includes:

- Increase by 50 percent the number of referrals received from government and community organizations.

Sample short-term objectives to support this strategy include:

- Contract with a public relations firm to assist in the development of a marketing campaign.
- Develop a brochure and other supporting data to be used by the board and staff to publicize services.

Sample Governance Strategy   The board of directors of a volunteer-run organization played both an administrative and a governance role—

they ran the organization (made all the day-to-day decisions) and governed the organization (protected the public interest by making sure that charitable dollars were used effectively and efficiently to support the organization's mission). The board made the decision to start to hire staff to run the programs and change from an administrative and governance board to a primarily governance board.

Sample long-term objectives to support this strategy include:

- Focus board committees primarily on governance (i.e., fundraising, finance, planning) as opposed to program operation.
- Increase the board to 18 members, with particular attention to individuals with fundraising experience and interest.

Sample short-term objectives to support this strategy include:

- Train board members on the roles and responsibilities of a governance board.
- Develop a decision-making grid to clarify decision-making roles of the staff and board.

In each case, the organization made a clear choice among competing options about how best to pursue its mission. Strategies either affect every department or use a considerable amount of the organization's resources. It is easy to see how each of these core strategies might be translated into specific goals and objectives over a period of several years and for the immediate future, with sufficient resources allocated in the yearly budget to support the accomplishment of those strategies. What is not easy to see is how much effort, experimentation, and discussion were required to find these successful strategies. The strategic planning process helps organizations identify various strategic options and make intelligent choices in developing strategic directions and plans.

THE STRATEGIC PLANNING PROCESS

The fundamental phases of the strategic planning process, as outlined in this book and illustrated in Exhibit 1.1, are presented as a logical series of phases and related steps that allow for flexibility and creativity. These recommended phases are not the only recipe for cooking up a strategic plan —other sources might recommend different steps or variations on these phases—but this book's strategic planning process describes the essential

EXHIBIT 1.1 THE STRATEGIC PLANNING PROCESS

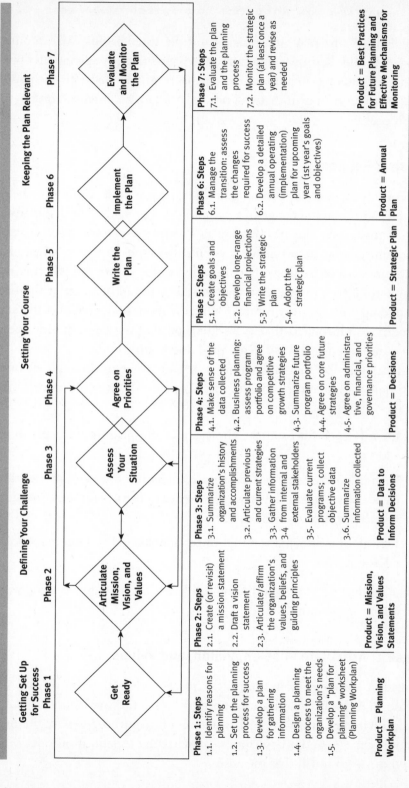

Source: © CompassPoint Nonprofit Services

ingredients of the planning process and the usual results. We encourage planners to add their own touches to the recipe (e.g., by spicing up opportunities for interaction among participants or giving elegance to the presentation, to create a plan that will not only sustain an organization but will help it prevail).

Phase 1: Get Ready

To get ready for strategic planning, an organization must first assess whether it is the right time to engage in a planning process and what that planning process might look like. Although several issues must be addressed in assessing readiness, that determination essentially comes down to whether an organization's leaders are truly committed to the effort and whether they are able to devote the necessary attention to the big picture at the time. If a funding crisis looms, or if the founder is about to depart, or if the environment is so turbulent that everyone is putting out fires, then it doesn't make sense to engage in strategic planning at this time.

An organization that determines it is ready to begin strategic planning must then complete the following tasks to pave the way for an organized process:

- Identify specific issues or choices that the planning process should address.
- Decide on the basic process to use, including roles and participation (who does what in the process, whether to use a planning committee, whether to hire a consultant, etc.).
- Identify the information that must be collected to help make sound decisions.

The product developed at the end of Phase 1 is a strategic planning workplan (plan for planning).

Phase 2: Articulate Mission, Vision, and Values

A mission statement communicates to the world what you do and why you do it. As such, organizations need to have a succinct and well-crafted mission statement that has both a statement of purpose—why the organization exists—and a description of what the organization does—and for whom—to fulfill that purpose.

Whereas the mission statement summarizes the who, what, and why of an organization's work, a vision statement presents an image in words of what success will look like if the organization achieved its purpose:

> A vision is a mental model of a future state . . . built upon reasonable assumptions about the future . . . influenced by our own judgments about what is possible and worthwhile. . . . A vision is a mental model that people and organizations can bring into being through their commitment and actions.[9]

Finally, most nonprofit organizations are driven by—and grounded in—values and beliefs about why they exist and how they want to operate in support of those values. The more those values are made explicit, the more likely it is that those values will be put into action.

With mission, vision, and values statements in hand, an organization knows what it is doing, why it is doing it, and what it hopes to achieve. The next phases of the process discuss how to get the job done. The products developed at the end of Phase 2 are draft statements of mission, vision, and values.

Phase 3: Assess Your Situation

Once an organization has established some clarity on why it exists, what it does, and what it hopes to achieve, it must take a clear-eyed look at its current situation. This step requires gathering up-to-date information about the organization's internal strengths and weaknesses and its external opportunities and threats (SWOT)—assessments that will refine and possibly reshape the list of strategic questions the organization faces and seeks to answer through the strategic planning process. In this phase, information is gathered from both internal and external stakeholders about their perceptions and expectations of the organization and empirical data are collected to inform the decisions made in the next phase. The product of Phase 3 is a database of concrete information that will support planners in making decisions about an organization's future priorities. At times, an organization may choose to reverse Phases 2 and 3, gathering data about the organization's situation before having a discussion regarding mission, vision, and values.

Phase 4: Agree on Priorities

Once an organization's mission has been affirmed and its critical issues identified, it is time to make decisions about the future direction of the organization: the broad approaches to be taken (strategies) and the general and specific results to be sought (the long-term and short-term goals and objectives). Strategies, goals, and objectives may emerge from individual inspiration, group discussion, or formal decision-making techniques, but the bottom line is that, in the end, leadership agrees on its top priorities.

This phase can take considerable time. Discussions at this stage may require additional information or a reevaluation of conclusions reached during the situation assessment. It is even possible that new insights will emerge that change the thrust of the mission statement. In order to create the best possible plan, it is important that planners are willing to go back in the process to an earlier phase to use new information. The product of Phase 4 is an agreement on the organization's priorities: the general strategies, long-range goals, and specific objectives.

Phase 5: Write the Strategic Plan

The mission has been articulated, the critical issues identified, and the strategies and goals agreed on. This step involves putting the pieces together into one coherent document. Usually one member of the planning committee, the executive director, or a designated writer, will draft a final plan document and then submit it for review by all key decision makers (usually the board and management staff). The reviewers should make sure that the plan answers the key questions about priorities and directions in sufficient detail to serve as a guide for the organization's members. Revisions should not be dragged out for months, but action should be taken to answer any important questions raised at this juncture. The end result will be a concise description of where the organization is going, how it should get there, and why it needs to go that way—ideas that are widely supported by the organization's staff and board. The product of Phase 5 is the strategic plan.

Phase 6: Implement the Strategic Plan

All of the work described so far is for naught if it doesn't align the day-to-day work with the strategic priorities that have been so carefully chosen. The interface between the strategic directional thinking embodied in the strategic plan and day-to-day work is a concise and easy-to-use operating plan. It should coincide with the organization's fiscal year and accommodate the need for other, more detailed program-level planning related to funding cycles or other reporting cycles.

An organization's strategic priorities, its organizational structure, and its previous planning process will influence the nature of a particular organization's operating plan. The essence of the operating plan, though, remains the same: a document that defines the short-term, concrete objectives leading to achievement of strategic goals and objectives and that is easy to use and monitor. Ironically, the level of detail is not the deciding factor in how useful the operating plan is; the most important factors are the clarity of guidelines for implementation and the precision of results to be monitored.

In addition, we need to be aware that confusion and resistance may surface during implementation of the plan, especially regarding the changes that need to occur. As part of ensuring successful implementation of the plan, management needs to pay attention to managing the changes required and supporting organization members in successfully executing those changes. The products of Phase 6 are a detailed annual operating plan.

Phase 7: Evaluate and Monitor the Strategic Plan

The strategic planning process is never really finished. There are cycles and periods of more and less intense activity, but the process of responding to a changing environment is ongoing. Each organization needs to choose the appropriate length of time for planning and reevaluating. Many nonprofits use a three-year planning cycle. The first strategic plan is completed with a three-year time horizon and a one-year annual operating plan. At the end of years one and two, progress toward the priorities of the strategic plan are assessed and adjusted as necessary, and a new annual operating plan is developed. During year three, a renewed strategic planning process is undertaken. Depending on the extent of change in the organization's internal and external environment, the strategic planning workplan is more or less intensive. By the end of year three, a new three-year plan, as well as a new annual operating plan, is approved and the cycle begins again. What is important is that the planning process is ongoing and responds to the changing environment. If the core strategies and priorities agreed to for the future remain valid, which is not uncommon, then the time frame previously outlined works well. However, if the environment changes in ways that are fundamentally different from the assumptions underlying the strategic plan, then it is necessary to regroup and restrategize earlier. The product of Phase 7 is a current (quarterly or annual) assessment of the ongoing validity of the decisions made during the strategic planning process and revision to the plan as needed.

Exhibit 1.2 describes the phases in detail, with all the related steps necessary to complete the plan.

The Language of Strategic Planning in the Nonprofit Sector

In professions such as accounting and law, the language is fairly well-defined. Every accountant knows what a debit is. Every lawyer knows what a tort is. There is no such agreement on the definitions of planning words used by planners, however, and there are differing definitions of planning words as used by the nonprofit sector as opposed to the for-profit sector. Is there a difference between mission and purpose? Why distinguish between external and internal vision? What is a strategy? What distinguishes goals from objectives and programs from activities?

We believe two things are important about strategic planning terms. The first is that it doesn't really matter what you call certain concepts, as long as everyone in your group uses the same definitions. The definitions we use are spelled out in the next couple of pages. The second point is a fundamental distinction between means and ends. In our view, it is critical not to confuse means and ends—and one of the key purposes of language clarity is to support this conceptual clarity.

A successful strategic planning process supports an organization involving its stakeholders in reaching consensus about what end results they are trying to achieve (external vision, purpose, goals, and objectives), and the means to accomplish those results (internal vision, core services, specific programs and administrative functions, and activities).

An organization's strategic plan is not an end, but rather a means of achieving its purpose. Tom Peters (*In Search of Excellence*[10]), John Carver (*Boards That Make a Difference*[11]), and many others have emphasized the need for the people implementing a strategic plan to have enough flexibility and authority to be creative and responsive to new developments—without having to reconstruct an entire strategic plan. This flexibility is required most in adjusting means. In other words, the purpose of an organization and the priority goals are much less likely to change than are the programs and activities necessary to achieve them.

EXHIBIT 1.2   DETAILED PLANNING ACTIVITIES THAT AN ORGANIZATION MIGHT ENGAGE IN DURING THE PLANNING PROCESS

Phase	Planning Activities	Key Products
Phase 1 Get Ready	1.1 Identify the reasons for planning	Articulation of desired outcomes
	1.2 Set up your planning process for success	Go/No go decision
	1.3 Develop a plan for gathering information from internal and external sources	Clarity about information needed
	1.4 Design a planning process to meet your organization's needs	Decision about process design
	1.5 Develop a planning workplan that articulates the outcome(s) of the planning process, strategic issues to address, roles, planning activities, and time frame	Planning workplan
Phase 2 Define Your Mission, Vision, Values	2.1 Write (or revisit) your mission mission statement	Affirmation of current mission statement or revision of current mission statement
	2.2 Draft a vision statement	Vision statement
	2.3 Articulate/affirm your values, beliefs, and guiding principles	Values statements
Phase 3 Assess Your Organization's Situation	3.1 Develop your organizational profile: summarize organization history and prepare summary information regarding programs/services	Board and staff are up to date regarding history and current scope and scale of programs
	3.2 Articulate previous and current strategies	Context for future decisions
	3.3 Collect perceptions of internal stakeholders regarding organization's strengths, weaknesses, opportunities, and threats	Data to inform planning decisions

(continues)

EXHIBIT 1.2   DETAILED PLANNING ACTIVITIES THAT AN ORGANIZATION MIGHT ENGAGE IN DURING PLANNING PROCESS *(Continued)*

Phase	Planning Activities	Key Products
	3.4 Collect perceptions of external stakeholders regarding organization's strengths, weaknesses, opportunities, and threats	Data to inform planning decisions
	3.5 Collect empirical data to better understand the choices to be made during the strategic planning process. Evaluate current programs.	Data to inform planning decisions
	3.6 Summarize findings from data gathered from internal and external sources: organization's strengths and weaknesses; trends in the environment that are or will impact the organization; organization's competitive advantage, needs in the community	Report that summarizes data and is used as part of the discussion below
Phase 4 Agree on Priorities	4.1 Analyze data: review progress to date and update the workplan if necessary	Shared understanding of common themes emerging to date and plan for completing the planning process
	4.2 Assess your program portfolio	Data to inform planning decisions
	4.3 Agree on programs' future growth strategies and develop program portfolio	Outline of future scope and scale of programs
	4.4 Confirm your future core strategies	List of 3 to 5 future core strategies
	4.5 Agree on administrative, financial, and governance priorities. Summarize the revenue potential and resources required to support the organization's long-term vision	Long-term goals and objectives

Phase	Planning Activities	Key Products
Phase 5 Write the Plan	5.1 Create goals and objectives	Goals and objectives
	5.2 Understand the financial implications of your decisions	Information for long-range fundraising plan
	5.3 Write the plan • Introduction to the plan/executive summary • About the strategic planning process (summary of process used) • Mission statement • Vision statement • Values statement • Summary of SWOT (included in appendix of plan) • Core future strategies • Program goals and objectives • Administrative goals and objectives, revenue potential, and resources required	Written strategic plan, approved by the board of directors
	5.4 Adopt the plan	Adopted plan
Phase 6 Implement the Plan	6.1 Manage the transition period between the old and the new: Assess the changes that need to happen (skills, systems and structures, and organization culture) to support the strategic plan	Plan for managing the transition between the old and the new way of doing things
	6.2 Develop a detailed implementation plan for upcoming year (first year's goals and objectives)	Annual plan
Phase 7 Evaluate and Monitor the Plan	7.1 Evaluate the strategic planning process	Best practices for future planning
	7.2 Monitor the strategic plan (at least once a year) and affirm, update, and revise as needed. Develop next year's detailed implementation plan	Effective mechanisms for monitoring the plan and ensuring that the plan is relevant and is implemented

For example, an organization decides it wants to achieve a particular goal and sets up a program to achieve that goal. If another organization has decided simultaneously to set up a similar program, the first organization may collaborate with the second organization or adjust its program plan without changing its original goal.

Peters calls this being "tight on ends" (i.e., building strong commitment to the purpose and goals of an organization), while allowing the people in the organization to creatively adapt their methods to best achieve the goals, or staying "loose on means."[12]

The planning process presented in *Strategic Planning for Nonprofit Organizations: A Practical Guide and Workbook* is built on the important relationship between ends and means. Because different individuals use different terminology, Exhibits 1.3 and 1.4 define the language to help make the thinking behind this process clear and useful.

Key terms can be defined as follows:

- *Core strategies.* Broad, overall priorities or directions adopted by an organization
- *Mission statement.* A succinct statement that articulates what the organization does (its programs) and why it does it (the purpose for providing those programs)
- *Values and beliefs.* The basic, guiding principles that guide and inspire the board and staff

Remember, when implementing your strategic plan, you should be "tight on ends and loose on means."

HOW MUCH TIME AND MONEY DOES IT TAKE TO DO STRATEGIC PLANNING?

The answer is: It depends. A useful strategic plan can be sketched out in a few hours at no cost, completed at a one- or two-day retreat for several hundred or a few thousand dollars, or take over a year to write and cost more than $100,000. On what does the answer depend? Many factors influence the cost and time frame for an organization to do strategic planning. Taken together, these factors can be weighed and balanced to develop an appropriate planning process.

It sounds obvious, but the thing to consider is how much time and money is, or can be, available for planning. It pays to be realistic. There are usually relatively narrow ranges for available money and time. These ranges need to be respected and used as meaningful constraints. If a board and staff are heavily involved in a labor-intensive project or other immediate issues, they will not have the time or energy to devote to an intensive planning process. Although strategic planning is often supported through technical

EXHIBIT 1.3   THE LANGUAGE OF PLANNING IN THE NONPROFIT SECTOR—KEEP FOCUSING ON ENDS AND MEANS

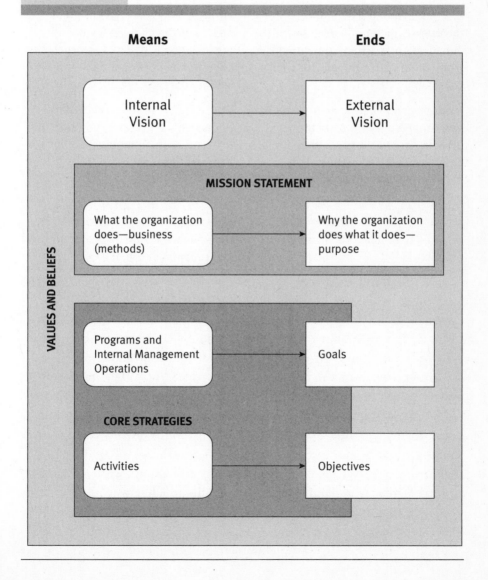

EXHIBIT I.4   WHAT ARE THE DIFFERENT MEANS
AND ENDS CONCEPTS?

Means	Ends
Internal vision: A description of the organization operating at its most effective and efficient level	*External vision:* A statement that describes how the world would be improved, changed, or different if an organization is successful in achieving its purpose
Business: What the organization does; the primary method(s) used by the organization to achieve its purpose (sometimes called the organization's "mission")	*Purpose:* Why; one sentence that describes the ultimate result an organization is trying to achieve; answers the question, "why—and for whom—does the organization exist?"
Programs and internal management functions: A description of the programs that an organization offers, and the internal operations that support the delivery of services or products	*Goals:* Outcome statements that define what an organization is trying to accomplish both programmatically and organizationally
Activities: The specific actions required to produce services and products	*Objectives:* Precise, measurable, time-phased results that support the achievement of a goal

assistance grants, it is more appropriate for some organizations than others to invest a lot of money in strategic planning. One 50-year-old organization with a multimillion-dollar budget had not deeply examined its mission and program mix in decades. It received a $100,000 grant to support a two-year planning process that also covered the cost of staff time devoted to the planning process. A small and/or young organization may not be comfortable spending even $3,000 for a planning process lasting a few months when its entire operating budget is less than $100,000.

The experience level of the leaders of the planning process is another critical factor. It generally takes more time and requires more outside assistance to complete this process if the organization's leaders have little experience with strategic planning. However, if an organization has a well-developed annual program and budget planning routine, much of the information needed for strategic planning may be readily available, thus shrinking both the time and cost of a strategic planning effort.

Other factors that will affect the amount of time needed to do strategic planning include:

- *The degree of commitment to the current mission statement.* Is there a fundamental agreement about the purpose, mission, and guiding principles of the organization? Is there a shared vision of the impact the organization wants to have in the world and what the organization would need to do to accomplish that result? If so, the mission statement may only need polishing; if not, a full day or more may need to be devoted to this task.

- *The amount of new information that needs to be gathered in order to make informed decisions.* How well do planners currently understand the strengths, weaknesses, opportunities, and threats facing the organization? How current is feedback on the organization's programs and services from outside stakeholders: clients, funders, community leaders, etc.? What information is needed to assess the competitive environment and the effectiveness of current programs?

- *The level of agreement on priorities.* How much agreement or disagreement currently exists regarding overall direction and allocation of resources? Is there agreement about which clients to serve and which services are most important? Or are there power struggles over competing internal resource needs for program services, facilities, development, staff, etc.?

- *The level of trust among and between the staff and board.* The level of trust among all of the key stakeholders involved in the planning process can significantly hinder, or greatly support, the discussion of differences and the management of conflict.

- *Involvement of key stakeholders.* How much time and energy needs to be spent involving key stakeholders in the planning process in order to get both their input and their support for decisions made during the planning process?

- *The size of the organization.* Is there only one service provided, or does the organization provide a variety of services that need to be assessed? Does the organization have one department or do many departments need to be involved in the planning process?

What If I Have Only One or Two Days for Strategic Planning?

It is important to choose the right level of intensity for the planning questions facing your organization. An organization doesn't need to spend 12 months doing planning in order to have it been effective. As illustrated in Exhibit 1.5, an organization can engage in one of three levels of strategic planning: an abbreviated, moderate, or extensive process. There is no wisdom in choosing the path of an extensive process when the organization requires only an abbreviated or moderate process. At best, an organization will spend more resources than it needs to in developing a plan. More likely, the process will stall in the middle and leave some people feeling frustrated and defeated, rather than inspired and energized; sometimes that is worse than no planning process at all.

There are always trade-offs to be made in selecting a planning process. Even in a 6- to 12-month process, hard choices have to be made concerning which issues to explore and which to leave alone. Use Exhibit 1.5 to help you choose; don't be afraid to adjust the process as you go along if you find that a more, or less, intensive process will serve the organization.

See Appendix B for sample workplans for each of these planning processes.

EXHIBIT 1.5   LEVELS OF THE PLANNING PROCESS

Level of planning process	Abbreviated	Moderate	Extensive
Time available	One or two days	One to three months	Six months or more
Who will be involved	If the organization is smaller, usually entire board and staff If the organization is larger, usually entire board and staff representatives (usually only internal stakeholders)	For smaller organizations, usually entire board and staff For larger organizations, usually entire board and staff Some external stakeholders provide input (such as clients or funders)	Large number of people, including extensive input from all major internal and external stakeholder groups

EXHIBIT 1.5   LEVELS OF PLANNING PROCESS *(Continued)*

Level of planning process	Abbreviated	Moderate	Extensive
Depth of analysis/amount of new information to be gathered	Abbreviated or no new research conducted Depth of analysis limited to time available	Moderate amount of new information gathered Depth of analysis with existing and new information varies	Extensive amount of new information gathered: at a minimum includes data from stake-holders and objective data about operating environment Depth of analysis is extensive
Primary outcomes sought from strategic planning process	Consensus among board and staff on mission, future strategies, list of long-term and short-term priorities Guidance to staff on developing detailed annual operating plans	Consensus among board and staff on mission, future strategies, list of long-term and short-term priorities Articulation of program and management/operating goals and objectives Greater understanding of the organi-zation's environment Guidance to staff on developing detailed annual operating plans	Consensus among board and staff on mission, future strategies, list of long-term and short-term priorities Articulation of program and management/operating goals and objectives Greater understanding of the organi-zation's environment Guidance to staff on developing detailed annual operating plans

ENDNOTES

1. Warren Bennis, *On Becoming a Leader* (New York: Perseus Publishing, 2003).
2. George Steiner, *Strategic Planning* (New York: The Free Press, 1979), pp. 14–15.

3. Paul C. Light, "The Case for Capacity Building and the National Infrastructure to Support It," Working paper, Wagner School of Public Service, New York University, 2004.

4. Ibid.

5. David Osborne and Ted Gaebler, *Reinventing Government* (Reading, MA: Addison-Wesley, 1992).

6. Thomas J. Peters and Robert H. Waterman, *In Search of Excellence* (New York: Warner Books, 1982).

7. Although the for-profit, nonprofit, and government sectors sometimes use different words to describe planning concepts.

8. Boris Yavitz and William H. Newman, *Strategy In Action— The Execution, Politics, and Payoff of Business Planning* (New York: The Free Press, 1984), p. 4.

9. Burt Nanus, *Visionary Leadership* (San Francisco: Jossey-Bass, 1995), p. 25.

10. See note 6.

11. John Carver, *Boards That Make a Difference* (San Francisco: Jossey-Bass, Inc., 1997).

12. See note 6.

CHAPTER 2

Phase 1: Get Ready

HOW DO WE GET STARTED?

Strategic planning is a good idea in theory, but it is only a good idea in practice if the right people in an organization believe it is a good idea and the organization is ready. The initial worksheets to be used in Phase 1 specify prerequisites for successful planning, as well as potential pitfalls to avoid. Chief among the prerequisites is a true commitment to the planning process by the executive director and board leadership. In other words, regardless of how much an organization needs to do some strategic planning, a sole program manager or member of a board will not be able to initiate a planning process alone or see that it happens successfully. Top leadership must spend significant time and energy on the process or it will merely amount to going through the motions.

Does this mean that a lonely visionary on the staff or board has no opportunity to initiate a strategic planning process? No, but it does mean that such an individual must actively recruit support from leaders by identifying the potential benefits to the organization and helping them see the need for planning. For example, is the staff aware of big changes happening in the program environment? Does the board shy away from seeking community support for the organization because it's unclear what the organization has accomplished and how it should measure the success of its efforts? Has the organization grown, or shrunk significantly over the past few years? If the answers to these kinds of questions are "yes," then a compelling case for doing strategic planning can be made to the organization's leadership. Similarly, an enthusiastic executive director working with staff and board members who are reluctant to commit time, energy, or money to strategic planning must look for ways to understand the organization's needs from their perspective. It is important to take the time to build board and staff commitment for the process upfront, because it will pay off down the line.

Whoever initiates the strategic planning process must recognize that its success lies in getting involvement from all parts of the organization. Therefore, the executive director and board president must be committed to planning and be willing to participate fully and to invest the necessary organizational resources (time and money) to support the planning process. These two individuals, at a minimum, need to be clear on what they would like the planning process to accomplish and then assess the organization's readiness to conduct successful planning. If it makes sense to go forward, then proceed with forming a planning committee and get ready to succeed!

STEP I.I: IDENTIFY THE REASONS FOR PLANNING

An organization considering a strategic planning process is usually facing one or more important issues or choices, such as the following: Are our services still relevant? What do we do about a potential loss in funding? Should we close down a program, change its focus, or explore a collaborative partnership? Should we buy a building or should we lease more space? Sometimes the need for a plan is more vague (we don't really know where we're going), and sometimes more concrete (our biggest funder is requiring a three-year plan). The reasons for planning—and the issues or choices that need to be addressed during the planning process—have a major impact on how to go about planning, whom to involve, and even whether a strategic plan is needed.

The questions highlighted in Worksheet 1 (see process notes in Exhibit 2.1) provide a framework for determining planning outcomes and issues. It is okay for the key issues and choices to be somewhat vague and/or overlapping; the planning process is designed to help bring clarity to the questions as well as to create answers to the questions. If, however, the reasons for planning are not important ones, then the process will probably fizzle for lack of commitment. If the goals for planning are not clear in the beginning, it will be difficult at the end to determine if the process was successful.

Once these issues and questions are drafted, it is important to make sure that strategic planning is the appropriate way to deal with them. A pressing need to hire a new executive director or addressing a cash shortfall may well have strategic implications, but the urgency of the decisions requires immediate executive action by the board and/or senior staff. Therefore, it is necessary to sort the issues into one of the following categories: (1) *strategic*

EXHIBIT 2.1	WORKSHEET 1: IDENTIFY PLANNING PROCESS OUTCOMES AND ISSUES

Process Notes

How to do this activity	Use the Planning Process Outcomes and Issues worksheet to
	• List your expectations—what success would look like at the completion of the planning process, what you hope to accomplish by the end of this process
	• Identify the strategic (longer-term) questions that need to be addressed during the planning process
	• List any operational short-term issues that need to be addressed in the near future (Consider that not every strategic issue will have a related operational issue.)
	• Clarify whether any issues are non-negotiable
Why do this activity	You have to agree on ends (what you wish to accomplish during the planning process) before you can agree on means (how you will go about doing planning)
	The planning process is one of identifying strategic questions and then gathering information to answer the questions
	This worksheet helps to sort out—and make explicit—the issues and outcomes that are often assumed to be clear in everyone's mind
Who to involve in the process	Executive director and board president (plus other key board and staff members if their input would be helpful)

See ASO/USA's example of this worksheet at the end of this chapter. Blank worksheets are provided in Appendix A and on the CD that accompanies this book.

issues, questions that have a longer range focus (one to three years) and are more geared to fundamental questions regarding organizational ability to meet the needs of the community; and (2) *operational issues,* the questions that are primarily shorter-term (less than one year) in focus and implementation oriented. *Crisis situations,* which have to do with the immediate survival of the organization, would be placed in the operational category.

Both strategic issues and operational issues are important and will need to be addressed by the organization. However, separating them out can help determine whether certain operational issues need to be addressed before serious attention can be paid to the strategic issues (or whether they can be handled concurrently). Any crisis situation will have to be brought under control before a strategic planning process is initiated.

Finally, if certain decisions are not up for discussion, then those issues or decisions should be put on the table at the beginning of the planning process as non-negotiable. The non-negotiable issues may be program-oriented ("we are not going to expand our geographic boundaries") or business-oriented ("any new program effort must be revenue-generating"). Articulating non-negotiable issues upfront will help avoid wasting people's time or setting them up for unrealistic expectations about what they can and cannot change.

In Worksheet 1 we have suggested four types of strategic issues to consider. Most issues will fall under one of these headings, and the worksheet provides a simple way to see if you have identified all of the key issues you will want to address, such as the following:

1. *Mission.* How well are we achieving our mission with our programs and how could we have a greater impact?

2. *Finances.* Are our operations financially viable, and how can we ensure the long-term financial stability and sustainability of our organization? Do we have effective financial management systems in place to monitor our finances?

3. *Administrative capacity.* Do we have the administrative capacity to effectively and efficiently support our programs and services? What would it take to maximize our organizational capabilities in terms of planning, human resources and leadership, organization culture and communication, and our technology and facilities infrastructure?

4. *Governance.* How effective is the board at protecting the public's interest—ensuring that charitable dollars are used effectively and

efficiently and that the organization is fulfilling its mission? What can we do to ensure that our board is able to fulfill its governance role now and for the future?

STEP 1.2: SET UP YOUR PLANNING PROCESS FOR SUCCESS

As with any major effort, a strategic planning process has its proper time and place in the life of an organization. Certain conditions must exist if strategic planning is to be a creative, collaborative successful endeavor, so it is important to be honest when analyzing an organization's readiness to plan. It is not uncommon for a planning process to be initiated before an organization is truly ready to meet the challenges and demands of the job. When an organization initiates a planning process before being ready and able to do so, that organization may either go through an inadequate process (with unsatisfactory results) or have the planning process stall abruptly or stop completely.

In thinking through the conditions that encourage an effective planning process, the two most important components are committed leadership and sufficient information. However, several other important criteria should be considered in determining readiness. The following conditions for success are highlighted in Worksheet 2 (see process notes in Exhibit 2.2) and form the readiness assessment.[1]

Conditions for Success

Before embarking on a strategic planning process, leadership needs to assess whether it is the appropriate time for the organization to initiate a planning process and, if so, whether the conditions are present for a successful process. If the conditions for success are not present, then what steps need to be put in place to ensure a successful planning process? Or, should the organization consider doing something other than a formal strategic planning process?

An organization should make sure the following conditions are present before deciding to initiate a strategic planning endeavor:

- Commitment, support, and involvement from top leadership, especially the executive director and board president, throughout the entire process

EXHIBIT 2.2   WORKSHEET 2: SET UP YOUR PLANNING PROCESS FOR SUCCESS

Process Notes

How to do this activity	Before embarking on a strategic planning process, make sure the conditions for successful planning are in place. Check yes or no in the conditions checklist. Explain any negative responses.
	Decide whether to proceed with planning: Go or no go. If significant barriers exist that might impede the process, deal with those barriers before continuing.
Why do this activity	Helps you decide whether you are ready to embark on a planning process or whether strategic planning is the appropriate management tool to use
Who to involve in the process	Executive director and board president (plus other key board and staff members if their input would be helpful)

See ASO/USA's example of this worksheet at the end of this chapter. Blank worksheets are provided in Appendix A and on the CD that accompanies this book.

- Commitment to clarifying roles and expectations for all participants in the planning process, including clarity as to who will have input into the plan and who will be decision makers

- Willingness to gather information regarding the organization's strengths, weaknesses, opportunities, and threats; the effectiveness of current programs; both current and future needs in the community; and information regarding competitors and (potential) collaborators

- The right mix of individuals on the planning committee—strategic thinkers and *actionaries* (individuals who are in a position to see things through to completion), as well as big-picture visionaries (conceptual) thinkers and detail-oriented (perceptual) thinkers

- Willingness to be inclusive and encourage broad participation, so that people feel ownership of and are energized by the process

- An adequate commitment of organizational resources to complete the planning process as designed (e.g., staff time, board time, dollars spent on the process for market research, consultants, etc.)

- A board and staff that understand the purpose of planning, recognize what it is and is not able to accomplish, and have clarity about the desired outcomes of the process and issues to be addressed

- A willingness to question the status quo, to look at new ways of doing things; a willingness to ask the hard questions, face difficult choices, and make decisions that are best for the organization's current and future constituencies, as well as a willingness to support organizational change as a result of the planning effort

- The organization has the financial capacity to sustain itself for the immediate future without a financial crisis appearing to detract from strategic planning

- Top management's commitment to carefully considering recommendations made during the planning process rather than disregarding decisions in favor of intuitive decisions

- No serious conflict between key players within the organization (although a healthy dosage of disagreement and perhaps some heated discussions can be expected during a strategic planning process)

- No high-impact decision to be made in the next six months by an external source

- No merger or other major strategic partnership effort is under way

- A board and top management that are willing to articulate constraints and non-negotiables upfront

- A commitment to tie the strategic planning process to the organization's annual planning and budgeting process—to create a detailed annual operating plan for the upcoming year and monitor/revise the strategic plan as needed

- A commitment to allocating sufficient resources to support the implementation of core strategies

These conditions should be in place before an organization commits to a strategic planning process.

What If Some of the Conditions for Success Are Missing?

If some of the conditions for success are missing, then an in-depth strategic planning process may not be appropriate at this time. Even if an organization is halfway through the planning process before realizing that it isn't really ready to plan, it should stop and reassess how to proceed. Consider the following situations:

- "Fall is our busiest time of the year; we should wait until spring." This is easy: Wait.
- "We won't know what is going to happen to our most important funder (competitor, constituency, customer base, etc.) until X happens next year." In this case, program planning for the coming year is appropriate, but a longer-range plan will be difficult to create without serious work on contingency planning.
- "As a result of some initial planning discussions, we have initiated merger discussions with another organization." The initial strategic planning process has already defined a core future strategy—merge. The organization should wait until the merger discussions are completed, and then the new entity's board and staff should engage in a joint effort.

If the lack of readiness has to do with a lack of commitment to planning, lack of commitment to inclusiveness, or lack of willingness to consider new possibilities, then the situation is more difficult. Sometimes it is possible to influence the individuals in question regarding their orientation to strategic planning. However, sometimes it just doesn't make sense to conduct strategic planning until the players change. An executive director might wait until after the next board election, or a board might have to assess whether lack of leadership by an executive director in this area is enough of a problem to find a new executive director. In these situations, the readiness assessment is a judgment call, as is the decision about how to respond to a suspected lack of readiness.

If current problems exist that might interfere with the ability of top leadership to focus on the future, then either delay the strategic planning process or choose an abbreviated planning process that allows some overall strategic thinking to take place but doesn't require in-depth data gathering or discussions at the current time. Alternately, two parallel planning processes could take place: one that addresses the immediate issues and one that focuses on the larger strategic issues; the top leadership must be involved with the strategic issues.

In most cases, though, the assessment serves as a guide to potential problems in the process. The value in discussing the readiness criteria lies in focusing a prospective planning group's discussion around the commitment and concerns of its members, developing a planning process that addresses those concerns, and setting up the planning process to be successful.

An Alternative to a Formal Strategic Planning Process — The Strategic Learning Agenda

Because of limited time, limited commitment, and past dissatisfaction with previous strategic planning processes, Evergreen Services' board and staff were reluctant to engage in a formal strategic planning process. However, the organization was facing some important issues—issues that have both long-term and short-term implications. To address these issues, the board initiated a six-month strategic learning agenda. Three strategic learning topics were identified:

1. How can we have a greater impact in the region?
2. Under what circumstances should we collaborate?
3. Should we take our informal research efforts and grow those efforts into a major research program?

Interested Board and staff members volunteered to participate in one of the three strategic learning agenda committees, and after no more than six months, present their findings to the board of directors. By the end of six months, each committee had finished its work and presented its recommendations, including detailed action steps, to the board of directors. The board approved those recommendations, and the staff took on the responsibility of implementing the decisions.

Step 1.3: Develop a Plan for Gathering Information from Internal and External Stakeholders

Considerations for Participation in the Planning Process

Strategic planning should be an inclusive effort that engages a broad array of stakeholders at the appropriate phases in the strategic planning process. Who are stakeholders? A *stakeholder* is simply defined as anyone who cares, or should care, about the organization—anyone who has a stake in the success of its mission. This encompasses those who must implement the strategic plan, those who benefit from its implementation, and those who could significantly help or hinder its implementation.

Part of the thoughtfulness and creativity of the strategic planning process is identifying those individuals and groups who traditionally might not be regarded as stakeholders to involve in the process. This might include those who could contribute unique and valuable perspectives (not to mention those who should be included because of other substantive or political reasons). A truly inclusive process can accomplish the following:

- Help build internal and external enthusiasm for and commitment to the organization and its strategies. Those who feel they have contributed to the planning process then feel invested in it and are more likely to take ownership of the organization's goals and efforts

- Add objectivity to the process. Outsiders can identify jargon or ask critical questions about issues that insiders might assume common knowledge of or simply take for granted.

- Develop foundations for future working relationships.

- Establish a continuous exchange of information among staff, management, clients, and other key stakeholders.

- Ensure an adequate depth and breadth of data from which to make informed decisions.

Determining how to include all of these internal and external stakeholders can prove trickier than identifying who they are, because there are many different kinds and levels of participation and roles in the planning process, such as the following:

- *Leadership.* Taking the initiative to see that decisions get made and things get done

- *Decision making.* Deciding on strategies, goals, objectives, and the like

- *Facilitation.* Paying attention to the process rather than content (a role played, for example, by an outside consultant or neutral participant)

- *Input.* Providing information and opinions

It is especially important to delineate between those stakeholders who provide input and those who make decisions. Being asked an opinion is not the same as having a final say in related decisions, but stakeholders some-times lose sight of that distinction. It is the decision makers' responsibility to let participants who provide input know what was done with their information and the rationale for decisions that were made.

The nature of stakeholders' participation will depend on several fac-tors—an organization's size, culture and management style, range of con-stituents, breadth of services, and so on—but following are some general understandings of specific stakeholders' roles in the strategic planning process.

Internal stakeholders include:

- *Executive director.* The executive director (chief executive officer) is usually the chief planner and prime mover of the plan through the entire process. Even if she or he is managing the planning process, the executive director works closely with the chair of the planning committee and often serves as the prime liaison between the staff and the planning committee. Sometimes the executive director writes the plan, but larger organizations may delegate that responsibility to someone else. Finally, the executive director plays the crucial role of being ultimately responsible for implementation of the plan.

- *Board of directors.* Strategic planning is one of the primary functions for which the board–staff partnership can ideally work the best. Both the board and the staff have different contributions to make and perspectives to bring to the process: the staff know individual clients' needs, understand day-to-day operations and other service providers, but may not always be willing or able to think big picture or long term. The board, in its governance capacity, has the respon-sibility to think about what is important for the entire community and not just one particular client. The board has within its gover-nance role the responsibility to practice what Harvard Professor Retina Herzlinger has referred to as "intergenerational equity" (i.e., the needs of both current and future clients are responded to within the strategic plan). The board must make sure that the plan's goals are consistent with resources and that the organization is sustainable.[2]

  An appropriate role for the board is to make sure an effective planning process is in place. The board should provide input into the organization's mission statement and approve any changes that need to be made. Either as a whole or through their representation on a strategic planning committee, the board should be involved in strategy discussions, setting long-term program and administrative priorities, and setting goals for the board. Individual board members may be able to gain access to external stakeholders for input.

Regardless of board members' level of involvement, the board needs to be kept informed throughout the planning process, not just at the end when they are presented with the final planning document. This can happen through reports at board meetings, written updates, a committee structure, or in other ways.

SIDEBAR

Board of Directors' Participation in a Planning Retreat

The process of holding an annual planning retreat has benefits far beyond even the significant advantage of giving a clear idea of where you're going. For instance, the very nature of the session provides the [board] with a common grasp of existing commitments and resources . . . and their participation will help them feel a commitment to the goals for the year. . . . Planning retreats are not easy sessions; properly organized, they should be designed to decide what not to attempt to accomplish or what should be assigned a low priority. . . .

Source: Brian O'Connell, *The Board Member's Book* (New York: The Foundation Center, 1985), p. 79.

- *Staff members.* Paid and volunteer staff have programmatic expertise and familiarity with the field and clients, information that is vital to shaping a relevant and workable strategic plan. Their involvement not only ensures buy-in to the organizational goals and strategies but is also the link between the plan's vision and the realization of that vision on a day-to-day basis. As such, staff members should be involved in identifying current and future client needs and able to give their perceptions regarding the organization's strengths, weaknesses, opportunities, and threats, and possible short-term and long-term program and administrative priorities.

Staff members may also be asked to collect data (do market research) and evaluate programs. Program managers should have significant input into setting long-term program objectives and should assist in the development and monitoring of operational plans. Ideally, staff members should be represented on the planning committee and kept informed throughout the planning process.

- *Advisory boards.* If you have an advisory board, you might want to involve these people in some of the strategic conversations. They are an important bridge between your internal and external stakeholders—closer to the organization than other outsiders and yet still likely to be more objective than board or staff members.

External stakeholders include people you serve, those with whom you partner, and people or organizations whose support is required to move the organization's vision forward. Identifying how and when to involve external stakeholders is an important activity when designing your planning process. Involving external stakeholders can accomplish two objectives: (1) these people have perspectives that inform your strategic decisions, and (2) and sometimes just as importantly, asking for input from external stakeholders invites them into a closer relationship with your organization. Everyone likes to feel that their opinion is important to others.

External stakeholders include the following:

- *Clients.* The sole reason for most nonprofits' existence is the betterment of society, whether that means providing a top-notch and well-rounded education, enriching cultural life, feeding the hungry, protecting the environment, providing quality health care, or defending the freedom of individuals. In a planning process, then, it is critical to evaluate how well intended beneficiaries are being served. Directly involving past and present clients (and perhaps potential clients) in the planning process, soliciting their unique firsthand experience of the organization, is one of the best ways to gain such insight into the organization's performance and to receive guidance on how to improve services. Some organizations include client representatives on the planning committee.

- *Funders.* Past, current, and potential institutional funders provide another valuable perspective on client needs and how others in the community are either meeting or failing to meet those needs. They may be able to shed some light on the funder community's inclination to fund a specific new program and their own interest in particular programs. Funders' input should be sought primarily during

Phase 3, Assessing Your Situation. Current and prospective funders should also receive an executive summary of the strategic plan.

- *Government funders and regulators.* Local (and sometimes state and national) officials can have a great influence on the external environment within which an organization operates. Asking their perspective about trends in the environment and their perception of what role your organization plays in the provision of services can help inform your future decisions.

- *Community leaders and partner organizations.* Community leaders, including elected officials, can also offer a valuable opinion of an organization's strengths and weaknesses, as well as insight into the needs of the community and knowledge of the competition. Their buy-in and support may be needed to secure funding and other forms of support; therefore, their input is valuable. Some organizations include a key community leader on the planning committee, thereby building in community commitment to the organization and its mission.

- *Individual donors.* An individual donor base is one of your most important resources. As such, keeping in regular contact with these people and asking them questions about why they support you and what they expect from your organization is critical. The strategic planning process is an invitation to get them involved in creating—and therefore being more willing to support—your future.

- *Competitors and potential collaborators.* Competitors (those who compete for funding as well as those who compete for clients or other customers) might also be approached to contribute to an organization's assessment of its environment—not just to get another outside opinion, but also to garner information to help the organization be more competitive or develop collaborative relationships.

- *Other agencies in parallel or related fields.* When individuals from related fields are involved in an organization's planning process, their knowledge and experience can be leveraged not only for the benefit of the clients being served, but also to foster cooperation and decrease unnecessary competition.

- *Previous staff and board members.* Staff members who were previously employed with the organization or former board members sometimes are considered unofficial alumni, and they offer a historical perspective that can be helpful in informing the future choices facing the organization. How valuable this perspective is may depend on just why their relationship is former.

Identifying Documents that Would Help Provide Important Background Information

In addition to outlining whether and how to involve internal and external stakeholders, it is helpful to gather all in one place any documents or other background information that would help inform your strategic questions. If you have already collected data about your situation, there is no need to duplicate your efforts.

Not every document needs to be given to every member of the planning committee. The following is a list of the types of documents that you might want to gather:

Mission-Related Documents
- Mission, vision, values statements; strategic plan; annual plans
- Program descriptions/workplans
- Needs assessments
- Client satisfaction surveys
- Previous evaluation designs and results
- Evidence of innovation or reputation in the field
- Other data (such as government reports, etc.)

Financial Documents
- Fundraising materials
- Fundraising plans
- Budget reports
- Audits
- Sample financial reports
- Internal controls procedure manuals

Administrative Capacity Documents
- Organizational chart
- Internal newsletters or other communication vehicles

- Personnel policies and performance appraisal forms
- Previous organizational effectiveness surveys and/or climate surveys (or other formal review of culture and staff satisfaction)
- Volunteer management plan
- Information technology plan
- Visual survey of facilities and equipment

Governance Documents
- Board development plan
- Board minutes
- Board roster and committee structure
- Previous board self-evaluations
- Board manual

Worksheet 3 (see process notes in Exhibit 2.3) can help you develop a preliminary plan for gathering information from internal and external stakeholders and other documents. Although you won't be actually gathering the information until Phase 3, by starting to develop an initial information-gathering plan, you will be better able to design your planning process and develop a strategic planning workplan.

STEP I.4: DESIGN YOUR STRATEGIC PLANNING PROCESS TO MEET YOUR ORGANIZATIONAL NEEDS

When designing a strategic planning process, a series of choices needs to be made regarding whom to involve, the role of those participants, and how the process will be structured. As part of getting ready, the initial planners need to make decisions regarding the design of a strategic planning process that will work for them. Whether you are working with a planning consultant in designing your strategic planning process or designing the process in-house, it is critical that you design a planning process that meets your organization's specific needs and establish a time frame that makes sense given all that is going on in your day-to-day operations. When designing the planning process, you first want to reflect on previous strategic planning endeavors: what has worked or not worked in the past that might inform the design of the current planning process. Next,

EXHIBIT 2.3   WORKSHEET 3: DEVELOP A PLAN FOR
GATHERING INFORMATION FROM
INTERNAL AND EXTERNAL STAKEHOLDERS

Process Notes

How to do this activity	Using the strategic planning outcomes and issues identified in Worksheet 1, brainstorm a list of internal and external stakeholders whom they wish to get input from. After identifying all the possible stakeholders, clarify what you wish to accomplish by involving each stakeholder group, as well as ideas for how to best involve them.
Why do this activity	While you won't actually do the information gathering until Phase 3, developing an initial plan during Phase 1 is important because it helps define the scope and scale of the data collection process. With a better understanding of the information gathering needs, you will be in a better position to decide on the level of your strategic planning process (abbreviated, moderate, extensive) and also whether it makes sense to start off your planning process with information gathering rather than start off with a discussion of mission.
Who to involve in the process	Strategic planning committee identifies the internal and external stakeholders and suggests processes to use to get the information that is needed. Sometimes, once the initial brainstormed list of stakeholders is created, additional input into the data gathering process is sought from board and staff members who are not on the committee.

See ASO/USA's example of this worksheet at the end of this chapter. Blank worksheets are provided in Appendix A and on the CD that accompanies this book.

the initial leaders of the planning process need to look at the various design choices, including:

- How to involve internal stakeholders (i.e., top-down, bottom-up, or hybrid)

- How (and whether) to involve external stakeholders
- Time and level of intensity of the process (i.e., abbreviated, moderate, extensive)
- Leadership of process (e.g., whether to use a strategic planning committee)
- Division of labor of assessment and planning discussions at department/unit level (e.g., use existing committees, department structure, form ad hoc committees)
- Who will serve as primary author/compiler of the strategic planning documents
- Use of large-group retreats
- Whether to hire a consultant
- How to inform stakeholders who are not deeply involved with the planning process about the process and resulting plans

Who Makes What Decisions?

The first choice has to do with decision making. Should there be a top-down or a bottom-up process? A top-down process assumes that those with the highest level of responsibility in an organization are in the best position to be big-picture thinkers and plan what is best for the organization. This approach is more expedient and can be an appropriate exercise of leadership. The main drawback to this approach is that it often results in plans that do not have the understanding and support of line staff (those most directly involved in providing services to clients), and the plan may not prove feasible or in the best interests of the clients. A bottom-up planning process starts with input from individual staff members or departments, thereby addressing the need for staff input and investment. Such a process, however, can produce a patchwork plan that lacks coherence for the organization as a whole and results in an uncoordinated, even wasteful, use of resources.

For most organizations, the best approach seems to be a hybrid approach, one that strikes a balance between the need for decisive leadership and productive collaboration, featuring the open communication of a bottom-up planning process as well as the clear coordination of a top-down process. The net result is an effective combination of the best of both models of participation—the planning process described in this workbook is such a hybrid.

Regardless of the flow of decision making for the organization, the board in its governance role approves the final planning document. The following are some of the choices regarding who decides and what degree of input is sought from board and staff:

Choices	Factors to Consider in Selecting the Best Choice for Your Organization
The board decides strategic direction for the organization. The staff has little involvement in developing the plan.	When the board feels that members of the board are the most appropriate and knowledgeable judges of the organization's strengths and weaknesses and opportunities and threats, that they alone should decide the long-term priorities, and that the staff will be willing and able to support their decisions (or there is no staff)
Board and staff together decide strategic direction for the organization.	When there is the recognition of the contribution that both board and staff can bring to the strategic planning process—a commitment to a true board–staff partnership
Staff, by itself, decides strategic direction for the organization. The board has little involvement in developing the plan.	When the board and staff agree that staff members are the most appropriate and knowledgeable judges of the organization's strengths and weaknesses and opportunities and threats, that they should lead in determining the long-term priorities for the organization, and that the board is willing to support their recommendations

Whether to Involve External Stakeholders in Addition to Internal Stakeholders

In certain circumstances, the only participants would be internal stakeholders. Internal stakeholders include the management team, all other paid and volunteer staff, the board of directors, and an advisory board if the organization has one. Internal stakeholders can be involved through meetings, surveys, and interviews.

Planners may also choose to gather data from external sources: This includes doing formal research, as well as surveying, interviewing, or meeting (through focus groups, etc.) with constituents/clients (current, past), grantors (foundations, corporations, government agencies), government officials, nonprofit and for-profit entities with which the organization partners, donors, and ex-staff or ex-board members.

Choices	Factors to Consider in Selecting the Best Choice for Your Organization
Only gather data about the organization from internal stakeholders (board and staff).	When staff and board do not need, or do not have time to solicit, outside perspectives in order to make informed strategic choices
Gather data about the organization from both internal stakeholders (board and staff) and external stakeholders (including but not limited to clients, ex-staff, funders, community leaders, etc.).	When there is a need or desire for an outside perspective and/or when building relationships with key outside stakeholders is one of the desired outcomes of the strategic planning process

How Long a Process to Have

As previously discussed in the introductory section of this workbook, there are various levels of planning, and each level requires a different amount of time and a different level of planning activities. These levels are determined by both the amount of discussion that is needed to address key issues as well as the extent of data that needs to be gathered before making decisions about the strategic direction of the organization.

Choices	Factors to Consider in Selecting the Best Choice for Your Organization
Abbreviated Process (One- or two-day retreat)	Extent of external data to be gathered—usually none Amount of discussion needed about key issues: little
Abbreviated Plus Process (One- or two-day meeting with additional follow-up meetings)	Extent of external data to be gathered—minimum or none Amount of discussion needed about key issues: abbreviated
Moderate Process (One to three months)	Extent of external data to be gathered—some Amount of discussion needed about key issues: moderate

Choices *(Continued)*	Factors to Consider in Selecting the Best Choice for Your Organization
Moderate-Extensive Process (Three to six months)	Extent of external data to be gathered— moderate Amount of discussion needed about key issues: moderate to extensive
Extensive Process (Six to nine months)	Extent of external data to be gathered— extensive Amount of discussion needed about key issues: extensive

Use of Strategic Planning Committee and/or Task Forces

When designing a planning process, two early decisions are (1) whether to use an existing committee or a strategic planning committee to *coordinate* the planning work and *assist* with information-gathering activities, and (2) whether to have the strategic planning committee or ad hoc issue-focused task forces be charged with the responsibility to *discuss* future program or administrative options and *make recommendations* to the board.

The authors of this workbook recommend that there be, at the very least, some group that takes responsibility for coordinating the planning process. Whether it is a special strategic planning committee or another group, an effective committee can ensure appropriate involvement and perspective in discussing strategic issues. Usually, a planning committee spearheads the planning process; this does not mean that committee members are responsible for doing all of the work, but they are responsible for ensuring that the work gets done. Basically, a planning committee decides (with appropriate input from other board and staff) which stakeholders to involve and how to involve them, coordinates and makes assignments to staff or board members, provides linkages and liaison with constituencies, and prioritizes or narrows information for the organization to discuss and evaluate.

In addition, the planning committee might discuss some of the strategic issues, make recommendations regarding strategies and priorities, create initial drafts of planning documents for approval by the board, and critical tasks. However, the organization may decide to use ad hoc issue- or program-focused task forces to discuss and make recommendations regarding specific planning issues. These ad hoc task forces would be made up of interested board and staff members and perhaps other external stakeholders, and the task forces' recommendations would then be presented at a board–staff planning retreat or directly to the board.

The executive director and the board president typically select the planning committee. The committee should be convened once a decision to go ahead with planning has been reached.

Choices (More than one choice may be appropriate)	Factors to Consider in Selecting the Best Choice for Your Organization
Do not use a strategic planning committee.	An individual—or individuals—are willing and able to coordinate the strategic process.
Use existing standing committee (i.e., executive committee or management team) to coordinate process and discuss some of the issues (including making recommendations).	There are current structures in place that are the appropriate venues for coordinating the strategic planning process. These workgroups may also be the appropriate venue to discuss some of the strategic issues.
Strategic planning committee delegated full responsibility for coordinating the SP process	When there is not an existing workgroup whose focus is on planning and strategy
Strategic planning committee in charge of discussing strategic issues and making recommendations to management team and board of directors	When the strategic planning committee has enough diversity of knowledge and experience to be able to discuss strategic issues and make sound recommendations
Use ad hoc task forces for discussion of strategic issues or program priorities and making recommendations to management team and board of directors or presentation at a board–staff retreat.	When there is a need for more focused discussions on certain strategic issues, and these discussions would benefit from having individuals with specialized knowledge or expertise (board, staff, and or external stakeholders) discuss these issues

Strategic Planning Committee Membership

If the organization does decide to create a planning committee, that committee should:

- Consist of approximately six to eight individuals (could be larger if need exists to include broader representation of stakeholders;

however, too large a committee—more than 15—may make it more difficult to coordinate meetings and have discussions)

- Be a combination of visionaries (people who see what the organization can be and can rally the organization around that vision) and actionaries (people who will ensure that the projected goals and tasks are realistic)
- Be a group that has informal power and the respect of the entire organization
- Be a diverse group of stakeholders who are committed to a vision for the common good, rather than just advocating for the particular population they represent. Usually the committee is a combination of board and staff members, including the executive director, board president, and whoever has responsibility for writing the final planning document. If the board president is unable to fully participate in membership of the committee, then he or she needs to delegate authority and responsibility to the committee and ensure that he or she is kept informed of discussions in a timely manner.

Choices	Factors to Consider in Selecting the Best Choice for Your Organization
Board with executive director	When the board only—with the executive director—is deciding the strategic direction for the organization
Representatives of board and staff	When the strategic planning process is viewed as a partnership between the board and the staff and with a recognition that each can contribute valuable perspectives
Representatives of board, staff, and some external stakeholders	When the strategic planning process is viewed as a partnership between the board and the staff and with a recognition that each can contribute valuable perspectives and that an outside perspective would be helpful for coordinating the strategic planning process and managing discussions

Who Will Lead the Process?

Usually, either the board president or the executive director will lead the strategic planning process, but sometimes a board member may be appointed chair of the planning committee, or a senior staff representative may hold the leadership.

Choices	Factors to Consider in Selecting the Best Choice for Your Organization
President/chair of the board	President/chair has sufficient interest, time, and skill to lead the planning process
Board member as chair of strategic planning committee	There is a desire or need to share a leadership role and there is a board member who has the interest, time, and skill to lead the planning process. It is critical that the president/chair delegate authority to chair the committee and that the chair of the committee keeps the president/chair and the rest of the board informed about planning discussions taking place.
Executive director	The board has sufficient interest in the strategic planning process, but it is felt that the executive director has the time and skill to lead the process and would be in a better position to spearhead the planning efforts than a board member. The major caveat is that the leadership of a planning process can take considerable time, and if an executive director is already overextended, the planning process may not get the attention it needs.
Other	In larger organizations, a senior staff person may have the responsibility for leading the strategic planning efforts.

Who Will Be the Primary Writer of the Plan?

The primary writer of the plan should be the board or staff person who has the skill and time to do so. In certain circumstances, a consultant might assist in the writing of the plan, although this approach can be problematic if it results in staff and board members feeling that the plan is the consultant's plan and they do not have ownership of the words and concepts. At the very least, the role of the writer of the plan should be to summarize the discussions and conclusions reached during the strategic planning process.

Choices	Factors to Consider in Selecting the Best Choice for Your Organization
Executive director	If he or she is the best person to write the plan, based on skill and time availability
Chair of planning committee	If he or she is the best person to write the plan, based on skill and time availability
Designated member(s) of strategic planning committee	If he or she is the best person to write the plan, based on skill and time availability
Consultant	When there is no one on the board and staff with the skill and time available to produce a planning document in a timely manner (Based on issues of buy-in and ownership, we recommend this as the last choice to consider.)

Sequencing of Retreats and Discussions

Although this workbook outlines the seven phases of strategic planning, Phase 2 (Articulate Mission, Vision, and Values) and Phase 3 (Assess Your Situation) don't always need to follow that order and can be reversed. In addition, strategic planning processes don't always have to start off with a retreat; you get to decide the sequence of events.

Choices (Note: More than one choice is possible)	Factors to Consider in Selecting the Best Choice for Your Organization
Start with data collection	Useful when the organization needs a better understanding of its situation (strengths, weaknesses, opportunities, and threats) before starting to define the organization's mission, vision, and strategic issues
Start with a retreat	Useful when leadership wants to build commitment to the overall process and gather input on key questions and issues to be addressed

(continues)

Choices *(Continued)* (Note: More than one choice is possible)	**Factors to Consider in Selecting the Best Choice for Your Organization**
End with a retreat	Especially if the organization has started the planning process with data collection, having a retreat at the end of the planning process allows for presentation of the data and discussion of how to best respond to that information (i.e., what should be the organization's future strategies and program and administrative priorities).
Start with, and end with, board and staff or board–staff retreats	Retreats at the beginning and end of the planning process can be effective vehicles for both initiating the conversations and getting buy-in at the end regarding the organization's future.
Start with committee discussions	Useful when information available about the organization's performance and its environment requires some sifting in order to provide enough direction for a plan to take shape. Also useful when many different planning activities have taken place already (e.g., at the board, senior staff, department level), and a committee needs to determine what has already been done sufficiently to expedite the process.

See ASO/USA's example of this worksheet at the end of this chapter. Blank worksheets are provided in Appendix A and on the CD that accompanies this book.

Whether to Use a Consultant and How Best to Use a Consultant

Many organizations include an outside consultant in part or all of the planning process. For example, it is common to have a consultant facilitate retreats and meetings, serving as a neutral facilitator so that good ideas do not get lost among the emotions or personalities of the participants. A consultant can also provide objectivity by asking clarifying questions, challenging assumptions, encouraging the group to question the status quo, and seeing that organizational jargon is kept to a minimum. Organizations can also look to consultants for information or training on planning language, tools, and processes.

When working with consultants, it is important to clearly define the scope of the project, identify the benefits expected for each party, and agree on responsibilities and mechanisms for accountability. The relationship must be one on which you can depend. Different situations allow for different ways to involve consultants.

Choices (Note: More than one choice is possible)	Factors to Consider in Selecting the Best Choice for Your Organization
Do not use a consultant.	The organization has sufficient knowledge of strategic planning and strong facilitation expertise in-house; chair of strategic planning committee is skilled at both participating in discussions and ensuring an effective meeting process.
Consultant assists in designing the strategic planning process.	Organization lacks sufficient knowledge of strategic planning or wants outside perspective about strategic planning; chair of strategic planning committee is skilled at both participating in discussions and ensuring an effective meeting process.
Consultant acts as a facilitator of discussions.	Outside/neutral facilitator is needed for more productive and focused discussions so all stakeholders can participate fully in discussions.
Consultant helps as a researcher and/or evaluator.	An extra pair of hands is needed or an objective interviewer is needed.
Be a subject expert.	When the organization needs assistance from an expert in its field to help in framing the choices

When hiring consultants, consider the following tips:

- You may choose to have different consultants for some of the roles mentioned previously. For example, you may hire one consultant to facilitate the planning process and another to do some of the research.
- Interview at least two consultants. You will be able to explore different approaches to the project and may utilize the ideas of more than one consultant.

- For substantial projects, ask for references and a written price bid from each consultant interviewed.

- Agree on one person to whom the consultant will report. The process will get confusing if different people are asking for different things.

- Have a written memorandum of understanding or contract with the consultant, with payments based on the consultant's performance of agreed-on tasks.

- Throughout the project, give the consultant feedback about his or her work.

- If the organization is working with other consultants, make sure the other consultants and the planning consultant are informed of each others' work and coordinating each others' efforts.

- Do not expect a consultant to make tough decisions or value-based choices for you. A consultant can help articulate alternative courses of action and the implications of various choices, but the organization's decision makers should make the important decisions.

- Agree in advance on how you will pay the consultant's fees, including any overruns.

Other Considerations for the Strategic Planning Process

At the first meeting of the planning committee (or whatever group is leading the strategic planning process), the committee's responsibilities should be delineated and any milestones or deadlines confirmed. In addition, the committee should state the principles and values that will broadly govern the strategic planning effort as well as any meeting agreements about how the group will work together.[3]

Planning principles and values serve as a framework for assessing the integrity and responsibility of the planning process. Some typical planning process principles and values may include:

- *Inclusiveness.* Input will be sought from all levels within the organization.

- *Meaningful participation.* Staff should feel that their participation is substantive, with the potential for real influence on the outcome of the plan; if an individual is expected to implement a strategy, that individual should participate in shaping that strategy.

- *Share the work.* The successful completion of the planning process should not depend on one or two people.

- *Focus on the "big picture."* There should be no expectation that every concern or issue will be addressed by the strategic planning process; however, all critical issues should be addressed, regardless of how difficult those issues may be.

- *Ownership.* We will seek to develop deep ownership of our mission, vision, critical issues, and corporate strategies.

- *Strategy.* Our strategies should be responsive to the environment and based on our understanding of the probable future environment. Much of this understanding will come from in-depth market research.

- *Set benchmarks.* Our strategic plan must be used and results measured against set benchmarks; we must update and renew our planning efforts annually.

Worksheet 4 (see process notes in Exhibit 2.4) can be used by the initial leaders of the planning process to consider what the planning process might look like, as well as expected roles and authority of board, staff, external stakeholders, and consultant.

Other Considerations Before Initiating a Planning Process

Thought should be put into deciding how the board and staff will be kept informed of discussions and decisions during the planning process. It is not advised to wait until the last minute or keep everyone in the dark regarding the strategic decisions that are being made

Finally, everyone involved in the planning process should have a basic understanding of strategic planning, of what it can and cannot accomplish, and an overview of the language of planning. All members of the planning committee must talk the same planning language. As stated previously, words such as *purpose, mission, business, strategy, strategic, goal, objective, vision,* and *long-range* have different meanings to different people. Given that the language of planning is not consistent between the for-profit and nonprofit sector and even within the nonprofit sector, the committee should agree at the first meeting on the definitions they will use for such words as *purpose, business, mission statement, strategy, goal,* and *objective.*

EXHIBIT 2.4   WORKSHEET 4: DESIGN A STRATEGIC
PLANNING PROCESS TO MEET YOUR
ORGANIZATIONAL NEEDS

Process Notes

How to do this activity	Answer each of the questions on the worksheet, taking into consideration the thinking that went into the previous three worksheets: what planning processes will best help your organization achieve its planning outcomes, ensure a successful planning process, and involves appropriate stakeholders?
Why do this activity	By designing a process that meets your specific organizational needs, you will be able to develop a plan for planning that can be successfully implemented.
Who to involve in the process	Strategic planning committee—either on its own, or with a consultant—answers the planning process questions. Once a workplan is developed, the board of directors should approve it.

See ASO/USA's example of this worksheet at the end of this chapter. Blank worksheets are provided in Appendix A and on the CD that accompanies this book.

SIDEBAR

Barriers to Planning in Government Agencies

Government agencies have built-in obstacles to effective planning. Some of the obstacles are similar to those found in any large institution: entrenched bureaucratic procedures; dense and complex decision-making processes; the challenge of involving large numbers of staff in order to foster staff participation in planning; and the logistical difficulties of uniformly implementing a plan over time.

In addition, however, government has inherent practices, values, and structures that make long-term strategic planning particularly difficult:

- *The political arena.* All organizations operate in some form of political context. Government programs, however, are especially affected by the electoral process. Partisan politics drive the timing and types of policy-making in government. And, since policy drives strategic planning—in terms of an organization's identity, philosophy, values, and method of operation—then it is clear that strategic planning in government must reflect policy that has a political base. When partisan politics change, so too may an agency's policies and plans. The greater the visibility factor in the political environment, the more difficult it is to plan and execute for the long term because of the varying concern: (philosophies and values) of both the elected body and the stakeholders outside the agency.

- *The decision-making process.* Two factors make decision-making in government programs difficult. First, the uncertainties of the election process make it difficult to commit to strategies which will take longer to implement than the length of an election cycle Second, where policies are defined by statute, the flexibility of program level decision makers is strictly bounded. This makes it difficult to be responsive to changes in the environment.

- *Leadership.* The highest level of management in government is elected. It is not uncommon for newly elected officials to have no working knowledge of a government agency's purpose and programs, or for their views of what an agency should do to differ from those of agency staff. Elected officials may set policy, both administratively and through legislation, without involving the agency in planning for any changes. Obviously, agencies strive to continually educate elected officials about their activities in an effort to improve the quality of decisions that will come their way.

Despite these obstacles, agencies at all levels of government do strategic planning and many of them do it well. One government agency was able to overcome some of the barriers by adopting and implementing a planning process that incorporated the following planning principles:

- Top management shall exert strong leadership in valuing and committing to a planning effort.

- Management will participate in and support planning efforts with adequate time, budget, and staffing.

- Adequate background work or research will be done to include client or constituent needs, as well as a record of the public's use of agency services.

(continues)

- The planning effort must be inclusive of staff in some form that is both informative and meaningful to both staff and management.

- A good strategic plan must define the agency, clearly indicate goals and objectives, lay out a range of activities that meet the agency's mission, and benchmark success.

- A good strategic plan must be used and results measured against the benchmarks.

- Our agency must update and/or renew its planning efforts annually.

During this agency's initial getting-ready meeting, staff identified the following benefits of engaging in a strategic planning effort:

Effective planning that targets and achieves results can build a base of support with constituencies outside of the agency, who in turn can advocate for continuation of services, assuming that the constituents' needs are being addressed. The more our agency tracks client response and need and uses that information to build its programs, the greater the likelihood that elected officials, regardless of which party is in office, will have a reason to continue to support our plans. The more public our agency makes its plan and the more it involves client participation, the more client satisfaction will be realized in the long run.

STEP 1.5: WRITE A PLANNING WORKPLAN

Last but not least, the planning committee will need to develop an overall workplan for managing the planning effort (also referred to as a "plan to plan"). The workplan should outline the activities involved over the course of the entire planning process, the processes to be used for all activities (such as interviews, retreats, etc.), persons responsible for executing or overseeing those tasks, desired outcomes, resources required (e.g., time and money), and time frames.

At this point, the planning committee will need to decide the extent of the planning process. Exhibit 2.5 is a guide to developing the planning workplan. It describes the three levels of intensity in the planning process: abbreviated, moderate, and extensive. Use this guide to select the depth of the process appropriate for your organization. In Appendix B, sample workplans are included for each type of process.

Why develop a workplan? One might argue that failure to plan is planning to fail. The planning process is, after all, a process that can involve many people and take a considerable amount of time. The more clarity

EXHIBIT 2.5 THREE LEVELS OF INTENSITY IN THE PLANNING PROCESS

Abbreviated Workplan

Depth of analysis during the planning process: Abbreviated analysis

Personnel involved	Typical format	Typical time frame	Strategic plan: typical products to come out of the strategic planning process	Suggested worksheets
If a smaller organization, usually the entire board and staff If a larger organization, usually the entire board and staff representatives	Day-long retreat (plus time to plan retreat) Follow-up meeting(s) by staff to develop detailed annual operating plan to implement strategic plan	One day* Time for staff to develop annual plan	Strategic planning document that is 3–8 pages in length and includes: • Mission statement • Summary of strategies and list of long-term and short-term program and management/operations priorities • Detailed annual operating plan (as prepared by staff)	Homework assignment to be filled out and brought by all participants to the retreat: • Mission statement • Vision statement • Organizational history either filled out by one or two individuals before the retreat or done on wall using a large piece of paper • SWOT

*May need additional meeting(s) if more time is needed to discuss all issues and agree on priorities.

(continues)

EXHIBIT 2.5 THREE LEVELS OF INTENSITY IN THE PLANNING PROCESS (Continued)

Moderate Workplan

Depth of analysis during the planning process: Moderate analysis

Personnel involved	Typical format	Typical time frame	Strategic plan: typical products to come out of the strategic planning process	Suggested worksheets
If a smaller organization, usually the entire board and staff If a larger organization usually the entire board and staff representatives (management team) Usually includes some external stakeholders input (such as clients or funders)	One or two days of larger group meetings; smaller meetings of entire board and line staff may meet prior to larger group meetings A few planning committee meetings to discuss past strategies, current issues, and future priorities May include some collection of data regarding the external environment and stakeholder expectations and needs	One to three months to complete process Time for staff to develop annual plan	Strategic planning document that is usually 8–12 pages in length and includes: • Mission statement • Summary of strategies • List of long-term and short-term program and management/operations priorities • Program and management/operations goals and objectives (optional) • Summary of environmental assessment (optional) • Detailed annual operating plan (as prepared by staff)	For first retreat: Homework assignments to be brought by all participants to the retreat: • Mission statement • Vision statement • Organizational history either filled out by one or two individuals before the retreat or done on wall using large piece of paper • SWOT Other worksheets will depend on the issues facing the organization and the detail of information needed to assess the environment and set priorities, but at a minimum would include: • Long-term and short-term priorities • Previous and current strategies • Core future strategies Additional worksheets may be used, depending on the products that the organization wishes to produce as part of the strategic planning process

EXHIBIT 2.5 THREE LEVELS OF INTENSITY IN THE PLANNING PROCESS *(Continued)*

Extensive Workplan

Depth of analysis during the planning process: Extensive analysis

Personnel involved	Typical format	Typical time frame	Strategic plan: typical products to come out of the strategic planning process	Suggested worksheets
Entire board Entire staff Clients/customers Others, including funders, other organizations, community leaders, government officials, actual or potential competitors, and collaborators	Meeting(s) to assess strategic issues, organizational readiness, and participation in the planning process Meeting(s) to orient planning committee regarding planning process and planning language; review of organizational history and profile, previous and current strategies, and development of an information gathering plan Retreat(s) of board and staff to review organization's history, mission and vision statements, SWOT analysis, and discussions of issues, possible strategies, and priorities Planning committee meeting to identify external stakeholders and how to involve them in the process External stakeholder input through surveys, interviews, or focus groups; staff input through assessment of programs, and program evaluation; other data collection will depend on information needs Meeting(s) of planning committee to review external and internal environment information collected above, the interplay of SWOT, and competitive analysis of programs Meeting(s) of planning committee to discuss strategic issues and determine core future strategies and possible long-term and short-term priorities Meeting(s) of planning committee to review proposed future program portfolio and short-term and long-term program and management/operations priorities Meeting(s) of planning committee to develop and review goals and objectives Meeting(s) of planning committee to review and modify strategic plan Board of directors meet to approve strategic plan Follow-up meeting(s) by staff to develop detailed annual operating plan to implement strategic plan	Four to eight months to complete process	Extensive strategic plan that is usually 12–40 pages in length and includes: • Mission statement • Strategic issues and core strategies • Program goals and objectives • Management/operations goals and objectives • Summary of planning process • Appendices: summary of environmental assessment, in-depth analysis from client/customer surveys and stakeholder comments • Detailed annual operating plan (as prepared by staff)	All worksheets might be used in completing the extensive workplan

you have regarding what activities are needed, who is involved, who is the prime mover (person responsible for overseeing/ensuring that an activity happens), what process you will use, by when it should be completed, and products to deliver, the more your planning process can be managed effectively and efficiently.

The main thing to help groups with in this phase is deciding if strategic planning is the right thing to do at this time. Thus, the challenges focus on possible bad choices.

- *Going ahead when not ready.* The readiness assessment is a critical step, so take these issues seriously or the likelihood of failure looms ahead.

CAUTIONS TO FACILITATORS *(Continued)*

- *Taking too little or too much time.* Certainly not giving enough time to planning is a problem, but there is an unconscious bias for many people that more time equals more value. Be careful not to assume that more time is needed.

- *Time is not the same thing as attention.* Be realistic about the quality of attention required by senior leaders for valuable planning to take place.

- *Find the right consultant.* If you are using a consultant, or you are the consultant, take care to ensure that a good match is made between the skills and consulting style offered and the needs of the organization.

ENDNOTES

1. Adapted from George Steiner, *Strategic Planning* (New York: The Free Press, 1979), pp. 290–293.
2. Retina Herzlinger, "Effective Oversight: A Guide for Nonprofit Directors," *Harvard Business Review* (July–August 1994): 52–60.
3. See Appendix G for meeting guidelines.

CASE STUDY—ASO/USA

❏ What would success look like at the completion of the planning process? What does your organization wish to achieve from a planning process?

❏ What issues or choices do you think need to be addressed during the planning process?

❏ Are there any non-negotiables that need to be articulated up front? Any constraints regarding the planning process?

What would success look like at the completion of the planning process? What do you wish to achieve from a planning process?

- *A new 5 year strategic plan*
- *Increase sense of partnership between the board and staff.*
- *Figure out how to get board more engaged and involved in fundraising.*
- *Answer key questions about partnership with City Clinic.*
- *Decide whether to expand our services in any of three different directions: expand HIV prevention services, expand care services to serve more clients, and/or expand services to people with other life-threatening illnesses.*

Many of the strategic issues discussed during a strategic planning process address some or all of the following four questions:

1. *Mission.* How well are we achieving our mission and how could we have a greater impact?

2. *Financial.* Are our operations financially viable, and how can we ensure the long-term financial stability of our organization? Do we have effective financial management systems in place to monitor our finances?

3. *Administrative capacity.* Do we have the administrative capacity to effectively and efficiently support our programs and services? What would it take to maximize our organizational capabilities in terms of planning, human resources and leadership, organization culture and communication, and our technology and facilities infrastructure?

4. *Governance.* How effective is the board at protecting the public's interest, ensuring that charitable dollars are used effectively and efficiently and that the organization is fulfilling its mission? What can we do to ensure that our board is able to fulfill its governance role now and for the future?

What specific strategic questions or choices does your organization need to address during the planning process? (Note: Not every strategic issue will have a short-term focus question).

Strategic (longer-term) issues to be addressed—framed as a question:	Short-term focus? Are there some operational questions that need to be in the near future? If yes, list below:
• *HIV/AIDS treatment advances, and the changing nature of living with HIV are challenging us to change our services and our prevention efforts. What new or additional services should we offer?* • *How can we better integrate our services?* • *Could some of our current services be better done by other organizations?* • *How do we better serve traditionally disenfranchised communities?* • *Should we expand our services beyond people living with HIV and AIDS?*	*Our contract for employment support services was reduced 25% by the City Planning Council—we need to prioritize who remains eligible for these services.*
Our revenues are vulnerable—our current business model assumes major ongoing government funding. How do we decrease our over-dependence on federal funding? Should we start to charge for services?	*How do we deal with the decision by one of our regular corporate funders not to give us the $50,000 grant that was budgeted for this year? Individual donations are down from two years ago—how should we respond to an increased shortfall this year—we already were projecting a $15,000 deficit out of a reserve that is down to $95,000.*
Do we have the administrative capacity to support any additional growth or to be able to raise and manage new sources of revenue?	*How to improve our communication and increase teamwork among the various programs?* *What changes do we need to make to our current accounting system to be able to produce more useful financial reports?* *Staff turnover has recently become an issue.*
Our partnership with City Clinic has been a headache since the beginning. We need to fix this relationship or change it.	*The funder is beginning to look at this relationship more closely and demand accountability. How should we respond to this increased scrutiny of our outreach program?*

(continues)

Are there any issues that are non-negotiable (not open for discussion)?
Any constraints regarding the planning process?

We will not expand beyond our current geographic region. It is a given that we will continue to provide both prevention and care services, although the extent to which we focus on prevention versus care is up for discussion.

CASE STUDY—ASO/USA

❑ Are the conditions and criteria for successful planning in place at the current time? Can certain pitfalls be avoided?

❑ Is this the appropriate time for your organization to initiate a planning process? Yes or no? If no, where do you go from here?

The following conditions for successful planning are in place:	Yes	No	Unsure or N/A
1. Commitment, support, and involvement from top leadership, especially the executive director and board president, throughout the entire process	✔		
2. Commitment to clarifying roles and expectations for all participants in the planning process, including clarity as to who will have input into the plan and who will be decision makers	✔		
3. Willingness to gather information regarding the organization's strengths, weaknesses, opportunities, and threats; the effectiveness of current programs; needs in the community, both current and future; and information regarding competitors and (potential) collaborators	✔		
4. The right mix of individuals on the planning committee—strategic thinkers and actionaries (individuals who are in a position to see things through to completion), as well as big-picture (conceptual) thinkers and detail-oriented (perceptual) thinkers	✔		
5. Willingness to be inclusive and encourage broad participation, so that people feel ownership of and are energized by the process		?	*Need to clarify issues of input versus decision making*

(continues)

The following conditions for successful planning are in place:	Yes	No	Unsure or N/A
6. An adequate commitment of organizational resources to complete the planning process as designed (e.g., staff time, board time, dollars spent on the process for market research, consultants, etc.)			?
7. A board and staff that understand the purpose of planning, recognize what it is and is not able to accomplish, and have clarity about the desired outcomes of the process and issues to be addressed			?
8. A willingness to question the status quo, to look at new ways of doing things; a willingness to ask the hard questions, face difficult choices, and make decisions that are best for the organization's current and future constituencies as well as a willingness to support organizational change as a result of the planning efforts			?
9. The organization has the "financial capacity" to sustain itself for the immediate future without a financial "crisis" appearing to detract from strategic planning.	✔		
10. Top management's commitment to carefully considering recommendations made during the planning process rather than disregarding decisions in favor of his or her intuitive decisions	✔		
11. There is no serious conflict between key players within the organization (although a healthy dosage of disagreement and perhaps some heated discussions can be expected during a strategic planning process).	?		*Not a serious conflict, but, there are strong feelings regarding expanding beyond HIV/AIDS*

The following conditions for successful planning are in place:	Yes	No	Unsure or N/A
12. There are no high-impact decisions to be made in the next six months by an external source.	✔		
13. No merger or other major strategic partnership effort is under way (separate strategic planning conversations are not taking place while strategic restructuring negotiations are taking place).	✔		
14. Board and top management are willing to articulate constraints and non-negotiables upfront.	✔		
15. A commitment to tie the strategic planning process to the organization's annual planning and budgeting process—to create a detailed annual operating plan for the upcoming year, and monitor/revise the strategic plan as needed	✔		
16. A commitment to allocating sufficient resources to support the implementation of core strategies	?		*Sounds good, but we need to set realistic strategies?*

Comments to explain—and/or suggestions on how to respond—to "No" or "Unsure or N/A" answers

- *Not sure all board members are really committed to an inclusive process—need to discuss concerns and clarify decision making. Want board fully involved so they don't feel the planning process is "too staff driven" this time.*

- *It would be helpful to have a consultant facilitate some of our meetings and facilitate focus groups. If we can't get foundation support for strategic planning, need to adjust our expectations of the process.*

- *We have some board and staff who may be reluctant to look at new in different ways of doing things.*

(continues)

- *We need to plan carefully for resources. What level of time and commitment will we need from staff and board to participate in both the planning process and the implementation of the plan? We need to be realistic when developing the strategic plan.*

Other issues/concerns?

Is this the appropriate time for your organization to initiate a planning process? Yes or No? If no, what steps need to be put in place to ensure a successful planning process—where do you go from here? Or, should the organization consider doing something other than a formal strategic planning process?

Yes. We need to address the critical operational issues, but it is clear we need to engage in strategic planning as well. A key step that needs to be done up front is to have a meeting with the board to develop consensus on how the strategic planning process will proceed. Board buy-in will be critical to success. We also decided we need consultant support to be successful.

WORKSHEET 3 Develop a Plan for Gathering Information from Internal and External Stakeholders

☐ Using the strategic issues you identified in Worksheet 1, develop a plan for gathering information—from internal and external sources—to inform those questions.

Data Collection from Internal Stakeholders—Board and Staff

Internal Stakeholders	Outcome of contact with them? Questions they can answer? What information do you want to gather from this stakeholder?	How best to involve them (such as: surveys, discussions at regularly scheduled meetings, retreats, in-depth program evaluation worksheets, etc.)	Details (may be filled out when starting to implement data collection phase: time frame and who is responsible for implementation)
Staff—do you want to engage: • All of the staff ✔ • Management team ✔ • Some staff (list individuals)	Perceptions regarding quality of programs, administrative and financial capacity of the organization and program, and program priorities A plan for improving communication and teamwork among all the component parts	Have all staff fill out online assessment of organization (EEMO²). Program directors work with their staff to complete program evaluation. Solicit regarding future program and administrative priorities at staff meetings and at volunteer meeting. Management team to attend board Staff Retreats. Representatives of each of program meet to help solve the operational barrier of poor communication when a lot of teamwork will be needed for the process.	

(continues)

Data Collection from Internal Stakeholders—Board and Staff

Internal Stakeholders	Outcome of contact with them? Questions they can answer? What information do you want to gather from this stakeholder?	How best to involve them (such as: surveys, discussions at regularly scheduled meetings, retreats, in-depth program evaluation worksheets, etc.)	Details (may be filled out when starting to implement data collection phase: time frame and who is responsible for implementation)
Board of directors	*Perceptions regarding quality of programs, administrative and financial capacity of the organization and program, and program priorities* *Agreement on future board priorities*	*Board to complete online assessment of organization and board assessment* *Discussion of long-term and short-term board priorities at regular and/or special board meetings*	
Others—do you want to engage others (such as advisory board members, volunteer staff, etc.)		*Consultant to facilitate "town meeting" of volunteers to get their input regarding program priorities.* *Consultant to attend Client Advisory Board meeting*	
Departments/program units	*All relevant information will be captured by staff and management team.*		

Data Collection from Internal Stakeholders—Board and Staff

Internal Stakeholders	Outcome of contact with them? Questions they can answer? What information do you want to gather from this stakeholder?	How best to involve them (such as: surveys, discussions at regularly scheduled meetings, retreats, in-depth program evaluation worksheets, etc.)	Details (may be filled out when starting to implement data collection phase: time frame and who is responsible for implementation)
Specific individuals to be interviewed (such as director of finance, development director)		Consultant to interview all program directors and other members of management team	

Data Collection from External Stakeholders—How to Involve External Stakeholders

(List specific names if possible)	Why talk with them? Relationship building or information gathering, or both?	Outcome of contact with them? Questions to answer? What information do you want to gather from this stakeholder?	How best to involve stakeholder (i.e., questionnaires, interviews [face-to-face or phone], focus groups, meetings, etc.)	Details (may be filled out when starting to implement data collection phase: time frame and who is responsible for implementation)
Constituents/ clients (current, past)	Let them know we care, but mostly information gathering. Give clients a voice in the shaping of our services.	How well are we serving various client groups? What changes or new services would clients want to see?	Survey and a few focus groups	

(continues)

Data Collection from External Stakeholders—How to Involve External Stakeholders

(List specific names if possible)	Why talk with them? Relationship building or information gathering, or both?	Outcome of contact with them? Questions to answer? What information do you want to gather from this stakeholder?	How best to involve stakeholder (i.e., questionnaires, interviews [face-to-face or phone], focus groups, meetings, etc.)	Details (may be filled out when starting to implement data collection phase: time frame and who is responsible for implementation)
Institutional funders (foundations, corporations, government agencies)	Relationship building and information.	Plans for future funding. Trends in funding—what will be the focus of prevention and care funding over the next 5 years?	Interviews. (6)	(List of who to interview and their contact information to be developed by next strategic planning meeting. We may want to interview some of them earlier in the process than later).
Government officials	Relationship building and information.	Plans for future funding, service delivery.	Interviews, summarize recent city planning documents. (2)	(List of who to interview and their contact information to be developed by next strategic planning meeting).
Organizations we partner with	Relationship building and information.	Their plans and feedback on our performance.	Interviews. (2)	Staff to develop list of potential partners to interview.

Data Collection from External Stakeholders—How to Involve External Stakeholders

(List specific names if possible)	Why talk with them? Relationship building or information gathering, or both?	Outcome of contact with them? Questions to answer? What information do you want to gather from this stakeholder?	How best to involve stakeholder (i.e., questionnaires, interviews [face-to-face or phone], focus groups, meetings, etc.)	Details (may be filled out when starting to implement data collection phase: time frame and who is responsible for implementation)
Individual donors	Big donors: relationship building and information. Small donors: information.	What they like and don't like about us. What would be an incentive for them to donate.	Big donors: interviews. (3) Small donors: survey in annual appeal.	(List of who to interview and their contact information to be developed by next strategic planning meeting.)
Ex-staff, ex-board members	Information from the few folks involved in other agencies now.	Input on direction of the field.	Interviews. (3)	
Other:	Health experts: information.	Direction of the field.	Interviews. (2)	

(continues)

Which of the following documents would help provide important background information and/or inform your strategic issue decisions? (Check appropriate documents to assemble)

Mission-related documents

- ☑ Program descriptions/workplans
- ☑ Needs assessments
- ☑ Client satisfaction surveys
- ☐ Previous evaluation findings
- ☐ Evidence of innovation/reputation in the field
- ☐ Other data (such as government reports, etc.)

Administrative capacity documents

- ☑ Mission, vision, values statements; strategic plan; annual plans
- ☑ Program descriptions/workplans
- ☐ Organizational chart
- ☐ Internal newsletters or other communication vehicles
- ☐ Personnel policies and performance appraisal forms
- ☐ Previous organizational effectiveness surveys and/or "climate surveys" (or other formal review of culture and staff satisfaction)
- ☐ Volunteer management plan
- ☑ Information technology plan
- ☐ Visual survey of facilities and equipment

Financial-related documents

- ☐ Fundraising materials
- ☑ Fundraising plans
- ☐ Budget reports
- ☐ Audit
- ☑ Sample financial reports
- ☐ Internal controls procedures manuals

Governance documents

- ☐ Board minutes
- ☐ Board roster and committee structure
- ☑ Previous board self-evaluations
- ☐ Board manual

CASE STUDY—ASO/USA

❏ What has been your previous experience with strategic planning?

❏ Consider some of the choices to be made when designing your strategic
planning process

❏ Other considerations for the strategic planning process

What has been your previous experience with strategic planning—what has
worked or not worked in the past that might inform the design of your strategic
planning process?

*Staff has usually been much more involved than the board—board retreats
generally get low turnout. The last planning document was not used to guide
some critical decision making—this time we want to develop detailed annual
plans to support the implementation of the strategic plan, and make sure that
every year we review the plan and make changes to reflect the changing
environment. We want to make sure this time that the board is much more
involved and has much more ownership and buy-in to the process.*

The following is a list of some of the choices to be made when designing a
strategic planning process:

• Who makes what decisions—who decides the strategic direction for the
  organization, and what degree of input is sought from the board and the staff

  *The board approves the plan. Staff input will be sought regarding program
  and administrative priorities. Since staff is extremely knowledgeable about our
  client population and are responsible for implementation. We need to make
  sure that the program managers are intricately involved in creating program
  and administrative objectives that they are willing and able to be held
  accountable for.*

• Whether to involve external stakeholders in addition to internal stakeholders
  (board and staff)

  *We should use the planning process as a way of building relationships with
  government officials, other funders, and community organizations. Also, it is
  absolutely essential to have input from clients. Perhaps through focus groups we
  can identify 10 to 15 clients who could become part of a community advisory
  board. We haven't talked to our long-term donors for a while—this is a great
  opportunity to do so.*

(continues)

WORKSHEET 4   *(Continued)*

- How long a process to have (abbreviated, moderate, or extensive)

  Moderate/extensive: no more than 6 months!

- Whether to use an existing committee or a strategic planning committee for such activities as coordinating the work and assisting with some of the planning activities (such as external stakeholder interviews, research, etc.)

  We should have a strategic planning committee to coordinate the planning process and help with external interviews. Last time the strategic planning committee was the primary place where strategic planning discussions happened. As a result we didn't get as much involvement of board and staff— this time let's consider having more of the discussions happen in some issue-focused ad hoc task forces that have additional board and staff representation.

- Whether to have a strategic planning committee—and/or ad hoc issue-focused task forces—charged with the responsibility for discussing future program or administrative options and making recommendations to the board

  Given what we stated in the fourth question we should try to maximize board and staff involvement through ad hoc issue-focused task forces that come up with recommendations that can be presented at a board/senior management team retreat.

- If using a strategic planning committee, deciding who should be on that committee. If using ad hoc task forces, deciding membership on those committees (including the decision as to whether nonboard members might be on those committees)

  The strategic planning committee should have both board and senior staff representatives. It's too early to decide what task forces to have, but any ad hoc task forces should have other board and staff members, and perhaps if appropriate some external stakeholders. For example, we should invite representatives from some community-based organizations serving the African-American community, because African Americans make up a substantial portion of our client base.

- Who will lead the process

  The president of the board will appoint a planning chair from the board.

- Who will be the primary writer of the plan (with guidance from a consultant if necessary)

  The executive director, with help from the consultant

- The sequencing of discussions (i.e., "do data collection first and then have a retreat" or "kick off the planning process with a board/staff retreat and then create issue focused board/staff task forces to collect and analyze data and make recommendations to the board of directors")

Last time we started off with a retreat in which we looked at mission and vision and brainstormed our strengths and weaknesses and opportunities and threats, and generated a list of possible program and administrative priorities. That worked fine, but some of our discussions at that retreat would have been better if we had been better informed about the external and internal environment. Let's start off with in-depth data collection (Phase 3!) Some of the examples of the information we need include: changes in federal HIV prevention priorities, information on possible reduction in care funding, what type of prevention programs have been successful in other parts of the country.

- Whether to use a consultant and if yes, how best to use a consultant/ expectations regarding the consultant's role

We need to hire a consultant to do some training to staff and board about planning (or, at the very least, copy the introductory chapter of the Allison and Kaye Strategic Planning for Nonprofit Organizations workbook). The consultant should facilitate all retreats, help with some of the more difficult task force discussions, assist us with designing an evaluation process, and help with the writing of the plan. Perhaps the consultant can also run some focus groups.

Other considerations for the strategic planning process:

Planning committee membership:

Name	Representing what key stakeholder
Sam Green	Board — long time member and board president
Juan Hernandez	Board, client
Tim Washington	Board — fairly new member
Joseph Chin	Executive director, management
Delores Molina	Program director, management
Jon Nguyen	Volunteer — long term volunteer
Lori Smith	Development director, management

Milestones and deadlines:

We are able to hand out an executive summary at our annual dinner in April — six months from now.

(continues)

WORKSHEET 4   *(Continued)*

Planning principles and values (e.g., we are committed to being inclusive of all key stakeholders; we are willing to look at new and different ways of doing things and face the hard choices regarding how to best use our resources):

- *The past has a vote, not veto power—just because we did things in the past doesn't mean these activities are guaranteed to be a part of our future.*
- *We want to develop a plan that has the buy in of staff and board.*
- *This planning process cannot succeed if it depends only on one or two people.*
- *We will use the strategic plan as a guide for the allocation of resources.*

Meeting agreements (e.g., when offering a dissenting opinion, be willing to offer a solution that meets your needs and the needs of others; show up at meetings and be prepared; seek first to understand, then to be understood; respect differences):

We need to develop some meeting agreements about participation behaviors at our first planning committee meeting. (The ones listed previously sound good.)

How board and staff will be kept informed about the strategic planning discussions:

This is really critical. Last time people did not feel informed about decisions until the end, and then there was a lot of resistance. Executive director and chair of planning committee will keep staff and board updated at monthly meetings.

CHAPTER 3

Phase 2: Articulate Mission, Vision, and Values

One of the primary reasons for undertaking a strategic planning process is to establish—or reaffirm—a shared understanding of why an organization exists and its aspirations for the future. The most succinct reflections of this shared understanding lie in the organization's mission, vision, and values statements, which can be defined as follows:

- *Mission statement.* Statement of purpose and business (primary methods)
- *Vision statement.* An image of the future we seek to create
- *Values statement.* Guiding concepts, beliefs, and principles

accessible, efficient, and effective. We strive to create and sustain an environment that inspires trust, stewardship, integrity, collaboration, and personal responsibility (values in last three sentences).

WHY DO WE NEED A MISSION STATEMENT?

Anyone coming into contact with your organization wants to know: "Who are you as an organization: Why do you exist? What do you do? Whom do you serve?" A mission statement should provide these answers. In just a few sentences, a mission statement should be able to communicate the essence of an organization to its stakeholders and to the public: one guiding set of ideas that is articulated, understood, and supported by the organization's board, staff, volunteers, donors, and collaborators. For example:

- The *American Cancer Society* is the nationwide community-based voluntary health organization dedicated to eliminating cancer as a major health problem by preventing cancer, saving lives, and diminishing suffering from cancer, through research, education, advocacy and service.

- *Lambda Legal* is a national organization committed to achieving full recognition of the civil rights of lesbians, gay men, bisexuals, the transgendered, and people with HIV or AIDS through impact litigation, education and public policy work.

- The mission of the *African American Tobacco Education Network* (AATEN) is to engage communities of color throughout California in campaigns that reduce the use of tobacco products by people of African descent. AATEN has made a commitment to the following goals in an effort to achieve this mission:
    - Increase awareness of the disproportionately adverse health consequences of tobacco use among people of African descent.
    - Increase the effectiveness of tobacco control programs targeting people of African descent.
    - Increase participation by community-based organizations, businesses and individuals in the campaign to reduce tobacco use among people of African descent.
    - Enhance leadership, develop key leaders and mobilize young people to reduce tobacco use.

Each of the previous mission statements helps the reader understand what these organizations do and why they do it. A mission statement not only clarifies to both internal and external stakeholders what you do and why you do it, but it can also help you decide what *not* to do: The American Cancer Society or the AATEN may very well consider a new education program aimed at reducing smoking among young women, but neither should consider a request to fund a major research project on reducing adult illiteracy.

In *Profiles of Excellence,*[1] Independent Sector's book about the best practices of nonprofit organizations, the researchers stress that a "clear, agreed-upon mission statement" is one of the primary characteristics of successful nonprofit organizations.

A WORD ABOUT WORDS

Words such as "mission," "purpose," and "mission statement" are not used consistently by people in either the nonprofit sector or the for-profit sector. The authors of this workbook recommend the definitions used in this section because of a bias toward being clear about both means and ends when focusing planning discussions. (See Chapter 1 for a review of ends/means differences.) Participants in the planning process should not get hung up on words, but they do need to understand the difference between the various levels of ends and means that are addressed during planning. Ultimately, it doesn't really matter what the concepts are called as long as the end product—the plan—clearly describes what the organization seeks to achieve, what it does, why it does it, and the overall priorities for the achievement of the organization's purpose. It is important that all participants in the planning process agree to call the concepts by the same name, and those definitions should be clarified during Phase 1, Get Ready.

STEP 2.1: WRITE (OR REAFFIRM OR REWRITE) YOUR MISSION STATEMENT

A mission statement should include two elements:

1. *Purpose.* One sentence that describes the ultimate result an organization is trying to achieve (answers the question "Why does the organization exist?"). A purpose sentence focuses on an end result.

2. *Business.* A statement that describes what the organization does (i.e., the primary methods (programs/services) used by the organization to achieve its purpose). Your programs and services are a means to an end. Many times within the statement of what the organization does will also be a description of for whom the service is provided.

Three examples of such mission statements are as follows:

1. *UNITY: Journalists of Color, Inc.* is a strategic alliance of journalists of color acting as a force for positive change to advance their presence, growth and leadership in the fast-changing global news industry. This alliance includes the Asian American Journalists Association, National Association of Black Journalists, the National Association of Hispanic Journalists, and the Native American Journalists Association.

    The goals of UNITY are:

    - To stem the exodus of people of color from the industry through fairer promotion practices, more representative media leadership and development of role models

    - To improve coverage of people of color by dispelling stereotypes and myths, and by increasing the understanding of other cultures

    - To educate mainstream media on the value and importance of diversity and to ensure inclusion of, and access by, people of color in diversity discussions and decisions

    - To serve as a working model of diversity and inclusiveness, and to promote UNITY's collective agenda and the individual agendas of its member organizations

    - To establish these issues as a public priority by sending a message to the news industry and to the American public.

2. Designed for three- to five-year-old children in Native American Head Start Centers and Preschools, *Native Child's* goal is to affirm the Indian child's culture and identity in a positive way through a curriculum that builds self-confidence and a sense of belonging. The resources are also developed to help non-native childhood professionals promote multicultural understanding of Native Americans for both teachers and children.

3. War causes wounds and suffering that last beyond the battlefield. The mission of *Swords to Plowshares* is to heal the wounds; to restore dignity, hope, and self-sufficiency to all veterans in need; and to significantly reduce homelessness and poverty among veterans. Founded in 1974, Swords to Plowshares is a community-based not-for-profit organization that provides counseling and case management, employment and training, housing, and legal assistance to veterans in the San Francisco Bay Area. The organization promotes and protects the rights of veterans through advocacy, public education, and partnerships with local, state, and national entities.

Create a Purpose Sentence by Identifying the Focus Problem

A purpose sentence may be developed by simply asking the question, "Why do we exist?" For example, when asked why their organization existed, members of a legal aid program responded: "to ensure equal access to legal protection under the existing laws of the federal and state government." Another organization, the Institute for Food and Development Policy—Food First, stated that they exist "to eliminate the injustices that cause hunger."

This direct approach to defining an organization's purpose may not be as easy for some organizations. Therefore, to define or clarify an organization's purpose—the ultimate result an organization is working to achieve—individuals may need to step back from the day-to-day activities and define the focus problem that the organization is trying to solve. The focus problem is the need or opportunity the organization exists to resolve, and the purpose statement describes how the world would be changed if that problem or condition were solved or improved. For example, the focus problem for a Big Brothers/Big Sisters chapter might be that "children from single-parent families are increasing in number without same-gender positive role models. These children are at a higher risk of developing adjustment/delinquency problems than children with same-gender positive role models." The ideal future impact if the problem was solved would be "that every little brother or sister will become a happy, productive member of society." The purpose of one Big Brothers/Big Sisters Chapter reads: "to decrease the problems experienced by children in single-parent families."

Why Is Clarifying Purpose Important?

Failure to state and communicate clearly an organization's purpose (in ends terminology) can lead an organization to inadvertently restrict its effectiveness. For example, one program whose stated purpose was "to provide counseling to youth ages 13–18" (a narrow means statement) inadvertently shut off any hope of innovation by too narrowly restricting the scope of its programs and vision. Because its focus was only on counseling, the staff and board were limiting the impact of the organization's work. They rewrote their purpose to reflect an end statement: "to increase the mental health of youth in our county." With a broader focus, they expanded their vision to include new programs such as a crisis hotline, after-school programs, and workshops on coping with stress.

A too broadly defined purpose can leave an organization unable to prioritize program activities. A local community organization had long owned a building within which it provided several small programs and a much-used large meeting room. By renting out the meeting room to other community groups, the organization received a small but steady income. As long as the purpose statement was vaguely defined as "meeting the needs of the community," renting out the room took a higher priority over new activities because it was a revenue-generating activity. A strategic planning process led the organization to sharpen its focus on meeting the cultural needs of the local South Asian community. As a result, many new uses were found for the meeting space involving youth groups, senior citizen cultural activities, and programs celebrating the South Asian culture targeted at the general public. Because of the importance of these activities to the organization's purpose, new funding was acquired to offset the loss of the rental income and in the process making much better use of one of the organization's primary assets: its building.

Different understandings of purpose can lead to confusion and conflict. A battered women's shelter was asked by a funder to develop a program for men who were batterers. The organization's board and staff were strongly divided into two camps: those individuals who wanted the new program and those who did not. When a consultant was brought in to facilitate the conflict, she asked the group to tell her what the purpose of the organization was. Some individuals stated that they felt that the purpose was "to provide shelter to battered women and their children." Others stated that the organization's purpose was "to eliminate the cycle of violence in the family." Not surprisingly, those who most felt that the new program fit within the organization's purpose were also the ones who stated that the end result of their work was the elimination of violence in the family and that it made sense to provide services to men who were batterers.

After much discussion, the battered women's shelter rewrote its purpose sentence to read: "our purpose is to reduce—and work toward the elimination of—violence in the family." Interesting enough, the group chose not to develop and implement the program for men who were batterers because they did not feel they had a core competence in that arena. They did, however, identify a men's organization and assisted them in the development of an antiviolence program for men who had been convicted of domestic violence.

Finally, an organization may not realize when it is time to go out of business or change its purpose. For example, the initial purpose of the March of Dimes was "to eliminate polio." Because the purpose statement was clear, once polio was eliminated, the organization had to choose whether to go out of business or to refocus its mission. The board of

SIDEBAR

The Example of Alice

Lewis Carroll's Alice's Adventures in Wonderland speaks indirectly to the importance of mission statements:

> Said Alice, "Cheshire Puss . . . would you tell me, please, which way I ought to go from here?"
>
> "That depends a good deal on where you want to get to," said the Cat.
>
> "I don't much care where—" said Alice.
>
> "Then it doesn't matter which way you go," said the Cat.
>
> "—so long as I get somewhere," Alice added as an explanation.
>
> "Oh, you're sure to do that," said the Cat, "if you only walk long enough."

Source: Lewis Carroll, *Alice's Adventures in Wonderland* (London: William Heinemann Ltd., 1907), 75–76).

directors of the March of Dimes chose to change the purpose of the March of Dimes to the broader effort "to eliminate birth defects."

Write a Purpose Sentence

The purpose component of the mission statement explains the solution the organization seeks to accomplish with respect to a focus problem. It describes, in one sentence, why the organization exists—the end result of its efforts (i.e., what the organization aspires to achieve). A purpose sentence usually includes two basic elements:

1. An infinitive verb that indicates a change in status (such as to increase, to decrease, to eliminate, to prevent, etc.)

2. An identification of the problem to be addressed or condition to be changed (such as access to healthcare, public policy on the environment, cultural assets in the community). For example: "to decrease (infinitive) infant mortality rates in our city (problem)."

Following are examples of purpose sentences:

- The purpose of The SETI League, Inc. is to encourage and support the search for extra-terrestrial intelligence.
- The Coral Reef Alliance (CORAL) promotes coral reef conservation around the world.
- The Restless Legs Syndrome Foundation is a nonprofit 501(c)(3) agency that is dedicated to improving the lives of men, women, and children who live with this often-devastating disease. The organization's goals are to increase awareness of Restless Legs Syndrome (RLS), to improve treatments, and, through research, to find a cure.

Note that these examples focus on outcomes and results rather than methods. They describe how the world is going to be different—what the organization intends to change. Thus, the purpose of an agency serving the homeless should not be described in terms of its method "to provide shelter for homeless individuals." The purpose should be described in terms of a broader end result, such as "to eliminate the condition of homelessness in our region."

SIDEBAR

From Focus Problem to Ideal Future to Purpose Statement

- *Identify focus problem.* Youth who are involved in the juvenile justice system, homeless, inner-city dwellers, poor, or otherwise at risk have special needs for their physical and emotional well-being. Among the issues these youth face in their environment are violence, racism, sexism, poverty, lack of education, and substance abuse. These factors are often obstacles to accessing and utilizing services effectively, as well as elements that affect their higher rates of morbidity and mortality.

- *Articulate ideal future impact if the problem were to be solved.* In concert with the constellation of service providers who work with these youth, it is necessary to have quality comprehensive health care designed to meet their special needs.

- *Draft the purpose sentence.* Improve the health of at-risk youth.

Summarize Your Business

"What business are you in?" is the way a colleague of ours raises this question. Where the purpose sentence is an ends statement, the business or statement of program methods should be a summary statement about means. Program statements often include the verb "to provide," or link a purpose statement with the words "by" or "through."

For example, if the purpose of a youth-serving agency is to improve the health of at-risk youth, the organization must define what methods the organization will use to pursue that purpose, such as "offer direct medical services, counseling, and health education to youth at Juvenile Hall."

An organization whose purpose is to eliminate homelessness might choose one or more of the following methods: constructing housing for homeless individuals, advocating for changes in public policy, and/or providing counseling and job training to homeless individuals.

Try the exercise in Exhibit 3.1 to help your organization determine the difference between ends and means.

EXHIBIT 3.1   DISTINGUISHING BETWEEN PURPOSE (ENDS) AND PROGRAM (MEANS)

Examine the statements in this table. Which are statements of purpose (ends) and which are statements of programs (means)?

Statements	Ends	Means
1. Eliminate the causes of birth defects		
2. Provide counseling and support to victims of crime		
3. Make a profit—increase shareholder wealth		
4. To assure that comprehensive, culturally acceptable personal and public health services are available and accessible to American Indian and Alaska Native people		
5. Conduct biomedical research		
6. Heal the wounds of crime		
7. Increase the mental health of our clients		
8. Provide leadership training and legal assistance to migrant workers		
9. Decrease the problems of single-parent children		
10. Provide food and shelter to the homeless		

If you identified statement numbers 1, 3, 4, 6, 7, and 9 as purpose statements, you understand the difference between purpose (ends) and programs/services (means).

Clarify Purpose (Ends) and Business (Means)

Logically, it makes sense to define your purpose before you define your program. However, sometimes it is easier for people to relate to what the organization does because that is more visible.

What Is the Means (Business)?	Why? To What End (Purpose)?
We build housing.	We build housing in order to decrease homeless.
We put on art shows featuring artists who are developmentally disabled.	Our mission is to increase the visibility of artists with developmental disabilities.

If it helps to talk about what you do and then why you do it as a way of helping to clarify your mission statement, then whatever order works best for your group is the right way to go!

Put the Components of a Mission Statement Together

The mission statement, when completed, should be a simple yet powerful and inspiring statement that communicates to both internal and external stakeholders what the organization is all about. The mission statement can be one or two sentences long, or it can be longer. Keep in mind that the briefer the statement, the easier it is for board and staff members to remember it. Some examples of effective mission statements include the following:

- *East Bay Habitat for Humanity.* Inspired by God's love, our mission is to create successful homeownership opportunities (purpose) for families with limited incomes (for whom) by building sustainable housing and revitalizing neighborhoods (business).

- *The John D. and Catherine T. MacArthur Foundation* is a private, independent grantmaking institution dedicated to helping groups and individuals foster lasting improvement in the human condition (for whom). The Foundation seeks the development of healthy individuals and effective communities; peace within and among nations; responsible choices about human reproduction; and a global ecosystem capable of supporting healthy human societies (purposes). The Foundation pursues this mission by supporting research, policy development, dissemination, education and training, and practice (business).

- *The Hispanic Chamber of Commerce (HCCAC)* seeks to improve the quality of life (purpose) by providing leadership and promoting Economic Development (business) for the Latino Community (for whom) through partnerships with other community, business, educational, and governmental organizations.

There is no simple formula for efficiently drafting a definitive mission statement for an organization. In *Reinventing Government,*[2] the authors state that "the experience of hashing out the fundamental purpose of an organization—debating all the different assumptions and views held by its members and agreeing on one basic mission—can be a powerful one. When it is done right, a mission statement can drive an entire organization from top to bottom. It can help people at all levels decide what they should do and what they should stop doing." The process of creating a mission statement usually takes considerable time, but the effort is almost always worth the end result.

What's the Difference between a Mission Statement and a Slogan?

A brief phrase, such as "the world on time," is something for-profit companies use frequently in their marketing communications. It is not necessary, but if you can develop such a phrase, it can be a helpful way of communicating the essence of an organization in a catchy way.

The purpose sentence for most organizations can serve as the short mission statement, or sometimes an organization has a slogan (which also may be known as a motto or tag line) that is used when a few words can say it all. For example:

Seeds of Peace works to secure lasting peace in the Middle East by bringing together Arab and Israeli teenagers, aged 13 to 15, before their fear, mistrust, and prejudices have permanently shaped their vision of their "enemy." Seeds of Peace begins where international agreements end, dispelling fear in the hearts and minds of the next generation and preparing them for the arduous task of peacemaking. By nurturing lasting friendships the program makes it possible for these youngsters to become the Seeds from which an enduring peace will grow.

Their compelling slogan is, "Empowering Children of War to Break the Cycles of Violence."

While a slogan may be compelling (e.g., "Caring for the Land and Serving People"), it is *not* a substitute for a mission statement. A slogan alone often leaves the reader with little understanding of what the organization actually does: "Caring for the Land and Serving People" is the motto of the U.S. Department of Agriculture's Forest Service.

Worksheet 5 (see process notes in Exhibit 3.2) can be used to create a mission statement—each question can be discussed in a larger group, or individuals can be asked to fill out the mission statement worksheet in advance and bring to a meeting for discussion.

Mission Statement	Slogan/Tag Line
The mission of Audubon-California is to conserve and restore California's natural ecosystems, focusing on birds, other wildlife, and their habitats for the benefit of humanity and the earth's biological diversity. By connecting people with nature, Audubon-California will be the leader in creating a powerful California voice for the environment, deeply rooted in and broadly drawn from all parts of our population. By informing and involving people with nature where they live, Audubon-California will equip the people of California to actively and effectively conserve their ecological heritage.	"Connecting people with nature."
The mission of the Haight Ashbury Free Clinics, Inc. is to increase access to healthcare for all and improve the health and well being of our clients. Haight Ashbury Free Clinics provides free, high quality, demystified and comprehensive health care that is culturally sensitive, non-judgmental and accessible to all in need.	"Health care is a right not a privilege."
The mission of the Alliance for Technology Access (ATA) is to increase the use of technology by children and adults with disabilities and functional limitations. Through public education, information and referral, capacity building in community organizations and advocacy/public policy efforts, the ATA enables millions of people to live, learn, work, define their futures, and achieve their dreams.	"Using the power of technology to transform lives, build communities, and expand opportunities."

EXHIBIT 3.2   WORKSHEET 5: CREATE A MISSION
                STATEMENT

Process Notes

How to do this activity	Two options:
	1. Have board and staff fill out Worksheet 6 in advance of a planning retreat and then discuss the key components at a retreat.
	2. Have one or two designated writers from the planning committee review the current mission statement (if the organization has one), redraft it as necessary, and present it first to the planning committee, then to board and staff for feedback.
Why do this activity	Clarity about your mission statement is vital. You need to know where you are going before you can figure out how to get there. Expect to go through a few drafts before getting one that everyone likes.
Who to involve in the process	Input from board and staff (and possibly other key stakeholders); one or two people write the draft(s). Formal approval of the mission statement by the board of directors.

See ASO/USA's example of this worksheet at the end of this chapter. Blank worksheets are provided in Appendix A and on the CD that accompanies this book.

SIDEBAR

Role of Groups in Crafting Mission Statements

Note: In writing a mission statement, it is useful to realize that although groups are good at many things, writing is not one of them. Staff, board, and planning committee members might all participate in generating and discussing ideas, but it usually proves most efficient to leave one or two planning committee members in charge of actually getting the words on paper.

One way to start the process is to discuss the key components of the mission statement (either revisions to the organization's current statement or the creation of a new one) at a board or staff retreat. A broad preliminary discussion of the concepts to be included in the statement will quickly demonstrate areas of consensus and disagreement.

The designated planning committee members might then write a first draft of the statement and redraft it as it goes through the process of review, discussion, refinement, and final approval by the board of directors. Furthermore, as a result of assessing the environment or discussing the strategic issues facing the organization, the mission statement may need to be revised. However, a draft of a working mission statement should serve as a basis for guiding the discussions and decisions.

While the planning committee is primarily responsible for hammering out the details of the mission statement's format and wording, the evolving draft should also be circulated several times through board, staff, and sometimes other stakeholders as well.

Some consultants also advise organizations to seek an outside opinion from someone who is unfamiliar with the organization to gauge how accessible the statement is to the uninitiated. The great advantage of hashing over the statement in this way is that the discussion and debate introduces newcomers to the nuances of the organization's mission, refreshes old-timers' understanding, fosters stakeholders' sense of participation and commitment, and results in a mission statement that genuinely expresses a collective intention and common ideas.

With a measure of passion, humanity, and an eye on the big picture, a planning committee can keep refining the mission statement until it has a version that stakeholders can actively support.

STEP 2.2: WRITE YOUR VISION STATEMENT

The word "vision" has almost lost its meaning over the last ten years, due to the faddishness surrounding vision and mission statements. But *vision* is not a new word. We are told in Proverbs 29:18, "Where there is no vision, the people perish." It is hard to see an idea from the Old Testament as just a management fad.[3] So writes best-selling author Peter Senge on the topic of vision statements.

A vision is a guiding image of success. In architectural terms, if a mission statement provides a blueprint for an organization's work—the what, why, and for whom—then the vision is the artist's rendering of the realization of that mission. Whereas a mission statement answers the questions about why the organization exists and what program(s) it offers, a vision statement answers the question, "What will success look like?" The pursuit of this shared image of success motivates people to work together. For example:

Hawai`i Community Foundation
Our Vision

We want to live in a Hawai`i where people care about each other, our natural resources and diverse island cultures—a place where people's ideas, initiatives, and generosity support thriving, responsible communities.

Our Mission

The Hawai`i Community Foundation helps people make a difference by inspiring the spirit of giving and by investing in people and solutions to benefit every island community.

Vision statements can and should be inspirational. Martin Luther King, Jr., said, "I have a dream," and then offered a vision that changed a nation. That famous speech is a dramatic example of the power that can be generated by a person who communicates a compelling vision of the future. Although John F. Kennedy did not live to see his vision for NASA come to fruition, he set it in motion when he said, "By the end of the decade, we will put a man on the moon." When it came time to appropriate the enormous funds necessary to accomplish this vision, Congress did not hesitate. Why? Because this vision spoke powerfully to values the American people held dear: America as a pioneer and America as a world leader.

An organizational vision statement might not put a man on the moon, but it should be compelling in the same way that Kennedy's and King's visions were: It should challenge and inspire the group to stretch its capabilities and achieve its purpose.

The *external vision* focuses on how the world will be improved if the organization achieves its purpose. Too often, vision statements merely focus on the internal vision—what the organization would look like some time in the future ("We will have doubled the staff we have now"; "We will have our own building"). But these statements avoid answering the question: "To what end?" Why should we have doubled the staff? Why do we need our own building?

The focus of an effective external vision statement should first be on the client to be served or the constituency whose lives are to be impacted by the organization. For example:

- All people in our state will have access to quality health care, regardless of ability to pay. (Health Care for All, Inc.)

- The Julia Morgan Center for the Arts seeks to change people's lives by making art a common experience of everyday life and learning.

- We, the citizens of Oakland, commit ourselves to creating a city of healthy, well-educated people; safe, vital neighborhoods, a dynamic economy; and a vibrant quilt of cultures where the future will work for all. (Oakland Sharing the Vision)

Whereas the external vision defines how the organization plans to change the world, the *internal vision* describes what the organization will look like when it is operating effectively and efficiently to support the achievement of that external vision. The internal vision describes the ultimate scope and scale of programs and services, the organization's image or reputation, funding, partnerships, use of technology, board, staff, and facilities.

Examples of internal vision statements are as follows:

- We will have a 100, 000-square-foot gallery that has all the great neon artworks of the twentieth century on display. (Museum of Neon Art)

- All victims of felony assaults in Oklahoma County will receive information and counseling from a staff member or volunteer within 24 hours of their assault. (Victim's Assistance Fund)

- The Chorus will be the best gay men's chorus in the world and the equal of any performing arts organization in San Francisco, and will be a leader in the development of gay culture and gay pride in the United States. (San Francisco Gay Men's Chorus)

- We will achieve a diversified funding base, which will adequately support all of our programs. (Every nonprofit organization the authors have ever worked with!)

Examples of vision statements that include both an external and internal component include:

- *CompassPoint Nonprofit Services*. Nonprofits serve as agents of democratic involvement, innovation, and positive social change. Our organization's leadership and services are local, regional, and national in scope, and support the growth of an effective nonprofit sector essential to health communities.

- *Alliance for Technology Access*
  External vision statement—ATA and its members strive to help create a world in which:
    ○ All people with disabilities have ongoing and effective use of critical technology tools that are adaptable, accessible, affordable, and available, along with the training and support necessary to integrate these tools into their lives.

- Tools for living, learning and working are being developed that accommodate the greatest range of users, including those with functional limitations.

- People with disabilities are equipped to advocate for and have access to quality, culturally-sensitive, consumer-directed, and co-ordinated technology services in their communities making it easy for them to select, acquire and use technologies.

- Technology is demystified and seen as a critical tool for people with disabilities.

- People with disabilities and the general public understand the power of technology for people with disabilities and functional limitations and the importance of universal design in the development of all tools, services, media, and environments.

Internal vision statement—what we strive to maintain or achieve:

- ATA supports a dynamic network of organizations, individuals and companies who work collaboratively to ensure that cutting-edge technology is adaptable, accessible, affordable, available, and widely used.

- ATA supports and encourages members to connect with needed programs, services, and providers in their communities, so that people can access coordinated, quality services.

- ATA members have the skills, expertise and resources to meet the needs of individuals in their communities for excellent, quality, and culturally-sensitive services. These programs assist people in finding out about technology tools and resources to acquire them, and give people opportunities to test them out and learn how to use them.

- ATA is a growing national organization that works to bring local and regional concerns to national audiences. It is sufficiently funded and well connected. It maintains a large membership base with wide geographic representation, and is well known and widely respected by diverse players such as: policy makers, technology developers, parents, people with disabilities, the media, professionals, funders, service networks, and the business community.

○ ATA is a learning organization that is growing as quickly as the technology is changing, influencing the use of universal design principles, building expertise, providing training to insure members stay on cutting edge of trends in access technology.

○ ATA is a respected and powerful voice in the development of policies at the national level that result in increased support for direct assistive technology services, and access to technology programs and supports that serve the public.

Draft a Vision Statement

Like the mission statement, drafting a vision statement begins with intuition and ideas, evolves through discussion, and results in a shared sense of direction and motivation. All board and staff members should be involved in initial brainstorming and some subsequent discussion; the planning committee should more fully engage in the process. As with any such process, differing ideas don't have to be a problem: People can spur each other on to more daring and valuable ideas—dreams of changing the world that they are willing to work hard for, encouraging each other to dream the possible. As with the mission statement, the organization will probably refer back to its vision statement throughout the planning process and may modify it as it becomes clearer where the organization can and should be in the future.

SIDEBAR

Headline News

A powerful exercise is to ask individuals to write a headline that describes their vision of success for the future. Examples of headlines include:

- "Curb Cuts Happen—local disability organization successfully advocates for the city to make it easier for people in wheelchairs to negotiate city streets"
- "Supreme Court Upholds Right of Same-Sex Couples to Marry"
- "Dropout Rate Decreases to All-time Low"
- "Audubon-California Celebrates Opening of 20th New Nature Education Center"

The following is a description of the process to use. Ask each participant at a planning retreat to answer or respond to the following questions.

It's five years (or ten years) from now and our organization has just been written up in a major publication:

- What would the headline be saying about our organization?
- What would be a featured quote about the organization, and who would be saying it?
- Write a headline and two or three bullets that would serve as the outline for a sidebar story about our organization.
- Draw a picture or describe a photo that would appear in the publication (include a caption).

The challenge is to create a vision that is grand enough to inspire people, but also a vision that is grounded in sufficient reality that people can start to believe that it can and will happen. No Olympic athlete ever got to the Olympics by accident; a compelling vision of his or her stellar performance helped surmount all of the sweat and frustrations for many years. Without that powerful, attractive, valuable vision, why bother? Sometimes organizations far surpass their initial visions; as progress happens, what is possible expands. Nonetheless, the picture we carry around to remind us of why we are working so hard continues to inspire this success.

The Value of Using a Visioning Process during the Strategic Planning Process

The creation of a vision statement and the process of visioning cannot only help inspire board and staff, but can also be used as a basis for setting priorities. The visioning exercise can be referred to during Phase 4 (Agree on Priorities) to provide guidance to defining the ideal scope and scale of services and products. Visioning can help the organization be better able to answer the following questions:

- What services and products should we be offering now and in the future that would best enable us to achieve our external vision of the future?

- Should we make changes in the services or products we are currently offering or how we go about doing our business so as to be better able to achieve our preferred future?

Likewise, the internal vision statement could be used to clarify what the organization would need to do from a management and operations perspective to ensure that an infrastructure was in place to support the effective and efficient provision of goods and services to meet the needs of clients and customers. The internal vision can be used during the setting priorities phase as a basis for looking at some of these questions:

- What should be our long-term and short-term priorities regarding staffing, benefits, board, facilities, funding, partnerships, management, and financial information systems?

- What do we need to do now and in the next three years to distinguish us from our competition and to ensure that we are known and respected by our clients and the community?

- What can we do to increase cooperation and networking with agencies doing similar work so that limited resources are used in the most effective and efficient way?

SIDEBAR

Suggested Visioning Exercise

During a retreat, put up a series of large, easel-size wall charts, scattered around the room. Pick three to six questions for the exercise—there should be one wall chart for each question. Sample visioning questions follow:

- How will the world be improved if we were successful in achieving our purpose?

- What are the most important services that we should continue to provide, change, or begin to offer in the next three years?

- What staffing and benefits changes do we need to implement to better achieve our purpose?

- How can our board of directors increase their value to our organization?

- What changes in resource development (fundraising) do we need to implement to better achieve our purpose?

- What facilities and technology changes do we need to implement to better achieve our purpose?
- What infrastructure, systems, or communication changes do we need to implement to better achieve our purpose?
- How could we more effectively or efficiently provide our services? If you could only make three changes to increase our ability to serve our clients/customers, what would those changes be?
- What makes us unique (distinguishes us from the competition)?
- What do our clients/customers consider most important in our provision of services? What do our clients/customers need from us?

Divide the retreat participants into groups of three to six members and give each group 30 three-by-five-inch sticky notes. Have each group fill out no more than three sticky notes for each question. When each group is finished, their responses to the questions should be posted on the wall charts. Individuals should be encouraged to walk about the room and read everyone's responses.

After some discussion, one or two people can begin to draft a vision statement.

Regardless of whether an organization is involved in an abbreviated, moderate, or extensive planning process, these questions need to be answered. The process of visioning can provide a framework for answering those questions and therefore provide guidance in making the choices as to how an organization might best accomplish its purpose. Worksheet 6 (see process notes in Exhibit 3.3) encourages you to dare to dream the possible by articulating your internal and external visions of success. ASO/USA's visioning process provides a good example of the creation of this framework.

STEP 2.3: ARTICULATE THE FUNDAMENTAL VALUES THAT GUIDE YOUR WORK

Nonprofit organizations are known for being values–driven. Spelling out the values the organization supports helps tap the passion of individuals

EXHIBIT 3.3   WORKSHEET 6: CREATE A VISION
STATEMENT

Process Notes

How to do this activity	Visioning is a powerful activity to do at a meeting of board and staff.
	Distribute the vision statement worksheet to participants in advance of the retreat and ask them to describe their external and internal vision of success. If the number of participants at the meeting is small, have people read their visions and record key ideas on easel paper (both where there is agreement and where there is disagreement); if a large group, break into smaller groups and work as teams.
	You may need to refine or change this initial vision statement after you have completed Phase 3 and Phase 4 of the planning process.
Why do this activity	An inspiring shared image of success will galvanize the efforts of your organization's staff and board and help start defining program and organizational strategies, goals, and objectives.
Who to involve in the process	Ideally, all board and staff should have some opportunity to give input into the organization's vision statement. The planning committee would review that input and designate one or two people to craft a powerful vision statement that could be included in your plan.

See ASO/USA's example of this worksheet at the end of this chapter. Blank worksheets are provided in Appendix A and on the CD that accompanies this book.

and align the heart with the head. Values usually focus on service, quality, people, and work norms. For example:

- Integrity, quality, and excellence in service provision must always be maintained.

- Individuals should be empowered to make educated decisions about their health choices.

- We are client-centered.

Values might also include related beliefs, such as a vegetarian association's assertion that "eating vegetables is more economically efficient and ecologically responsible than eating beef."

Other examples of values, beliefs, assumptions, and guiding principles include:

- Self-confidence is not taught or learned; it is earned by surpassing your own self-set limitations. (Outward Bound)

- Understanding the world geographically as a youth is a prerequisite to acting with global responsibility as an adult. (National Geographic Association)

- The vitality of life depends on the continued addition of new perspectives, new beliefs, and new wisdom. (Yerba Buena Center for the Arts)

Examples of Values Statements

People to People International is an organization whose mission is "enhancing cross-cultural communication within each community, and across communities and nations." Their stated beliefs include:

- We believe that greater understanding between individuals and peoples, worldwide, reveals universal values and aspirations.

- We believe international educational and cultural exchange among youth further ensures long-term friendship and understanding.

- We believe we all benefit from sharing different approaches to solving common problems.

- We believe that individuals can often be more effective than governments in promoting human relationships and world peace.

- We believe if people can better understand other cultures, they are more tolerant and accepting of differences.

- We believe that citizens of all countries need personal contacts with other peoples and cultures.

- We need to ensure the enduring legacy of People to People International.

- We believe that People to People is fun! We believe in people!

Planned Parenthood believes in the fundamental right of each individual, throughout the world, to manage his or her fertility, regardless of the individual's income, marital status, race, ethnicity, sexual orientation, age, national origin, or residence.

- We believe that respect and value for diversity in all aspects of our organization are essential to our well-being.

- We believe that reproductive self-determination must be voluntary and preserve the individual's right to privacy.

- We further believe that such self-determination will contribute to an enhancement of the quality of life, strong family relationships, and population stability.

Sustainable Conservation is committed to an approach that combines business strategies with environmental priorities to find common ground and forge long-lasting solutions that work for everyone, because the environment is everyone's business. Their mission statement is, "Sustainable Conservation advances the stewardship of natural resources using innovative, pragmatic strategies that actively engage businesses and private landowners in conservation."

- It is society's ethical imperative (responsibility) to protect the environment.

- Incentives are powerful motivators for shifting behaviors of businesses and private landowners to ones that achieve conservation.

- Partnerships across all sectors build trust between parties and provide support for implementing change.

- We are pragmatic, problem solvers with a commitment to innovation.

- Success for us is measurable results from our projects that improve the environment.

- We respect the perspectives and priorities of businesses, private landowners, government agencies, other environmental groups and one another.

Why Are Values and Principles So Important?

Be great in act, as you have been in thought. Suit the action to the word and word to the action.

—William Shakespeare

Core values of an organization exist, whether spoken or not, but in most successful organizations, they are made explicit and are debated and updated from time to time. Ideally, the personal values of staff, as well as external constituents and supporters, will align with the values of the organization. When developing a written statement of the organization's values, stakeholders can contribute to the articulation of these values and evaluate how well their personal values and motivations match those of the organization. This process will help build stakeholders' commitment to the organization and strengthen alignment between individuals and institutions. Explicit values also help in recruiting and selecting staff and board members who share the values of the organization.

One valuable exercise that can be undertaken during this phase is to perform a *gap analysis* between the organization's current values being modeled with the core values that an organization wishes to personify.[4] This is especially important if an organization's staff is operating with a different set of values than what they wish to personify in the future. The strategic plan then becomes the vehicle to bridge the gap between what is and what they wish to be.

SIDEBAR

Putting New Values into Practice

HOPE Rehabilitation Services, an organization whose purpose is "to enhance the quality of life of individuals with disabilities and their families," articulated within its strategic plan such values as "empowering clients to be the best they can be, valuing family, and placing high value of honesty, ethics, integrity, respect, equality, and commitment."

During a planning retreat, HOPE's planning consultant suggested a process that would support a fundamental shift in how HOPE did business. The process entailed board and staff members articulating

(continues)

old mental models, mindsets, and assumptions they would like to discard, and replacing them with the new mental models they would like to embrace.

Old mental models, mindsets, and assumptions we'd like to discard (abbreviated list):

- We'll do what we need to do to get by.
- We focus on disabilities rather than abilities.
- Government should give HOPE money because we run good programs.
- The staff knows what is best and makes decisions for clients.

HOPE's new mental models we'd like to embrace (abbreviated list):

- HOPE Rehabilitation Services is driven by a "quality first" mentality with regard to internal and external customers.
- We focus on abilities rather than disabilities.
- HOPE is more independent and self-reliant—it operates as a business.
- Clients are involved and make their own decisions.

The board and staff of one organization, *Support for Families of Children with Disabilities,* felt so strongly that they wanted to "practice what they believed in" that they wrote down the "practical impact—commitments to practice everyday" that would put their values into action. Some (three of six are included here) of their principles and behaviors in action include:

- *Diversity.* Disabilities cut across all ethnic, linguistic and socioeconomic groups. We will endeavor to bring together the different groups with the understanding that working together, we can make systems change.

  Practical Impact—What We Commit to Doing in Everyday Practice:

  ○ Reflect diversity, not only in the people we serve but also in our staff, our volunteers and our board.

  ○ Actively seek involvement from diverse groups in all of our activities.

  ○ Provide information, education and parent-to-parent services that are linguistically and culturally responsive.

  ○ Consistently provide written materials in the languages of the families we serve.

  ○ Consistently provide presentations and trainings in the languages of the families we serve.

  ○ Consistently provide interpreters at trainings, clinics, and so on.

- *Collaboration.* Whenever possible we will work with other individuals, agencies, and systems in order to broaden and enhance our ability to serve families.

  Practical Impact — What We Commit to Doing in Everyday Practice:

  ○ Take time to think about involving others when developing new projects and actively seek their involvement.

  ○ Provide information, education and parent-to-parent services with an attitude that diverging perspectives can work together.

  ○ Include the materials and activities of others in our newsletter, at our drop-in center, etc.

  ○ Keep our partners informed of our activities, and make an effort to seek their input.

- *Grass Roots.* We are committed to being family-centered, parent-directed, peer-led and volunteer-energized.

  Practical Impact — What We Commit to Doing in Everyday Practice:

  ○ Ensure that the Board has 51% representation of the community we serve (i.e., 51% parents and individuals with disabilities).

  ○ Ensure that the staff who provide direct support are representative of the community we serve.

  ○ Implement focus groups and surveys to ensure that families and professionals have input on current services as well as potential services.

Write Your Organization's Values, Beliefs, and Guiding Principles

It is always more difficult the first time around for a board and staff to define — and agree on — the values, beliefs, and guiding principles that many times had been implied. A strategic planning process is an excellent opportunity to make explicit those implied values, or to reaffirm the values, beliefs, and guiding principles that were previously developed in past strategic planning efforts. Worksheet 7 provides a framework for defining values, beliefs, and guiding principles, as well as for the behaviors that support those guiding principles being practiced (see process notes in Exhibit 3.4).

Be prepared to have some heartfelt debates during the discussion of the organization's values and beliefs. This activity evokes strong feelings and emotions; most people are not neutral about their beliefs, and this is not really about an organization's beliefs, but rather individuals' beliefs, and most individuals feel strongly about their core values. Take your time, clarify where there is agreement and where there is disagreement, and strive to reach agreement on your core values and beliefs. It is important to reach consensus on these guiding principles because they are the foundation of your work.

| EXHIBIT 3.4 | WORKSHEET 7: ARTICULATE YOUR ORGANIZATION'S VALUES, BELIEFS, AND GUIDING PRINCIPLES |

Process Notes

| How to do this activity | At either a retreat or separate staff and board meetings, distribute copies of the blank worksheet and ask individuals to write the values, beliefs, and/or guiding principles that they believe are the foundation upon which you do your work. If the number of participants at the meeting is small, have people read their list and record key ideas on butcher paper; if a large group, break into small groups and work as teams. Facilitate discussions to identify where there is agreement and if there is some areas of disagreement. Where there is disagreement, develop a process to discuss differences and what such differences mean for ability of staff and board to work together and support the mission. |

EXHIBIT 3.4	WORSHEET 7: ARTICULATE YOUR ORGANIZATION'S VALUES, BELIEFS, AND GUIDING PRINCIPLES *(Continued)*

Process Notes

How to do this activity	Once there is agreement as to values, beliefs, and guiding principles, a list of supporting behaviors should be developed, either at the meeting or by an ad-hoc task force.
Why do this activity	Making explicit values of the organization is important for building the board and staff's commitment to the organization as well as supporting alignment between behaviors of individuals and the values that the organization's staff and board professes to uphold.
Who to involve in the process	All board and staff members should ideally be involved in developing and supporting the organization's values.

See ASO/USA's example of this worksheet at the end of this chapter. Blank worksheets are provided in Appendix A and on the CD that accompanies this book.

SIDEBAR

Difference Between Values and Beliefs, Assumptions, and Guiding Principles

The purpose of Squeezebox Synthesis is to promote accordions as a vital cultural link between the past, present, and the future.

- *Value and belief statements.* Culture is essential to a fully lived life. It is a good thing for people to understand their roots.
- *Assumptions.* Accordions help people find their European roots. An accordion is a maligned and misunderstood instrument.
- *Guiding principles.* At every concert we will spend time teaching people about the historical roots of the accordion, even people who make fun of accordions are to be treated respectfully and kindly.

CAUTIONS TO FACILITATORS

- Mission, vision, and values discussions can stir as many debates about the way to say something as about the ideas. Depending on the organizational experience of different planning committee members (nonprofit, business, etc.), people may come into the process with conflicting expectations.

- People have different experiences regarding what should be included in a mission statement and definition of terms such as purpose, mission, and so on. Get agreement upfront on the use of language. Don't get hung up on what to call things, but do make sure that whatever you call it, you end up with a description of both what the organization does and why it does it.

- Agree on the format of the statements the committee will create before writing the final statements. There are numerous right choices including the following:

  - Expected length: Some organization's mission statements can be succinctly written in one or two sentences; some organization's mission statements are much longer.

  - Full sentences or phrases

  - Separate mission and vision statements

  - Separate page of values and beliefs statements

  - A mission statement that includes a statement of vision or a separate statement of vision

  Whatever format is chosen, the end product should be understandable, jargon free if possible, inspirational, and accurate.

- Another source of tension can come between people who want idealistic statements and those who prefer a more realistic orientation. There is no right answer; the facilitator can help by bringing to light these kinds of tensions so that the group may resolve them effectively.

- If an organization does rewrite a mission statement, pamphlets, Web sites, and other communications should also be updated. If an organization dramatically changes its purpose, its by-laws may need to be revised.

ENDNOTES

1. E.B. Knauft, Renee Berger, and Sandra Gray, for the Independent Sector, *Profiles of Excellence* (San Francisco: Jossey-Bass, 1991).

2. David Osbourne and Ted Gaebler, *Reinventing Government* (Reading, MA: Addison-Wesley, 1992), pp. 130–131.

3. Peter Senge, "Leadership in Living Organizations" (based on his best-selling book *The Fifth Discipline*) in *Leading Beyond Walls* (San Francisco: Jossey-Bass, 1999).

4. Karl Albrecht, *The Northbound Train: Finding the Purpose, Setting the Direction, Shaping the Destiny of Your Organization* (New York: American Management Association, 1994), p. 159.

CASE STUDY—ASO/USA

❏ Draft a mission statement for your organization (please write legibly if filling out by hand).

What is the focus problem(s) that our organization exists to solve?
(In considering the focus problem or need, you might want to consider the following questions: What need or opportunity does our organization exist to resolve? Who is affected by the problem? How are they affected? If we were successful, what impact would we have regarding this problem?)

AIDS and HIV have greatly impacted our society. Greater attention must be spent not only on educating and supporting people to prevent HIV infection, but also in helping people who are living with HIV. Many low income and homeless people, and injection drug users are not being reached, due to barriers to receiving health and social services, such as discrimination, lack of insurance, and the fact that meeting daily basic needs often takes priority over dealing with issues such as HIV prevention or HIV treatment. In addition, there is a continued need to do aggressive prevention work within marginalized communities. If we were successful, we would have substantially prevented the spread of HIV in our community, and people living with HIV/AIDS would be able to lead quality productive lives. Ultimately we would like HIV/AIDS to be eradicated and we would go out of business.

What are the assumptions upon which our organization does its work?

- *HIV-positive people from marginalized communities—low-income people, people of color, injection drug users, and other disenfranchised people — have the lowest access to treatment services.*

- *People living with HIV/AIDS have specialized needs that AIDS service organizations are in the best position to be able to meet.*

- *All of our programs must be culturally sensitive, linguistically appropriate, and accessible to individuals regardless of class, racial/ethnic background, sexual orientation, and physical abilities.*

- *We believe we can make a real difference in this epidemic through a focus on direct services (care and treatment for people living with HIV/AIDS), prevention activities, and advocacy.*

What is the purpose of our organization?
(A purpose sentence answers the question of why an organization exists; it does not describe what an organization does. The sentence should be a short succinct statement that describes the ultimate result an organization is hoping to achieve. When writing a purpose sentence, make sure to indicate outcomes and

results [e.g., to eliminate homelessness], not the methods of achieving those results, which is what you do [e.g., by constructing houses].)

The purpose of our organization is to increase the quality of life for people living with HIV/AIDS, and prevent the spread of HIV in our community.

What are the methods that our organization uses to accomplish its purpose? Describe our business or businesses—our primary services or activities:

- *Care services: Support services to improve the quality of life for people living with HIV/AIDS*

- *Prevention services: Information and education about preventing HIV*

- *Other services: Public policy and advocacy*

Combine your purpose sentence and description of primary services/activities in a compelling mission statement:

AIDS Service Organization/USA (ASO/USA) is a community-based nonprofit organization dedicated to improving the quality of life for people living with HIV/AIDS and preventing the spread of HIV in our community. We strive to achieve our mission by providing support services to people living with HIV/AIDS, education and information on preventing HIV, and advocating for responsible public policies. We envision a world in which HIV/AIDS has been eradicated and people living with HIV/AIDS are able to lead quality productive lives.

Develop a powerful tag line or slogan:

ASO/USA — Serving the Community and Making A Difference

CASE STUDY—ASO/USA

❑ Dare to dream the possible. What is your organization's realistic but challenging guiding vision of success? (please write legibly if filling out by hand)

External vision: Describe how the world would be improved, changed, or different if our organization was successful in achieving its purpose.

Our vision is that all people living with HIV/AIDS

- *Get the appropriate care they need in a comfortable, accessible setting*
- *Are not discriminated against*
- *Make informed choices*
- *Choose hope over resignation*

It is also our vision that people have access to the personal and community resources, social support, and information to prevent new infections.

We hope to see the day soon when HIV no longer devastates our community and AIDS has been eradicated.

Internal vision: Envisioning our organization's future

Programmatic vision:

- *A spectrum of the highest quality support services for people living with HIV/AIDS that responds to changing needs in the community*
- *An aggressive and highly successful prevention program that results in decreased number of people acquiring HIV*
- *Continued emphasis on the provision of services through collaboration*
- *Greater success in working with public officials regarding policies that shape the lives of people with HIV and AIDS*

Administrative vision:

- *An active and informed board of 18 individuals representing a cross section of the community we serve*
- *No more than 60 percent of our funding from government with steady, renewable income sources making up the remaining 40 percent*
- *Sufficient infrastructure resources, including space and technology resources and support to do our jobs well*
- *Continued community support and a powerful voice on behalf of people living with HIV/AIDS*

- *Sufficient staff that feels fairly compensated and supported and a staff that reflects the face of our community*
- *Board and volunteers will continue to be inspired and recognized for their contributions in supporting the organization's mission.*

CASE STUDY—ASO/USA

Articulate Your Organization's Values, Beliefs, and Guiding Principles

❏ Clarify your organization's belief systems: What are some of the values, beliefs, and/or guiding principles that do (or should) guide your board and staff's interactions with each other and with constituencies?

❏ Practical impact: What behaviors should you commit to doing in everyday practice to support your values and beliefs?

Clarify your organization's belief systems: What are some of the values, beliefs, and/or guiding principles that do (or should) guide your board and staff's interactions with each other and with constituencies?	Practical impact: What are the behaviors you should commit to doing in everyday practice in support of our values, beliefs, and guiding principles
Guiding principle: All people deserve quality health care.	• *Provide all support services at no cost to the individual.* • *Conduct regular surveys of clients to ensure we are providing quality services that meet their needs.* • *Encourage providers of health care to see people living with HIV/AIDS as the primary decision-maker in health choices.* • *Be vigilant in our public policy program's efforts to ensure that vital services and treatments not be cut from federal, state, and local budgets.*
Value: Diversity	• *This principle is to guide not only who we serve but also who we recruit to our board, staff, and volunteers.* • *Our education materials will at all times be linguistically and culturally appropriate for the specific group that we serve.*

Clarify your organization's belief systems: What are some of the values, beliefs, and/or guiding principles that do (or should) guide your board and staff's interactions with each other and with constituencies?	Practical impact: What are the behaviors you should commit to doing in everyday practice in support of our values, beliefs, and guiding principles
	• *We will promote cultural responsiveness and respect for the diverse languages, beliefs, attitudes, and styles of individuals.*
Value: Partnership	• *We can't accomplish all we care about on our own. We have to work well in partnership.* • *We will share credit for accomplishments as well as share the workload, engage in open and honest communication with our partners, and, when possible, help other agencies doing similar work succeed so that together we can make a difference.*
Belief: We can make a difference in this epidemic.	• *Maintain a positive and ambitious outlook for our leadership and our organization.* • *Ensure that we offer the services that can have the greatest impact on quality of life/preventing new infections, and ensure that we provide these services to communities where they can make the most difference.* • *Infuse a message of hope and empowerment into all the services we offer.*

CHAPTER 4

Phase 3: Assess Your Situation

No organization exists in a vacuum. The definition of strategic planning offered earlier stresses the importance of focusing on the future within the context of an ever-changing environment. In addition to assessing the external environment, it is important to understand the organization's internal operations—what resources and capacities the organization brings to the work of its mission.

At the conclusion of this phase, the planning committee will have a database of concrete information that can be used to make decisions about program and administrative priorities and to develop overall strategies. Part of the challenge of this information-gathering and analysis phase is that the information gathered may be incomplete, or information gathered from one source may conflict with information gathered from another source. During this phase, the planning committee members will have to continually assess whether they have sufficient and accurate information to make informed decisions regarding short-term and long-term priorities.

Information gathering and analysis can be time consuming, and it will be natural to jump to conclusions as issues, problems, and questions emerge and are clarified. Although a given issue may appear to require an obvious response ("We're running a deficit; we need to bring in more revenue and cut costs!"), most issues have more than one level of complexity ("If we cut costs, how will that affect the quality of our programs? If we want to bring in more revenue by charging for certain services, how will that affect accessibility?")

Phase 3 is a creative process of gaining new awareness and insight into your organization's internal and external context. Try to hold back from deciding how to respond until you have gathered most of the information with which you will work. If you think of each stakeholder and source of information as casting a vote for which issues are most critical, the value of the creative thinking that takes place in this phase will be reduced if decisions are made before all of the votes are in. Don't be afraid to begin discussing possible responses—just wait to decide how to proceed until Phase 4 (Agree on Priorities) of the planning process.

This phase has three major tasks:

1. *Review the history and current scope and scale of operations.* The following descriptive questions help outline where the organization is currently and how it got there:

   o What is our organization's profile (history and current scale and scope of operations)?

   o What have been our key guiding strategies to date?

   Regardless of the intensity of your planning process, answering these two questions is an important exercise to complete. Each question has an accompanying worksheet.

2. *Gather new information.* In these steps we decide on what new information to gather. For abbreviated processes, this step may be a simple brainstorm of the organization's strengths, weaknesses, opportunities, and threats (SWOT) at a retreat. However, for moderate and extensive processes, information will typically be gathered from internal stakeholders, external stakeholders, and objective data sources (e.g., program evaluations and financial statements). This chapter provides several options for gathering this information:

   o Gather input from internal stakeholders.

   o Gather information from external stakeholders.

   o Gather information from objective sources.

3. *Summarize your findings.* Finally, the new information needs to be organized in preparation for the priority-setting process in Phase 4. Again, planners have a few choices about how to summarize this information. The distillation of this information will help planners start to identify common themes and emerging priorities.

Although all planning processes will address each of these three tasks, assessing your situation can range widely from abbreviated (such as a planning group sitting down together and identifying strengths, weaknesses, opportunities, and threats) to extensive (gathering lots of new information from stakeholders about their views and conducting additional research).

This chapter describes an extensive situation assessment process. Several approaches and tools are included as resources. No single organization will use all of these tools; we offer them because they each have pros and cons that planners need to take into account.

Planners should familiarize themselves with the steps of this phase and the choices available in terms of activities and tools, as part of designing the overall planning process. The extent of information gathering and analysis in Phase 3 is the primary variable in differentiating an abbreviated process from an extensive process.

A WORD ABOUT WORDS

This phase of the process is called by many names in our field: situation analysis, taking stock, environmental scanning, or simply data gathering. Because we want to gather information about both the external environment and the organization's internal environment, we use the broad term "assessing your situation."

REVIEW HISTORY AND CURRENT SCOPE AND SCALE OF OPERATIONS

Part of the context for an organization's strategic planning effort is the organization's history: where it came from, how it arrived where it is today, and what lessons from history are either the keys to stability and growth or causes for organizational instability. The planning committee should have a common understanding of this historical context so that all committee members are building the plan on the same foundation and the lessons from history can be incorporated into everyone's thinking.

STEP 3.1: PREPARE A HISTORY AND DESCRIPTIVE PROFILE OF OPERATIONS

The first step in the organizational assessment for strategic planning is to prepare an organizational history and organizational profile using Worksheet 8 (see process notes in Exhibit 4.1). The history is simply a brief summary of the events that have shaped the organization. For example, it

EXHIBIT 4.1   WORKSHEET 8: SUMMARIZE YOUR
ORGANIZATION'S HISTORY AND
ACCOMPLISHMENTS

Process Notes

How to do this activity	• Summarize the organization's history using a timeline format.
	• List and group all program activities into broad program groupings (goals). Describe current scope and scale of services. Add related management and operations data (infrastructure).
	• Take advantage of any documents that already explain the organizational profile, such as annual reports or brochures.
	• This information should be distributed to all members of the planning committee at the first or second meeting.
	• After the information has been reviewed, board and staff should identify lessons from history: keys to stability and growth and recurring themes that show causes for instability.
Why do this activity	• Helps ensure that all members of the planning committee are operating from the same knowledge base about the organization.
	• Organizes and presents programs for discussion of mission statement.
Who to involve in the process	• Individual or individuals who have in-depth knowledge of the organization's programs and history. Alternatively, to construct a group member history timeline, have attendees at an initial planning retreat reconstruct the organization's history using chart paper hung on the wall.
	• Both board and staff should have the opportunity to review the lessons from history—the keys and obstacles to stability and growth.

See ASO/USA's example of this worksheet at the end of this chapter. Blank worksheets are provided in Appendix A and on the CD that accompanies this book.

typically includes when the organization started, a time line that shows when programs were first offered, milestones reached in the organization, important events in the organization's history, and shifts in priorities, as well as significant external events that affected the organization's course. An organizational profile is a summary of all of the organization's current programs and related infrastructure.

This can be accomplished in three basic steps (which might be accomplished even more quickly by using documents that already present this information, such as annual reports or brochures):

1. *List key events in the organization's development in a time line format.* For example, date of founding, key mergers or moves, new office openings, executive director transitions, departure of founders, date key programs began, formative or traumatic events, and so on.

2. *List all specific program activities and services.* For example, counseling and support, housing, information and referral, speaking engagements at corporations, public policy updates, and so on. Note current levels of activity and scale of current programs (including production data such as number of clients served, cost per unit of service, geographic locations serviced, total expenses per program, major sources of revenue, etc.).

3. *Prepare an infrastructure profile.* This will include information on basic management and operation functions that support the current programs, such as personnel management, fundraising, marketing, facilities, financial management, and board of directors. This information will include current paid and volunteer staffing levels for all programs and for the entire organization, as well as the size of the board of directors. Also, briefly summarize sources and use of funds, analysis of financial condition, and other related organizational and management data. Charts and diagrams are useful visuals to present data.

Exhibit 4.2 is an example of an organizational profile for a Red Cross chapter.

STEP 3.2: ARTICULATE PREVIOUS AND CURRENT STRATEGIES

What does it mean to be strategic and employ strategic thinking? Being strategic means making conscious choices about how you are going to use

EXHIBIT 4.2   ORGANIZATIONAL PROFILE
OF A RED CROSS CHAPTER

Program Activities Grouped by Common Outcome

1. Prevention of Disasters

Goal: To prevent disasters that are caused by lack of awareness

Courses:
- Sailing
- Alcohol abuse
- Canoeing
- Facts of life
- Vital signs
- Seat belt safety
- Parenting
- Food safety
- AIDS
- Swimming
- Baby-sitting
- Tornado/hurricane/flood

Information:
- Newsletter
- Exhibits
- Public speakers bureau

Service Level:
- 240 courses, 4,800 participants
- 10 newsletters
- 20 public speeches

2. Intervention in the Midst of Disasters

Goal: To decrease the impact of disasters when they are occurring

Direct Services:
- Life-saving CPR
- First-aid stations at public events
- Blood pressure screening
- Blood drives

Service Level:
- 100 courses, 2,000 participants
- 2 blood pressure screenings, 500 participants
- Ongoing blood drives at Red Cross office, and 52 blood drives at office sites.

3. Relief of Suffering After Disasters Occur

Goal: To decrease the human suffering caused by disasters after they have occurred

Direct Services:
- Services to military families and veterans
- Mass feeding
- Bone and tissue transplantation
- Transportation services
- Emergency communications
- Disaster damage assessment
- Service in hospitals and health centers

Service Level:
- 15 services to military families and veterans
- 280 bone/tissue units transplanted
- 1,000 persons transported
- 5,000 hrs. of volunteer service in hospitals
- 50 damage assessments
- 6 mass feedings
- 6 emergency communications operations

EXHIBIT 4.2   ORGANIZATIONAL PROFILE OF A RED CROSS CHAPTER *(Continued)*

4. Fundraising

Goal: To ensure donations are adequate to support programs

Production:
- Individuals $150,000
- Corporations $150,000
- Foundations $100,000

Volunteer usage:
- 1,000 = 10% of volunteer hours

Expenses:
- $100,000 = 10% of gross expenses

Income:
- $400,000 = 40% of income

5. Marketing

Goal: To increase public understanding of the organization

Production:
- 10 newsletters, 12 PSAs

Expenses:
- $10,000 = 10% of gross expenses% of income

6. Personnel

Goal: To have a knowledgeable and experienced staff to manage and deliver services

Production:
- 15 FTE (full time equivalent)

Expenses:
- $600,000 = 60% of gross expenses (subset of other expenses)

Goal: To maintain a pool of trained volunteers to deliver services

Production:
- Recruit 6,000 volunteers
- Train 4,000 volunteers
- Place 2,000 volunteers
- Produce 10,000 volunteer hours worth $200,000

Volunteer usage:
- 2,000 hours = 20% of volunteer hours

Expenses:
- $40,000 = 40% of gross expenses

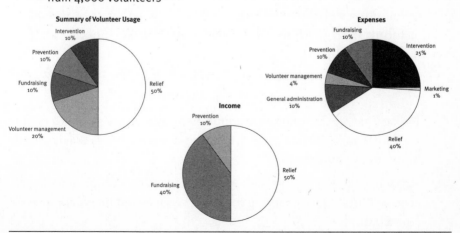

your limited resources to achieve your purpose in response to a dynamic environment. Strategic thinking therefore includes making decisions regarding what you will do and what you will not do, where you should focus your energies, and what your overall priorities should be.

A strategy is a broad overall priority or direction adopted by an organization to best achieve its purpose. A strategy defines your overall program and organizational priorities and therefore suggests where your organization should be investing its resources now and over the next few years.

A good place to start Phase 3 is to look at the previous and current strategies that the organization has either successfully or unsuccessfully used. The organization's history, developed using Worksheet 8, identified what was happening in the organization's internal and external environment during its history. What the organization did in response to its environment were strategic choices.

All organizations make strategic choices, although often these choices have been neither recognized nor articulated as actual strategies. Once an organization is in the process of strategic planning, however, it is important to make explicit these unspoken strategies and incorporate them into the deliberate consideration of the organization's future directions. As part of assessing your organization's situation, the planning committee should look for past patterns of operation or allocation of resources—these are the organization's previous strategies.

A question that can help prompt such thinking is: "Where have you primarily focused your energy and resources over the past few years; what efforts have gotten you to where you are now?" The planning committee should analyze whether the organization's past and present strategies were and are effective and then consider whether they should be part of future strategic thinking. Process notes for Worksheet 9 are presented in Exhibit 4.3.

Examples of strategic shifts that organizations could make over time include:

- *Program strategy*. From providing home-delivered meals only to people with HIV and AIDS, to providing home-delivered meals to any people homebound by illness

- *Revenue strategy*. From providing all free services with primarily government funding to charging for some services and increasing private contributions

- *Compensation strategy.* From paying low wages and low benefits (in order to maximize services) to providing competitive wages and benefits (to invest in long-term staff development and retention)

EXHIBIT 4.3	WORKSHEET 9: ARTICULATE PREVIOUS AND CURRENT STRATEGIES

Process Notes

How to do this activity	Review the history of the organization and articulate previous and current strategies. Discuss effectiveness of the strategy and implications for future.
Why do this activity	Understanding how your organization focused its resources in the past and present is critical to learning from your experience and setting future strategies.
Who to involve in the process	Planning committee

See ASO/USA's example of this worksheet at the end of this chapter. Blank worksheets are provided in Appendix A and on the CD that accompanies this book.

SIDEBAR

How the Arts Organization Changed Its Strategy

Storytelling Songbirds is a two-person performing arts group that tells dramatic stories through a combination of drama, dance, and song. Two years ago, both members of the group gave up their part-time day jobs to devote all of their time to the Songbirds. During this time, they have made a modestly successful CD and completed a national tour as well as a brief tour in Europe.

Storytelling Songbirds, centered on the artistic vision of the two writer/performers—Carlos and Fran—is nonetheless governed by a nonprofit board of directors. When the board of directors insisted on developing a strategic plan, an important insight emerged during the discussion about previous strategies.

They realized that an important part of their business strategy, and indeed a point of pride, is that they have never sought contributions to cover the cost of their performances. "We're making a decent living and paying all our expenses," says Fran, "with a budget

(continues)

purely from box office, performance contracts, and CD sales. For a performing arts organization, that's astounding success!"

Some of the board members of Storytelling Songbirds have been on other arts boards and felt a responsibility to warn Carlos and Fran about the financial unpredictability of arts income. When Carlos sprained his shoulder last month, the Songbirds realized that they had to reevaluate their long-term strategy.

"I hate it when I see other arts organizations begging for money," says Carlos. "But I've also realized how much we've just been scraping by. What we want to do—taking these stories to new audiences—just won't ever be completely supported by contracts. We need time to develop new concepts, work out collaborations with other artists, and explore our own boundaries and visions. I realize now that it costs more to put on a season than people can afford to pay."

Along with their board, Carlos and Fran are beginning to think about raising a modest proportion of their budget from grants and donations. "Moving away from a box office-only strategy has meant changing our self-image," comments Fran. Carlos is quick to add, "This new strategy will let us grow in new ways. I'm feeling good about it."

Overview of Information Gathering

In the following activities, the majority of new research is completed. Gathering information about your environment often consumes 50 percent or more of the time resources devoted to the entire strategic planning process. Begin this step by going back a few steps—remind yourself of what critical issues and questions prompted strategic planning in the first place. These were identified in Worksheet 1 (Exhibit 2.1). It is essential that your information-gathering activities provide the data you need to answer these questions. Next, review the initial thoughts about information gathering identified in Worksheet 3 (Exhibit 2.3).[1]

Assessing the situation is best done with information from the following sources:

- Internal stakeholders (board, staff, and volunteers)
- External stakeholders (clients, funders, strategic partners, community leaders, and other key informants)
- Objective data (internal financial statements, program statistics, data about trends in the environment, and interviews with experts)

In Step 3.6 we summarize the information gathered from these sources along four dimensions:

1. Mission accomplishment
2. Financial performance
3. Administrative capacity
4. Governance

The following table shows how these sources of information contribute to the summaries of information. As one can see from the table, internal and external stakeholders provide much of the information needed by planners. However, without objective data to support or correct the perceptions of internal and external stakeholders, planners risk working with incomplete and potentially inaccurate information.

In particular, objective information is required to assess financial performance. However, to understand mission accomplishment, some level of program evaluation is required, and to truly understand management/infrastructure and the governance functions, some objective information is necessary.

SOURCE	Internal Stakeholders	External Stakeholders	Objective Data
DIMENSION			
Mission Accomplishment	XX	XX	XX
Financial Performance			XX
Administrative Capacity	XX		XX
Governance	XX		XX

STEP 3.3: GATHER INFORMATION FROM INTERNAL STAKEHOLDERS

Your staff (paid and volunteer) and board typically have a very good idea of your organization's strengths, weaknesses, opportunities, and threats. In addition, in order to build the commitment you seek into the strategic plan, involvement of these internal stakeholders is essential. Thus, the first place to gather new information is from people who know your organization best: your board and staff members.

In an abbreviated planning process, this involvement could take place at a single retreat, during which the group goes through a SWOT analysis. The SWOT analysis is a broad overview of the most important internal strengths and weaknesses and the most important external opportunities and threats. However, in a moderate or extensive planning process, planners will want to gather more extensive input from these key internal stakeholders.

The SWOT analysis can be done at the level of the whole organization or of each program. Use the SWOT framework, Worksheet 10 (see process notes in Exhibit 4.4), to help gather and organize information in assessing the operating environment.

As can be seen in the case study, evaluating an organization's strengths and weaknesses typically includes gathering perceptions about several dimensions of organizational functioning.

Strengths	What are the organization's internal strengths? ("What do we do well?")
Weaknesses	What are the organization's internal weaknesses? ("Where can we improve?")
Opportunities	What external opportunities exist with respect to pursuing our mission? ("What changes are taking place in our environment that might allow us to better achieve our mission?")
Threats	What external threats might hinder the pursuit of our mission? ("What changes in the environment do we need to guard against or prepare for in doing our work?")

Evaluating an organization's strengths and weaknesses typically includes looking at what the organization is doing well, in addition to its weaknesses. Successful organizations are those that exploit strengths rather than just focus on weaknesses—in other words, this process isn't just about fixing the things that are wrong, but also nurturing what goes right.

The same should apply to how an organization approaches its opportunities and threats—the external forces that influence the organization. These are usually categorized into political, economic, social, technological, demographic, and legal (sometimes referred to as PESTDL) trends. These trends encompass circumstances such as changing client needs, increased competition, changing regulations, new interest in a particular

EXHIBIT 4.4   WORKSHEET 10: STAFF AND BOARD
PERCEPTIONS OF ORGANIZATION'S
SWOT

Process Notes

How to do this activity	• Brainstorm and record on flip charts a list of SWOT. This activity can take place at meeting(s) of staff and board; staff and board may meet separately or together (such as at a planning retreat). You may want to distribute the worksheet to staff and board ahead of time in order to get people thinking about the organization. • Alternatively, you may distribute Worksheet 10 and collect and summarize results. Participants should be encouraged to be as specific as they can and not generalize (e.g., "at least three-quarters of all staff have been with the agency for at least six years, rather than "great staff"). • Review the SWOT, sort into categories, select most important items, and summarize results. An optional activity is to assess the interplay of your strengths and weaknesses and your opportunities and threats. Make note of these interplays and refer to them in Phase 4. *For example: Are there any opportunities that we can take advantage because of a particular strength? Are there any threats that are compounded by a weakness?)*
Why do this activity	• Individuals' perceptions provide a starting framework for perceiving the organization's current situation. • One of the key aspects of strategic planning and management is being proactive—making decisions that take advantage of strengths and opportunities, overcoming weaknesses, and trying to turn threats into opportunities.
Who to involve in the process	Board and staff. The extent and format of their involvement to be decided by planning committee.

See ASO/USA's example of this worksheet at the end of this chapter. Blank worksheets are provided in Appendix A and on the CD that accompanies this book.

focus problem that the organization tries to address, and so on. These are forces that can help an organization move forward (opportunities) or forces that can hold an organization back (threats). Opportunities that are ignored can become threats, and threats that are dealt with appropriately can be turned into opportunities. During the strategic planning process, the organization wants to figure out how it can best use its resources to take advantage of strengths and opportunities, and to overcome weaknesses and threats.

During the SWOT review, planners may try to look at the interplay of strengths and weaknesses with opportunities and threats. Many times an opportunity can only be taken advantage of if the organization has a corresponding strength. For example, increased demand for services (opportunity) can only be met effectively if the organization has the necessary infrastructure and staff (strengths) to provide quality service. Conversely, if an organization is facing a significant shift in the political arena that could adversely affect its ability to get funding (threat), the organization could not respond quickly if it had poor relationships with government officials and a small and inactive membership (weaknesses). The planning committee should make note of any of these interplays of SW and OT and refer back to them in Phase 4.

The planning committee should involve as many staff and board members as possible in this process. As an alternative to a single retreat, their ideas and opinions might be collected through questionnaires, by telephone, or in-person interviews, facilitated organization-wide or in small group meetings, or a combination of these methods. Some organizations have board and staff in the same meeting to discuss these ideas, while others have them meet separately.

It may be helpful to examine individual dimensions of the internal organization in more detail than the SWOT assessment. The following tools have been developed to gather more extensive input from staff and board members.

Survey for Strategic Planning

A tool that can be used to identify how effectively the organization is managed and what specific areas need attention is Elements of an Effectively Managed Organization (EEMO$^{2™}$).[2] EEMO^2 is a framework for looking at what it means to be effectively managed, and it can be used by an organization's managers to identify areas that are perceived as assets and that are real or potential weaknesses. EEMO^2 looks in depth at the four dimensions of an organization:

1. *Mission.* How well are we achieving our mission and how could we have a greater impact?

2. *Finances.* Are our operations financially viable, and how can we ensure the long-term financial stability of our organization? Do we have effective financial management systems in place to monitor our finances?

3. *Administrative capacity.* Do we have the administrative capacity to effectively and efficiently support our programs and services? What would it take to maximize our organizational capabilities in terms of planning, human resources and leadership, organization culture and communication, and our technology and facilities infrastructure?

4. *Governance.* How effective is the board at protecting the public's interest, ensuring that charitable dollars are used effectively and efficiently and that the organization is fulfilling its mission? What can we do to ensure that our board is able to fulfill its governance role now and for the future?

This survey can be used with both staff and board members, although typically board members are not sufficiently familiar with internal operations to answer all of the questions.

An EEMO^2 assessment tool is included in Appendix C.

Self-Assessment of Governance

The effectiveness of the board is of major strategic importance for any organization. The board is expected to assess its own work on an ongoing basis, so the strategic planning process may or may not provide an appropriate opportunity for assessing its effectiveness.

One example of a board self-assessment survey is included in Appendix D. Each board member can complete this or a similar assessment anonymously. The results for each question then can be tallied and presented using bar graphs to show the spread of the board members' opinions.

STEP 3.4: GATHER INFORMATION FROM EXTERNAL STAKEHOLDERS

Gathering input from external stakeholders always improves the quality of a strategic planning process. Even if internal stakeholders are 90 percent correct about their assessment of their organization's SWOT, getting the input from outsiders will provide either much-needed confirmation or new perspectives that will make the difference in developing sound plans.

Making a few phone calls to funders or partner organizations can give new insight. Alternately, using a standard interview or survey instrument with external stakeholders can update assumptions. An added benefit of gathering input from external stakeholders is the opportunity to develop more honest and productive relationships with clients, funders, and partners.

Just as the SWOT assessment allows an organization to garner a wide variety of perspectives from internal stakeholders, a SWOT assessment by those outside the organization can also add a great deal to the assessment of the environment. Relying only on internal stakeholders will provide an incomplete picture of the organization's situation. Refer to Worksheet 3 in which the planning committee identified external stakeholders from whom to gather input.

General Comments Regarding External Stakeholder Interviews

There are two reasons why we involve external stakeholders in the strategic planning process:

1. *Information.* They have information (outside perspectives) that will help us make better strategic decisions. A stakeholder may have insights into the opportunities or threats that affect the organization (e.g., new data revealing that 60 percent of all nonprofit organizations in the city are facing serious rent hikes). If the stakeholder has heard about the organization—or has had some contact with the organization—then his or her perceptions regarding the organization's strengths and weaknesses can be compared to perceptions of internal stakeholders. (e.g., staff and board members think that the organization has a positive reputation in the community, but stakeholders comment that they hear there is a long waiting list and people are going elsewhere).

A stakeholder's expectations can also inform an organization regarding unmet or growing needs in the community (e.g., a community leader interviewed might reveal an expectation/hope, not previously considered internally, that the organization expand services to a neighboring community or to add a different type of program).

2. *Relationship building.* We wish to maintain, improve, or build a better relationship with them. If a stakeholder does not know about the organization, then the interview can be an opportunity for the person doing the interview to explain what services are offered or how the organization is making a difference in the community.

   If the organization has a good relationship with the interviewee, then the conversation can be the vehicle to affirm that partnership and find out how to expand that relationship. If the organization does not have a good relationship with the person being interviewed — or doesn't have a relationship with the individual—then the interview can be a vehicle to build (or rebuild) such a relationship.

Although it is useful to have a preset and agreed-on protocol for each stakeholder group, the actual discussion should be somewhat free-flowing, and the interviewer should be willing to ask follow-up questions to comments he or she hears. Those questions might deviate somewhat from the preset questions. Appendix J provides suggested questions for stakeholder interviews. Clearly you would not ask all of the questions listed, and not all of these questions would be appropriate for all of the stakeholders we have identified.

SIDEBAR

Animal Rights Now Responds to Its Stakeholders

Animal Rights Now had outgrown its old facility. The board and staff convinced themselves that a large new building was the answer to their facility problems. As the visions of the new building became grander, extensions of the program were planned. The board president, Jon, was particularly enthusiastic. "In addition to our advocacy work and our work with stray animals, if we build a theater/conference center, we can expand our education work. And we can

(continues)

generate extra income by renting out the space when we're not using it!"

A site was located, preliminary designs were invited, and the train seemed ready to go. As part of their planning process, the board and staff sought input from the external stakeholders whose support they would need: funders, individual donors, other organizations in the community, and neighbors. To their shock and ultimate benefit, the organization learned that three other organizations in the area had recently expanded their educational activities and that the theater/convention space would sink the building.

"It was tough," says Jon now. "We were so excited about the possibilities for growth and expansion. We even had a donation for lights in the theater. But in the end, our plan is much more realistic, and I am glad we didn't find out *after* we had put down a lot of money that our original vision just wasn't going to fly."

With a scaled-down facilities plan and a mission focused on needed services where there was no unnecessary duplication, the organization completed its strategic planning process and built a smaller building with extensive community support behind them.

Other ways of collecting data from external stakeholders include client-satisfaction and client-needs surveys, as well as focus groups. Ideally you have ongoing processes in place for assessing client satisfaction and needs. The strategic planning process can be an opportunity to do an in-depth analysis of what constituents think of your services and their current and future needs. If you are going to gather information from your constituents using a survey, make sure to pretest the survey for clarity and brevity. You might want to consider using an online survey; if so, give people the option of filling out the survey by hand so you don't bias your results toward those who are more comfortable using a computer.

Focus groups can be an invaluable tool for finding out more about your constituents experience with your organization and about their needs. Appendix F provides guidelines for conducting focus groups.

STEP 3.5: GATHER INFORMATION FROM DOCUMENTS AND OTHER SOURCES

Stakeholders' opinions about the organization and the environment are informed and critical. In addition, particularly in the areas of mission and finances, objective data (as opposed to subjective data from stakeholders) is needed to complete the situation assessment.

Sample Types and Sources of Information for Strategic Planning

Type	Source	Comment
Key trends in the field in which the organization operates	Industry journals; notes from latest conferences; local or state planners for the field/experts or advocates (lobbyists) and client advocates (consumer groups)	Information from individuals can be gathered via interviews or inviting key individuals to speak to the Planning Committee
Plans and attitudes of major existing funders	Personal interviews or annual reports	Some funders may be reluctant to talk about future funding commitments or give feedback to current grantees about their performance
Demographic changes within the target population	Census data; public health data; housing stock studies; city, state, or national planning offices	Staff and volunteers can often provide additional informal perspectives
Regulatory changes	Journals, conferences, slate associations of nonprofit organizations, independent sector, state regulators	Presentation should focus on the impact such changes have on the organization
Financial trends for the past five years	Organization's audited financial statements	Preferred presentation mode is through use of graphs that delineate trends and key ratios
Client data trends for the past five years	Program reports, annual reports, funder reports, and other internal records	Presentation should clarify key relationships among programs, shifts in characteristics or needs/wants of clients
Client satisfaction	Client surveys and/or focus groups	Such feedback should ideally be built into the organization's ongoing commitment to quality and meeting client needs
Quality indicators	Existing evaluation data, surveys of referral sources, consumer satisfaction, and staff perceptions	Such evaluation should ideally be built into the organization's ongoing commitment to quality and meeting client needs

(continues)

Sample Types and Sources of Information for strategic Planning *(Continued)*

Type	Source	Comment
Future program opportunities	Information from sources above; focus groups among potential consumers; market studies or needs assessments done by organization or others; interviews with other service providers	Once data has been collected, staff will need to put together a business plan with two- or three-year demand projection; staffing pattern; equipment and space needs; and first year financial pro forma

In Worksheet 3, objective sources to be consulted were anticipated. What follows is additional discussion of how to gather more information regarding your ability to accomplish your mission and your financial capacity.

Gather Information about Mission: Program Evaluation

Beyond the general input collected from internal and external stakeholders, the planning committee should make sure that current programs are assessed in some detail as part of the strategic planning process.

Which of our programs or services make the most difference to the community? Which are responding to growing needs? Which are the most cost effective? Which will face funding cutbacks in the future? Which will face influxes of funding in the future? Program planning needs to look both to the past (to learn whether our programs have had the impact we want) and to the future (to assess future needs, funding opportunities, and emerging new ways to meet the needs).

Ideally, program evaluation is an ongoing process for an organization. Client feedback mechanisms should be built into programs so that client satisfaction and progress are monitored continuously. Formal evaluations should be done regularly by outside evaluators or by staff or volunteers to help an agency consider how to improve a program, the degree to which a program is making a difference, and whether the program is cost effective. In this case, planners will be able to use relatively current program evaluation information.

For many organizations that do not have well developed program evaluation systems, the strategic planning process provides an opportunity to comprehensively look at program effectiveness. For some organizations, the single most important decision about programs in the strategic plan

CLARE DISCOVERS THE DIFFICULTY OF WORKING AT THE NATIONAL ORGANIZATION OF CLONED PEOPLE.

may simply be deciding to develop an ongoing feedback and evaluation plan in the future.

Program evaluations can use subjective and objective information, as well as quantitative and qualitative data. Objective data consists of fact-based information such as a review of records, descriptive statistics, and the like; it is more easily collected and less easily disputed because it translates experience into quantifiable data that can be counted, compared, measured, and manipulated statistically. Subjective, qualitative data consists of what people say about the programs based on interviews, focus groups or other meetings, direct or field observation, reviews of written materials, informal feedback, satisfaction surveys, and questionnaires.

Involve Staff in Assessing Programs and Client Needs   One of the places to start program evaluation may be with the program staff. Because program staff are usually the closest of the internal stakeholders to the clients, staff will have a definite perspective on client needs, strengths and weaknesses of the program, and the quality of the program in comparison to the competition. Asking staff members to evaluate their own programs, as well as the agency as a whole and its ability to serve specific populations, will not only allow program staff to have meaningful input into the planning process, but will also provide useful data and perspectives to make future decisions. ASO/USA put this into practice when they completed Worksheet 11 (see process notes in Exhibit 4.5). In order to complete the worksheet, program staff may need to dig into program records or other objective sources.

EXHIBIT 4.5   WORKSHEET 11: EVALUATE CURRENT PROGRAMS

Note: This worksheet expands on the work done with Worksheet 10. It asks staff to assess individual programs in detail, as well as to look at implications for the entire organization.

Process Notes

How to do this activity	Have each program's staff meet and discuss the questions on the Staff Assessment of Programs worksheet. The program manager should summarize the discussions and complete Worksheet 11.
Why do this activity	Information about the needs and perceived effectiveness of your programs is necessary, and program staff are some of the most informed regarding client needs and how their programs actually operate. Especially if there is a need to reallocate resources or cut costs for particular programs, it is helpful to involve staff in suggesting new and different ways of doing things and making suggestions for the future.
Who to involve in this activity	Appropriate program staff. Summary of findings presented to planning committee.

See ASO/USA's example of this worksheet at the end of this chapter. Blank worksheets are provided in Appendix A and on the CD that accompanies this book.

How the Program Is Doing Depends on Who You Ask!

The board of an established tutoring organization that worked with children whose native language was not English had great confidence that their program was doing a splendid job. Many of the board members had previously volunteered as tutors, and a local newspaper article printed a few years ago had lauded the program. The part-time program director collected reports regularly from the tutors, and it appeared that the number of children served was gradually increasing. The tutors consistently provided anecdotes of success stories they heard from parents and teachers.

As part of a strategic planning process, the board decided to gather more extensive feedback from their clients. They hired an outside evaluator to assess the effectiveness of the program and customer satisfaction. The evaluator put together a simple survey for the parents of each of the children enrolled and telephoned all of the teachers who referred children to the program for feedback. The evaluator, along with two board members, attended a few tutoring sessions to observe the program in action and to casually ask some of the children what they thought. The evaluator also talked to the principals of all three elementary school program sites.

What the board found out from the evaluator's report surprised them greatly. In the first place, new tutoring programs had begun recently at two of the schools. In each case, the new group was serving many more children than was the established tutoring program. In the second place, many of the parents and teachers reported that some volunteers from the established program rarely showed up for appointments with the children and that the use of the program's materials was inconsistent at best. It seemed that a few of the volunteers saw their role more as a "big brother/big sister" than that of an educator/tutor. The teachers and parents had been reluctant to complain because, "after all, they weren't paying for the program."

The program evaluation information collected easily and over a period of only weeks allowed the board and the director to identify these critical issues and to respond. The program director immediately began much more active training, coaching, and monitoring of the volunteer tutors. A few tutors were informed that their services were no longer necessary. The group also quickly moved to develop closer relationships with the two new local programs, sharing materials and referrals, and helping the new groups find out about other

(continues)

resources available to tutoring programs. Biannual surveys of parents, teachers, children, and volunteers were instituted.

The dark cloud of the news about the program had another silver lining: One year after the strategic plan was completed, the tutoring program had developed such a positive word-of-mouth reputation for its tutor training program that it was repeatedly asked to provide training to other tutoring programs and was expanding, carefully, its training services into a new program.

Techniques Used in Program Evaluation   Appendix E outlines nine techniques used in program evaluation, such as surveys of client satisfaction and outcomes, focus groups, interviews, and tests. These techniques can easily be adapted to help any organization answer the basic program evaluation questions noted previously.

Gathering Information about Financial Performance and Systems

Organizations have several sources of data with which to assess financial performance. Most organizations have audited financial statements to review. In addition to the statements of revenue, expenses, and assets and liabilities, the management letter included with an audited set of financial statements can be a source of information about systems and structures that support effectiveness and efficiency. The audit is useful for looking at a whole year's activity, but organizations typically have monthly and/or quarterly reports prepared showing revenues and expenses compared with the budget. The following questions may be helpful in suggesting the dimensions of financial performance relevant for your organization:

- Is the organization living within its means and maximizing its program services within its available resources?

- How much does the organization spend per unit of service?

- Are financial reserves available for hard times or to take advantage of new opportunities? (A reserve of three months of operating expenses is a relatively prudent goal.)

- Given comparison of current financial data to similar data for prior periods, is the organization better or worse off than before, and what are the possible future trends?

- To what extent are services being subsidized from other revenue sources, and what does this mean for future ability to provide services?
- How diversified are the organization's funding sources?
- What is the organization's overall financial health? Are financial management systems and personnel adequate?

STEP 3.6: SUMMARIZE INFORMATION INTO A SITUATION ASSESSMENT

By the completion of Phase 3, the planning committee should have sufficient data collected so that its members can make informed discussions during Phase 4. Before leaving Phase 3, the planning committee should summarize the data collected. Worksheet 12 (see process notes in Exhibit 4.6) provides three different lens for summarizing the data from your situation assessment:

1. Organizing the data around the framework of mission, finances, administrative capacity, and governance
2. Organizing the data around the strategic issues identified at the beginning of your planning process
3. Using SWOT structure to summarize your findings

In addition, Worksheet 12 not only reviews the data collected but also starts to make sense of that data by identifying emerging themes and/or priorities. Based on the information gathered

- Are there things that the organization should consider doing differently, more of, less of, the same?
- Are there things that the organization should consider starting or stopping?
- What discussions still need to happen? How and when will those discussions happen?
- Are there additional strategic issues that need to be addressed? For example, it may not be until after all external stakeholders have been interviewed that the planning committee realizes that the organization has a serious public image problem.

Phase 3 and Phase 4 are actually not separate processes; they are two points on a continuum of information gathering and decision making.

EXHIBIT 4.6   WORKSHEET 12: SUMMARY OF
DATA AND ANALYSIS OF POSSIBLE
CONSIDERATIONS FOR THE FUTURE

Process Notes

How to do this activity	Decide which of the three ways of summarizing data (1. Mission/finances/administrative/governance framework, 2. Strategic issues framework, or 3. SWOT structure) would be best for the strategic planning committee to understand and be able to make sense of the information collected. One or more members of the committee (or a consultant) should draft a summary of the findings, and present to the planning committee as a whole. Alternatively, the board chair might take the lead on the governance findings and the executive director or a member of the management team take the lead in summarizing the rest of the data.
	After reviewing—and discussing—the data findings, the committee would then discuss possible considerations for the future.
Why do this activity	If you have collected a lot of data during Phase 3, it is important to be able to distill it in a format that is easy to understand and not overwhelming. In addition, if some emerging themes are already apparent, you don't have to wait to Phase 4 to start to articulate those priorities.
Who to involve in the process	The planning committee is usually the prime mover for this activity. The planning committee might ask the management team to summarize findings and present their impressions of possible themes and priorities.

See ASO/USA's example of this worksheet at the end of this chapter. Blank worksheets are provided in Appendix A and on the CD that accompanies this book.

By now some themes and priorities have already become evident. With this thorough understanding of your situation and the beginning articulation of the themes and priorities, you have already started the work of Phase 4.

SIDEBAR

An Alternative Approach to SWOT

The most common approach to assessing an organization's situation has always been to look at the organization's internal environment (i.e., strengths and weaknesses) and the external environment (i.e., opportunities and threats). An alternative approach is to describe the organization's situation in terms of

- What are the organization's *assets*—the organization's strengths and core competencies (what it does best)?
- What are the organization's *opportunities*—trends in the environment that the organization could take advantage of?
- What are the organization's *vulnerabilities*—the organization's weaknesses and threats that work against achieving its mission?

CAUTIONS TO FACILITATORS

- *Collecting too little information.* By relying on what people already know (especially only information from internal sources), a danger is that the group will make decisions with a distorted perception of the current situation. Often we find that planners are actually more negative about the organization's position and prospects than are outsiders. The judgment call to make here is: Do we have enough confidence in our analysis of the situation to go forward with making decisions based on our current information? If not, get more.

- *Collecting too much information.* This is the other end of the spectrum. Paralysis by analysis is a common complaint of people getting lost in the information—losing the forest for the trees. In this case, someone needs to take the lead in paring down the information; returning to the original reasons for planning is often a good place to start.

(continues)

CAUTIONS TO FACILITATORS *(Continued)*

- *Failing to achieve a consensus assessment.* Quite often, either one source will contradict another source or information can be interpreted in different ways. Too little internal debate about the meaning of the information collected and organized in the assessment can leave unsettled key questions about your situation. Without a shared perspective about the situation, a risk is that board, staff, funders, and other stakeholders will not fully support the strategic plan.

ENDNOTES

1. Figuring out where to begin with this phase can be confusing. It is possible to organize information gathering along three different dimensions. The first would be to look at the list of *planning questions* and figure out what information is needed to answer these questions. The second would be along *organizational lines* (mission, financial, infrastructure, governance). We suggest using the third dimension, which is to organize by *information source*. We find that because the activity of information gathering involves interacting with sources, this is the most efficient approach. However, while the approach to information gathering is by source, the information should be summarized along the other two lines, which contain the questions to be answered.

2. Our original version of EEMO™ from the first edition of this book defined eight elements that make up an effectively managed organization: mission, priorities, structure, people, systems, program evaluation, leadership, and relationships. Our revised EEMO^2 organizes these eight elements into four dimensions: mission, financial, administrative capacity, and governance.

CASE STUDY—ASO/USA

Summarize Your Organization's History and Accomplishments

☐ Summarize your organization's history, listing the appropriate span of years such as 1-year, 5-year, or 10-year increments, depending on the organization's age. Identify lessons from your history.

☐ Summarize what has or has not been accomplished since your last strategic planning process. Optional: Describe your programs, staffing levels, and financial capacity (or attach a document that describes what you do and how it is supported).

Presentation of Organization's History

Timeline	1988	1989	1993	1995	1997	1998	2000	2001	2002	2003

List key organizational events and shifts in priorities (use the timeline to place events in chronological order)

1988 *Organization founded; Ken Brown, director*

1989 *First federal grant for prevention—hotline and outreach started*

1993 *First federal care grant—Case management services and support groups begun*

1997 *Satellite office opened to serve southeast section of the city*

2000 *Joseph Chin, new executive director*

2000 *First strategic plan completed*

2001 *Collaboration with City Clinic begins—prevention outreach expanded*

2002 *Federal care award increased—care services expanded to include transportation vouchers, benefits counseling*

2002 *City Health Department Award received to fund employment support services*

(continues)

153

Presentation of Organization's History

Timeline	1988	1989	1993	1995	1997	1998	2000	2001	2002	2003

List external events impacting the organization (use the timeline to place events in chronological order)

1995 *First HIV prevention community planning group and Title I CARE Council convened*

Late 90s dramatic medical treatment advances

2000 *city population decreasing along with rising unemployment*

2003 *Federal policy changes and funding cuts*

Lessons from history: Keys to stability and growth

- *Consistent and excellent staff leadership*
- *Steady involvement of volunteers (until recent years)*
- *Good relationships with government funders*
- *Collaborative relationships with other health service providers*

Lessons from history: Recurring themes that show causes for instability

- *Heavy dependence on federal funding since late 90's*
- *Few new board members in last several years*
- *Constant change in city politics and service planning*

What have we accomplished since our last strategic planning process?

- *Expanded services city-wide*
- *Increased investment in staff development and training*
- *Acquired new funders, and increased annual campaign*

What have we not accomplished since our last strategic planning process?

- *Didn't solve problems with City Clinic*
- *Haven't reduced dependence on federal funding*

Summary of Programs

Name of program/department: *Support Services*

Program/department purpose: *Improve the individual and community health of HIV-infected and affected individuals.*

Description of current scope and scale of activities: *This program includes five components: 1) case management, 2) support groups, 3) transportation services, 4) benefits counseling, and 5) employment referral.*

12 FTE staff and 30 volunteers provide all the services. Case management is provided to 300 individuals (all of whom are eligible for the other four service components). We have 12 ongoing support groups for people living with HIV/AIDS and for caregivers, and we offer transportation vouchers to individuals accessing care, employment referrals for those seeking work, and benefits counseling to those needing assistance in this area.

Name of program/department: *Public Education*

Program/department purpose: *Educate the general public about the risks of HIV, ways to prevent its spread, and the advantages of early treatment. Provide education to specific high-risk groups about HIV transmission.*

Description of current scope and scale of activities: *4 FTE staff and 20 volunteers do outreach/education in public schools (100 presentations annually), bars (20 "visits" monthly), on the street (one night a week), businesses (work with 10 local companies on their internal programs), and neighborhoods (support to 7 local neighborhood organizations). This is the work done in collaboration with City Clinic—they provide the HIV testing and referral component to the outreach that we do.*

2 FTE and 30 volunteers run the hotline, which receives 5,000 calls per year.

(continues)

Summary of Programs

Name of program/department: *Public Policy and Communications*

Program/department purpose: *Advocate for public funding for HIV prevention and care services (especially controversial programs, such as needle exchange), and promote positive media coverage of HIV related issues.*

Description of current scope and scale of activities: *1.5 staff and .5 FTE paid policy intern participate in local HIV prevention and CARE community planning groups and regional/statewide legislative and policy initiatives. Provide monthly updates to local media (neighborhood and city newspapers and local TV stations).*

Summary of Operations

Number of staff and board: *18 board members*
20 FTE paid staff members
80 core part-time volunteers

Summary of Operations

Financial data: (sources of revenue, budget, etc.)

	Total	Support Services	Public Policy and Communications	Public Education	General and Administration
Revenue					
Government					
Federal/State*	900,0000	800,000			100,000
City	400,000	200,000		200,000	
Foundations	200,000		150,000	50,000	
Other Contributions	85,000			50,000	35,000
Total	1,585,000	1,000,000	150,000	300,000	135,000
Expenses					
Personnel	1,275,000	765,000	100,000	300,000	110,000
Operating	335,000	200,000	10,000	50,000	65,000
Total	1,600,000	965,000	110,000	350,000	175,000
Excess (Deficiency)	(15,000)	35,000	40,000	(50,000)	(40,000)

*Although all of this money originates from the federal government, it is distributed by the state health department; therefore, our contracts for these dollars are with the state health department.

CASE STUDY—ASO/USA

❏ Identify and assess your organization's previous and current strategies.

Previous and current strategy	Was or is the strategy effective? Why or why not? Should it be considered as the strategy for the future? Why or why not?
Be a grass roots organization, with many volunteers.	This has been an important part of our uccess because the people we are trying to reach trust us and can relate to us. We should continue this strategy overall, but improve coordination and efficiency of our operations, and assess whether (1) some programs and services should be done better by paid staff, and (2) all programs should have paid program managers.
For prevention, focus on the people at greatest risk for HIV.	While we are increasingly serving people who are at greatest risk, we have not made as much progress as we could. First, we need to look at current epidemiologic and needs assessment data to see who is at greatest risk. Then we need to identify barriers to services for these populations in order to better reach them. Focusing on the highest risk groups is sound strategy and is in line with what government funding priorities.
Go after large federal and state grants so that we don't have to spend all of our time fundraising.	This has been successful to date, but it now leaves us in a vulnerable situation. Due to changes in federal government policy, the future of prevention and care funding is uncertain — how much will be available and what will be the focus? It is not clear how we can quickly change this basic strategy. We've had some success in raising money from individuals, but given rough economic

Previous and current strategy	Was or is the strategy effective? Why or why not? Should it be considered as the strategy for the future? Why or why not?
	times it may be a challenge to sustain our current individual supporters at a time when there's less federal, state, and foundation grant making.
Provide services based on available funding (an opportunistic approach), rather than focusing on building our services based on client needs and then seeking funding to support the programs that will meet these needs (a proactive, needs-based approach).	*We never wanted it this way, but basically that is what we've been doing. As a result, our programs have grown in unpredictable ways, and we are not getting funded for the full costs of the services we are providing. We need to make sure all our programs still fit together and support our mission, and make sure we are not duplicating efforts that can be done better by other organizations. We also really need to focus on who are client base is and should be, what services they need, and which of those services can be provided best by us.*
Be collaborative at all costs.	*Collaboration is one of our guiding principles, but some of our collaborative efforts have been excruciatingly difficult. We need to continue to have a commitment to collaboration when it benefits our clients and/or our agency, but get better at clarifying roles, expectations, and accountability.*
Be a full-service center, providing a spectrum of programs that meet every HIV-related need in the community— the comprehensive ASO that provides both prevention and care.	*This really raises the issue of whether or not we can really be effective at meeting all needs in both prevention and care. (It is interesting, though, that one of the nonnegotiable parameters for this process is that we will continue to do both prevention and care.)*

CASE STUDY—ASO/USA

Staff and Board Perceptions of Organization's SWOT

❑ List our organization's primary (program and administrative) strengths and weaknesses—internal forces working for and against our organization achieving its mission.

❑ List our organization's key opportunities and threats—political, economic, social, technological, demographic, or legal trends that are or may impact our organization's ability to achieve its mission.

❑ (Optional) Indicate any possible connection between an opportunity or threat and a strength or weakness? (Are there any opportunities we can take advantage of because of a particular strength? Are there any threats that are compounded by a weakness?)

Internal Forces	External Forces
Strengths:	**Opportunities:**
• *Strong track record of results in direct services*	• *We have been approached by other community organizations that work with homebound populations about expanding our scope of service to people other than AIDS and HIV.*
• *Good reputation in the community*	
• *Solid volunteer program*	• *Increased need for housing—not that we could really respond to this*
• *Dedicated, talented, experienced staff*	
• *Well-respected and highly developed case management program*	• *Increased volume of calls on our hotline looking for information on treatment options*
• *Good relationship with the city and state government officials*	• *New drugs allowing people to go back to work and need less direct service—other people with terminal illnesses (e.g., cancer) could benefit from our services*
• *Successful transition from a founder to a new executive director*	
Weaknesses:	**Threats:**
• *Our financial and information management and reporting systems are not giving us the information we need.*	• *Increased monitoring of some of our more controversial education programs*
	• *The economy*
• *We are not able to document impact on prevention.*	• *The complexity of new AIDS treatments and our ability to help our clients understand their choices*
• *Our board is not as active as it could be.*	
• *Recent program data are showing that our educational programs are not having significant effect on behavior.*	• *Increasing demand from funding community to document success*

Internal Forces	External Forces
Weaknesses:	**Threats:**
• Our staff can't keep up with new treatment options.	• Issues of homophobia and perceptions that AIDS is still primarily a gay problem
• People with AIDS are not integrated with our HIV prevention efforts.	• Continued evidence of new HIV infections among men and women in the African-American community and immigrants from Southeast Asia.
• We do not have sufficient bilingual staff.	• Changing policies and funding priorities at the federal level
• We have high staff turnover: staff feel overwhelmed and line staff salaries have not kept up with the cost of living in our city.	
• We do not have sufficient ethnic diversity in staff.	
• Our prevention outreach and education	

CASE STUDY—ASO/USA

❏ Evaluate each of your programs in terms of community needs, results, competitive position, and potential for increased efficiency.

Note: If you are filling this out by hand, please write legibly.

Program/service name: *Support Services (includes case management, support groups, transportation vouchers, benefits counseling, and employment referrals)*

Name of person(s) filling out this assessment: *Delores Molina*

Date: *September 5, 2004*

Description of program service: *Support services for people living with HIV/AIDS are designed to help them live full and productive lives. Case management is a service that links and coordinates assistance from multiple agencies and caregivers who provide psychosocial, medical, and practical support. The purpose of case management is to enable clients to obtain the highest levels of independence and quality of life consistent with their functional capacity and preferences for care. Support groups provide peer psychosocial and emotional support, transportation vouchers provide the practical means for clients to get to their health care and other appointments, benefits counseling helps clients access the most appropriate public and other programs that help pay for their care, and employment referrals help clients to secure work if and when the client has this as a goal.*

Units of service/number of people served including demographic information (if applicable)

We have a caseload of 300 clients. One hour of service is a unit of service, and each client receives an average of 70 hours per year. Therefore, 21,000 units of service are provided annually at a cost of $45.95 per unit of service (program expenses = $965,000 divided by 21,000 units of service).

Total Annual Expenses: *965,000*   Total Annual Revenue: *1,000,000*

What is the need in the community that this program exists to meet? *Many people in the community living with HIV/AIDS do not have adequate health insurance or experience other barriers to service, and therefore do not have regular access to the health care and support services needed to live healthy and productive lives.*

Who is the target audience(s) that this program serves to reach? *Low-income individuals who are not otherwise being reached by public or private health and social services*

What impact does this program currently have, or intend to have, on addressing the need articulated above? What is the outcome(s) of this program's work?

The people who receive services in our Support Services program have demonstrated increases in their access to services, improvements in basic health indicators, and improvements in quality of life indicators.

Measures of success: What evidence do you have to show that this program is having the impact you want it to have? How do we know we are being successful? What do this program's customers/clients consider value? How do we currently measure success: What are the indicators of success (benchmarks) we currently use to measure success?

- *We count the number of people served and the hours of service provided.*
- *We measure their access to services based on levels of access when we enroll them and at periodic points of service.*
- *We measure basic indicators of health (as established by the City Department of Public Health for people living with HIV/AIDS).*
- *We administer a quality of life survey to clients every six months.*

How should we measure success? Are there other indicators of success we should use in measuring success? How should we measure results/impact/outcomes of this program in improving the quality of constituents' lives and making a difference in the world?

We should include a client satisfaction survey to assess our clients' satisfaction with their level of access to needed services, and to determine whether our clients find our services culturally appropriate.

What are the greatest strengths of this program?
- *Staff*
- *Reputation*
- *Training process*
- *Relationships with clients*

What are the greatest weaknesses of this program?
- *Inadequate facilities for case managers*
- *Improving, but still inadequate internal record-keeping systems (too much on paper!)*
- *Lack of formalized policies and processes for documenting and reporting on our successes*

What are the trends in the environment—political, social, economic, technological, demographic, legal forces—that are or will be impacting this program in the future: trends either potentially moving the program forward (opportunities) or holding it back (threats)?

- *More working-poor people are losing health insurance*
- *Increased demand on the system of care, making it harder for our case managers to get people into the programs they need (e.g., substance use treatment)*
- *Increasing number of people with limited English language skills*
- *Increasing service needs among the population due various economic and political factors—including needs for mental health and substance use treatment*

(continues)

How could we improve the cost effectiveness of this program?

- *Make better use of computers.*
- *Provide administrative support to case managers (e.g., clerical tasks and scheduling appointments).*

How could we improve the quality of this program? How could we improve our ability to deliver this product/provide this service? If we were to reinvent this program, what changes would we make in how the service/product is delivered?

- *Update information on all available community resources more frequently (i.e., monthly versus every six months).*
- *Arrange for more consistent intake procedures with the services to which we refer our clients.*
- *Find ways to provide services onsite (e.g., mental health treatment, substance use treatment) when community resources cannot be identified, or community resources cannot handle the demand.*

How might we better market this program (i.e., increase the public's awareness of this program)?

Develop and enhance relationships with other ASOs and health and social service agencies, so they know they can refer clients to us.

Is there potential for (starting/increasing/improving) collaboration? How? With whom?

Within the organization:

- *Need better support from finance department to know how we are doing on our units of service*
- *Need better coordination between Support Services and Public Education to consider how we are meeting the unique prevention needs of HIV-positive people and how we can better incorporate prevention into Support Services*
- *Would like to give more input to public policy folks*

Outside of the organization? In what ways? With whom? Why?

- *Our voice should be stronger in the HIV prevention and CARE planning bodies.*
- *We need to identify agencies (e.g., ASOs and other health and social services agencies) that work with the same target populations so that we can maximize our collective effect, create better referral networks, and not duplicate services.*

If the budget for this program were suddenly cut, what would you recommend we do?

Close the southeast satellite office that we opened in 1997 and focus on only the clients on the north side of town; they are the people who have absolutely no other options.

If the budget for this program was suddenly increased, what would you recommend we do?

Create a formal prevention with positives component for this program, hire more bilingual/bicultural staff, and increase both the number of people served and the intensity of service (e.g., regular follow-up with people who don't come in for their appointments).

Competitive Analysis of This Program

Program fit:

How is this program congruent with the overall purpose and mission of our organization?

Core to what we do!

How does/could this program draw on existing skills in the organization and share resources/coordinate activities with other programs?

It already does quite well. As mentioned earlier, Support Services could better collaborate with the Public Education Unit (our prevention program), drawing on the expertise there to create a prevention with positives component.

Ability to Attract Resources:

(*Note:* The ability to attract resources deals with issues of market demand; stable funding or ability to provide current and future support; appeals to volunteers; measurable, reportable program results; complements other programs; low exit barriers—ability to discontinue program or abandon past commitment without alienating supporters.)

Does this program have the potential to attract resources and enhance existing programs?

___X___ Yes   _____ No

Because our services cover both our direct and indirect costs (our share of general and administration) we are in good shape. Not much ability to increase support though.

Competitive Position:

(*Note:* A program with a strong competitive position is one that meets the following criteria: good logistical delivery system; large reservoir of client, community, or support group loyalty; past success in securing funding; strong potential to raise funds; superior track record/image of service delivery; large market share of the target clientele; better-quality service/product/service delivery than competitors; superior organization, management, and technical skills; cost-effective delivery of service.)

(continues)

Are there many groups, or few groups, providing similar services in the community? Who else is doing the same or similar work to address this need in our geographic area?

___XX___ Few Groups   _____ Many Groups

List names of groups here: *City Clinic (but they don't do all that we do). Also, Two Trees Medical Clinic and the Asian AIDS Clinic. The Resource Center for Positives has a more comprehensive employment referral and training program than we do.*

Do you think your program is in a strong competitive position in relation to the above groups?

___X___ Yes, strong competitive position   _____ No, not a competitive position

With the exception of the Resource Center for Positives.

Why do you think it is important for our organization to address this need (as opposed to another organization)? What is your program's competitive advantage? What makes your program unique in comparison to the competition?

Our staff and volunteers have strong and longstanding relationships with our clients, and the community trusts us. We also have great capacity to do this work compared with our competitors—we have smaller caseloads per case manager, we have a larger program budget, and we have a more ethnically diverse staff. However, we are at a competitive disadvantage with Resource Center for Positives—they provide a more comprehensive service, as it is their main focus.

Suggested future growth strategy for this program:

___X___ Increase   _____ Maintain   _____ Decrease   _____ Eliminate

If we can attract more resources, we can definitely serve more people and improve the program by adding a prevention-with-positives component.

Why this strategy? Include the implications if we were to ignore this strategy.

This program is the core of what we do, and we do it best out of all the agencies providing similar services. There is also an increasing demand for these services, and if we do not grow this program, marginalized individuals living with HIV/AIDS in our city could fall through the cracks.

What impact would this growth strategy have on our resources (staff time and other expenditures) and revenues?

If we grow the program, we have to grow the resources and the number of staff. This means seeking out more revenues—and probably not from government, since we want to reduce our reliance on this potentially unstable funding source.

Analysis of Competitive Position (fill this in only if applicable)

Name of organization	Ability to provide service				Quality of service				Why did you rate the ability to provide service the way you did? Why did you give the rating on quality of service
Our program:	4 ✔ Excellent	3 Good	2 Fair	1 Poor	4 ✔ Excellent	3 Good	2 Fair	1 Poor	We have below-average caseloads per case manager and clients keep coming back.
Competitor: City Clinic	4 Excellent	3 Good	2 ✔ Fair	1 Poor	4 Excellent	3 Good	2 ✔ Fair	1 Poor	They have high turnover and staff is not up to date on health issues for people living with HIV/AIDS.
Competitor: Two Trees Medical Clinic	4 Excellent	3 ✔ Good	2 Fair	1 Poor	4 ✔ Excellent	3 Good	2 Fair	1 Poor	This is a private clinic that serves a high-income population on the west side of town.
Competitor: Asian AIDS Clinic	4 Excellent	3 Good	2 ✔ Fair	1 Poor	4 Excellent	3 Good	2 ✔ Fair	1 Poor	This is a small, understaffed AIDS health and social services clinic that primarily serves Chinese immigrants.

Other competitors not assessed:

CASE STUDY—ASO/USA

❏ Summarize the data you have collected during your strategic planning process; summarize your findings. You can summarize your data either by the categories of mission, money, administration, and governance, or, if you gathered data according to your strategic issues, use the issue summary page to summarize your findings.

❏ You may wish to compile a summary of all of your findings regarding your organization's strengths, weaknesses, opportunities, and threats on the last page.

Summary of Findings—Mission: How well are we achieving our mission and how could we have a greater impact?

What did you find out regarding current and future needs of your constituencies? How well is the organization meeting the needs in the community?

- *While the population in the city is decreasing, we have seen a dramatic increase in demand for our services by 28 percent in the last three years.*

- *Housing referrals—as well as coverage for the high cost of drug treatments and access to dental services—continues to be a major unmet need.*

- *Those who live in the southeast corner of the city value having access to our services at our location there, but they report frustration at having to take long bus rides to access the services we refer them to; and the lack of sufficient bilingual staff at the southeast site is hampering our efforts to work with immigrant communities.*

- *Our education programs in schools and businesses are well regarded. Our education programs in communities most impacted by HIV/AIDS have not been as effective as we would like, partly because the efforts are not targeted enough to the highest-risk groups.*

- *Our employment referral program, while in alignment with our mission, is our least-used service. Only 5 percent of our case managed clients used this service in the last three years.*

- *We are well respected by organizations with whom we collaborate within the policy arena.*

- *Our support groups get high satisfaction ratings but have recently not been well attended.*

- *Regarding expanding beyond HIV/AIDS work, our extensive interviews resulted in a split of opinions about people's feelings as to whether it was a good idea or not, but there was fairly consistent agreement that right now is not the right time to expand services*

Who else is providing similar products/services—potential and real competitors/collaborators? What distinguishes our organization from others doing similar work?

The City Clinic tries to serve our population, and we have tried to help them do a better job. Two Trees Social Services Center and Asian AIDS Clinic are small entities that have a local following with a limited client base. Another AIDS Service Organization—Community Cares—that was 30 miles from our office, recently closed its doors and as a result their clients are starting to ask to use our services. While they don't technically meet our funding guidelines, we have in the past been committed to not turning anyone away who has a need.

Is the organization providing services/products effectively and efficiently? Is the organization valued for offering high quality, innovative and effective services/products? Is the organization well known and respected in the community? What evidence do you have to support your answer?

Client satisfaction surveys and focus groups confirm that we are providing quality services to our constituencies. However, economically disadvantaged and disenfranchised individuals—those who are at greatest risks for HIV and who have the least access to services in the community—gave lower marks to easy access to service. Our hotline staff is having trouble keeping up with all the new treatment information that is available. The funders and community leaders who we spoke with gave high praise for our organization as a place that provides quality services.

Possible Considerations for the Future—Program: How well are we achieving our mission and how could we have a greater impact?

Emerging themes and/or priorities:

- *We need bilingual and multicultural staff.*
- *Given the number of individuals we are seeing from the southeast side of the city and those from the now-defunct Community Cares, we need to explore options for providing increased services in those areas or collaborating with other organizations. We do not currently have the capacity to expand our services beyond people living with HIV/AIDS—we will revisit this topic in two years.*
- *We need greater policy and advocacy at a federal and city level regarding housing for people with HIV/AIDS.*
- *We need to revamp our education program to be more effective and more focused on high-risk populations.*

(continues)

Based on the information gathered, are there things that the organization should consider doing differently, more of, less of, the same? Are there things that the organization should consider starting/stopping? Does the mission or vision need to be revisited? How or why? What is the unique niche that the organization fills? How does or should the organization distinguish itself from the competition?

- *New programs are needed: housing voucher program, prevention with positives program.*

- *Increase HIV-prevention work with high-risk populations—perhaps move beyond the outreach and hotline to doing more risk reduction/harm reduction services.*

- *Discontinue the employment referral program and refer those interested in employment assistance to Resource Center for Positives, the main employment and job-training program for people living with HIV/AIDS in the city.*

- *Maintain or decrease support groups pending further investigation as to why attendance is declining.*

- *Increase policy and advocacy work, particularly around housing for people living with HIV/AIDS.*

- *Consider spinning off treatment calls to the hotline and having those calls handled by a national organization such as Project Inform.*

- *Our unique niche is that we are the only full-service AIDS Service organization in the county. If we did have competitors, we would have to explore in more detail the core competencies that keep us ahead of the competition. But just because we are almost the only place in town to provide services, that is not an excuse for not continually looking at how can we ensure quality services to our clients.*

What discussions pertaining to program still need to happen? How and when will those discussions happen?

- *How can we modify our education program to provide better service to high-risk populations, and how are we going to identify the high-risk populations we should be reaching? The education director and staff are scheduled to present a proposal to the planning committee in one month.*

- *Our board has stated that expansion to another county is not an option. Given that Community Care clients are showing up at our door, we need to figure out how to ensure that their clients can find services. The Support Services director will convene/spearhead a task force, with recommendations due by board/staff planning retreat.*

Summary of Findings—Finances

Are our operations financially viable, and how can we ensure the long-term financial stability of our organization?

This year is the second year in a row that we have had to go into our reserves to support our programs. While the amounts are not large and we are not financially in jeopardy because of the negative $15,000 this year and negative $12,500 last year, we are going to have to develop an ambitious and yet realistic fund development plan to support this strategic plan. The fund development plan should be focused on increasing foundation, corporate, and individual support. In our planning discussions where we set priorities, we may have to do some zero-based budgeting or scenario planning if the future numbers just don't add up.

Also, we have had to use Support Services funds to support other programs. This is an indication that our other programs are under-funded. Our fund development strategy must take this into account.

Do we have effective financial management systems in place to use our resources effectively, monitor our finances, and ensure accountability?

Our financial management systems do not have the ability to give us the detailed and up-to-date information we need. Improving our financial systems is a short-term priority, and our new chief finance officer/controller has been given a mandate to put a new accounting system in place within the next four months.

What are the emerging themes/priorities regarding our financial capacity?

Ensuring our long-term financial viability (resource development):

- *Increase development staff.*
- *Increase collaborative efforts in the public policy and advocacy arenas regarding funding for people with AIDS.*
- *Use the strategic plan as a fundraising vehicle.*

Ensuring effective financial management:

- *Implement a new accounting system and computers as soon as possible.*
- *Increase involvement of program managers in budget development and control.*
- *It's been six years since we changed auditors—good internal controls tells us it's the right time to do so.*

(continues)

Primary Strengths— organizational strengths that support the organization's long-term financial viability and financial accountability	Primary Weaknesses— organizational weaknesses that work against the organization's long-term financial viability and accountability	Primary Opportunities— trends that the organization could take advantage of so as to better ensure its long-term financial viability and financial accountability	Primary Threats—trends in the external environment that are working against the organization's long-term financial viability and accountability)
• *New finance manager* • *Some reserves (10% of operating expenses)* • *Some board members are increasingly active in fundraising and PR* • *We have a relatively large annual budget for an ASO, with multiple funding sources*	• *We rely too heavily on government funding—82%* • *Barely passed last audit by city* • *Deficit spending: past year and this year* • *Outdated computer systems that cannot run new software package we just purchased* • *Only one staff in fund development*	• *One funder is interested in a capacity building grant that includes assisting in technology upgrade and in hiring a grant writer* • *Renewed interest by regional AIDS organizations to increase resources in the public policy arena*	• *Increased competition for charitable funds* • *Current economic situation is not likely to dramatically change for a while* • *Changing funding priorities on a federal level* • *Continued high costs of AIDS treatment drugs* • *Funder fatigue—HIV/AIDS is not the hot issue of the day anymore among funders*

What discussions still need to happen regarding our finances? How and when will those discussions happen?

Develop long-term fund development plan—one that includes minimum and optimum estimated costs to achieve vision. Development director and resource development committee of the board to work with the executive director to draft a fundraising plan after a draft of the strategic plan is completed.

After the plan is adopted, staff will develop program scenarios that will anticipate changes one way or the other in the organization's financial situation.

Summary of Findings—Administrative Capacity

Do we have the administrative capacity to effectively and efficiently support our programs and services?

Yes, and no. Our administrative capacity has certainly improved over the past few years, especially in terms of communication, planning, and leadership development; however, our computer technology is far from adequate and our staffing and benefits continue to be a focus of dissatisfaction among staff.

Summary of Primary Administrative Strengths—organizational strengths that indicate a strong administrative capacity	Summary of Primary Administrative Weaknesses— organizational weaknesses that indicate a vulnerability in administrative capacity
• *Highly skilled and respected staff* • *Improved communication and meetings since last strategic planning efforts* • *Good working relationship among departments* • *Senior management team works well together* • *Strong clerical support for management*	• *Recently, high turnover of middle management staff* • *Staff salaries and benefits not commensurate with cost of living* • *Software/hardware not able to produce information we need* • *Location of central office is increasingly feeling unsafe* • *Not up-to-date employee manuals* • *Lack of policy and procedures manuals*

What are the themes that are emerging from our data collection regarding our administrative capacity?

• *We need to invest in our staff in terms of increasing salaries and benefits, especially a retirement plan. We also need to make sure that our technology is*

(continues)

able to support our growing financial management and client tracking requirements.

- *Our central office lease is up next year. We should start to explore now whether we should move to a safer location.*
- *There is increased attention to tracking clients through the electronic centralization of our recordkeeping.*
- *Update all policies and procedures manuals.*

What discussions still need to happen regarding administrative capacity? How and when will those discussions happen?

- *Convene a task force to look at options for moving our central office. Board treasurer will take the lead on this.*
- *Fiscal office will complete a wage and benefits survey and work with the executive director to develop a plan for improving salaries and benefits by the end of the year.*

Summary of Findings—Goverance

How effectively is the board protecting the public's interest—ensuring that charitable dollars are used effectively and efficiently and that the organization is fulfilling its mission?

The board has made great strides over the past two years to improve its capacity to govern. This includes formalized board structures and systems in terms of

Primary Board Strengths—indicators of a strong and effective board	Weaknesses—indicators of a vulnerability in the board's ability to govern and support the organization
• *Well-run meetings that are less report focused and more discussion oriented* • *Committees with clear mandates* • *Finance committee that regularly meets to ensure legal compliance and review of financial statements* • *Regular evaluation of executive director* • *Conflict of interest policy statement signed by each board member each year*	• *Lack of diversity* • *Lack of orientation program for new members* • *Not have 100% board giving* • *Inconsistent board representation at community meetings and fundraising events* • *Lack of collateral material for board members to use for public relations and fundraising* • *No medical doctor or CPA currently on the board*

committees, meetings, agendas ahead of time, and regular board self-evaluation. The board successfully transitioned from meeting every month to every other month, with committees meeting on alternate months.

How might the board's composition, responsibilities, and processes need to change to support the long-term goals and objectives of the organization?

- *Develop and implement a board-orientation program.*

- *Provide ongoing training to board members (e.g., how to ask for money, how to read financial statements, issues related to policy and legal compliance).*

- *Create a board contract/statement of agreement that outlines specific board responsibilities and is signed every year.*

- *Have each board member sign yearly an individual fund development plan that confirms their personal gift and specifies donor development activities that each member is committing to.*

- *The board development committee will develop a board composition matrix to assess current composition. After completion of the strategic plan, the matrix will identify gaps in the current board composition and the skills (e.g., fundraising experience, affiliation, and demographics) that are needed to help support the organization's future vision.*

- *Establish a community advisory board.*

What discussions still need to happen regarding board governance? How and when will those discussions happen?

Board discussion regarding when and how does the board sign off on policy statements issued by the staff—board president to ensure this discussion happens at next board meeting

(Optional) Summary of Data Collection by Strategic Issue

Strategic issue:

Our revenues are vulnerable. Our current business model assumes major ongoing government funding. How do we decrease our overdependence on federal funding? Should we start to charge for services?

Summary of findings—issue:

It has been our policy not to charge fees for service, based on a guiding principle that states: **All people deserve quality health care.** *We have always defined* **health** *care in the broadest sense to include all support services that ensure individuals stay healthy, including: case management, support groups,*

(continues)

transportation, and other services. An in-depth assessment of the economic status of our clients reveals that our clients are almost exclusively low income, many living below the poverty line. This makes them eligible to participate in programs supported by federal funds, which in turn is an incentive for us to continue to rely on federal funds; however, due to federal policy changes, the amount and focus of federal HIV/AIDS funding in the coming years is uncertain. Assuming that the federal HIV/AIDS money will always be there could have disastrous consequences.

Possible considerations for the future:

Explore opportunities for federal funding from other departments, such as SAMHSA and HUD. Although it would still be federal funding, at least it would be diversified. Also, build relationships with corporate and community foundations who share a commitment to improving health in underserved communities. Consider having a large annual fundraiser, such as a dinner or a talent show, to encourage individual donors to give.

What discussions still need to happen? How and when will those discussions happen?

Development director and resource development committee need to meet and develop a realistic short-term and long-term development plan that will allow us to operate with a break-even budget and enable us to support the strategies articulated in the soon-to-be-written strategic plan. This development plan needs to address the need to diversify our funding sources.

CHAPTER 5

Phase 4: Agree on Priorities

In this phase, the planning process takes an important turn. The first three phases encourage expansive, exploratory thinking. Phase 1, Phase 2, and Phase 3 all have to do with considering possibilities, gathering new information, and dreaming big dreams. In Phase 4 it is time to stop exploring and to ground the discussions in realism. The process at this stage is not linear. The discussions undertaken during this phase are frequently the most challenging — and the most rewarding — part of the strategic planning process. Possible choices have been identified; it is time to choose a course of action.

The easy part of planning is choosing what to do; the hard part of planning is in consciously choosing what you will not do. Simpler said than done. We provide several options for processes to assist with the choosing process precisely because it is a messy process. This phase is experienced as a combination of intuition and analysis, using both facts and hunches, hopes and fears.

A WORD ABOUT WORDS

- *Strategic planning* is a systematic process through which an organization agrees on, and builds commitment among key stakeholders to, priorities that are essential to its mission and responsive to the environment.

- A *strategy* is a coordinated, broad approach or direction that informs organizational resource allocation.

- A *goal* is an ends statement that guides a program or management function.

(continues)

A WORD ABOUT WORDS *(Continued)*

- *Program and management functions* are the means an organization employs to implement strategies and accomplish the mission.
- An *objective* is a precise, measurable, time-phased result that supports the achievement of a goal.

OVERVIEW OF PHASE 4

The flow of the strategic planning process suggests that an organization should be ready to establish its overall direction at this point because it has officially gone through the previous phases of developing a mission statement and assessing its situation:

- The mission statement has defined the purpose and should serve as a compass for setting the direction and identifying which programmatic and organizational strategies will best move the organization forward.
- The assessment of the organization's strengths and weaknesses, the evaluation of client needs and programs, and the external market data have produced information and analysis that will help align strategic choices with the most significant forces in the environment.

  - The strategic planning process now requires in-depth discussions about strategic issues and choices facing the organization and the appropriate long- and short-term priorities. The planning committee must devote sufficient time to these discussions. If an organization is looking for a shortcut to the strategic planning process, this is not the place to do it. The organization that hasn't sufficiently thought things out or tested the feasibility of certain ideas may make imprudent choices.

  - As Benjamin Tregoe and John Zimmerman, two strategic planning experts, write: "If an organization is headed in the wrong direction, the last thing it needs is to get there more efficiently. And if an organization is headed in the right direction, it surely does not need to have that direction unwittingly taken in a strategic void."[1]

One challenge lies in having to make the difficult business decisions regarding which programs to grow, how much to invest in your infrastructure, and what programs should be eliminated or fundamentally changed. During Phase 4, you are forced to confront the nonprofit sector's dual bottom lines of mission and financial viability:

- Does this program make sense from a *mission* point of view (meeting needs in the community)? Given limited charitable dollars available to support our work, are we the best organization to provide this service—or could our competitors do a better job?

- Does this program make sense *financially*? How much do we need to invest in our program and administrative capacity to ensure effective and efficient delivery of services?

Another challenge lies in the fact that strategic planning is not just about making decisions; it is also about making decisions that have the full commitment of leaders and ultimately all members of an organization. In other words, there are no scientifically correct answers to be discovered. Strategic planning is about making sense of things and deciding what to do as a group. If you don't have significant consensus about your plans, you don't have a strategic plan that has much chance of helping your organization succeed.

> Until one is committed there is always hesitancy, the chance to draw back, always ineffectiveness. Concerning all acts (and creation) there is always one elementary truth, ignorance of which kills countless ideas and splendid plans: that the moment one definitely commits oneself, then providence moves too. All sorts of things occur to help one that would never otherwise have occurred. A whole stream of events issues from the decision raising one's favor all manner of unforeseen incidents and meetings and material assistance, which no man could have dreamt would have come his way. I have learned a great respect for one of Goethe's Couplets: "Whatever you do, or dream, begin it. Boldness has genius, power and magic in it."[2]

In Phase 2, you started to define your ultimate vision. In Phase 3, you assessed your situation to determine the driving forces that would move your vision forward or hold you back. In Phase 4, you need to agree on the core directions toward that vision (strategies), as well as how far and how fast you will move toward that vision.

In the end, the reason this phase can be so rewarding is that insight is gained here, and from new insight new inspiration is born. Although the prospect of discussing all possible program and organizational options might seem overwhelming at first, planners usually find it fun and invigorating to hash out the answers to the most important questions facing the organization.

There are four key steps in this phase:

1. Make sense of the data, review progress to date, and agree on how to move the planning process to completion.

2. Use business planning: Assess the program portfolio and develop a future program portfolio.

3. Confirm the three to five core future strategies that will serve as the primary focus of the organization's resources for the next three years.

4. Agree on administrative, governance, and financial priorities.

Don't be surprised if at this point the planning process refuses to follow a straightforward path. During this phase, the planning committee may decide to revisit discussions held in previous phases. For example, the planning committee might recognize that additional research is needed regarding a new client group or alternative program design. If the planning committee starts to consider changing current program priorities, they might want to convene additional focus groups to get input on possible changes.

Sometimes the planning committee, as a result of such a shift in priorities, may even need to revisit the organization's mission statement. The planning committee must balance the desire to move the planning process forward to conclusion with the need to achieve sufficient understanding and consensus to move forward with confidence.

Remember that individuals on the planning committee, whether staff or board members, are likely to experience the process very differently: Some people will be feeling the most confused just when others are feeling the most clear, and then they might change places. There are two keys to minimizing confusion and maximizing buy-in. First, give yourselves permission to be confused. The process at this state is not linear, so the swirling of ideas is normal, not a problem. Second, try to keep other people appropriately informed as discussions unfold and try to anticipate the need various stakeholders have to give meaningful input.

Step 4.1: Analyze Data, Review Progress to Date, and Update Workplan

By this time, important levels of agreement and understanding have been reached, and our discussions in Phase 4 should build on what has been agreed on in Phases 1, 2, and 3. Worksheet 12, which you completed in Phase 3, is the bridge between Phases 3 and 4 (see Exhibit 5.1). Thus, by the time you have finished summarizing your situation and making sense of the data collected, several mission, financial, administrative, and governance priorities are emerging—some of the answers to the strategic questions you developed in Phase 1 (Worksheet 1) have become evident. While some priorities are emerging and common themes for the future becoming clearer, the data may have also revealed additional questions or need for different research.

- At this time, the planning committee should review the specific strategic questions or choices that your organization wanted to address during the planning process, as well as what you said you wanted to achieve from the planning process. Has your group learned anything

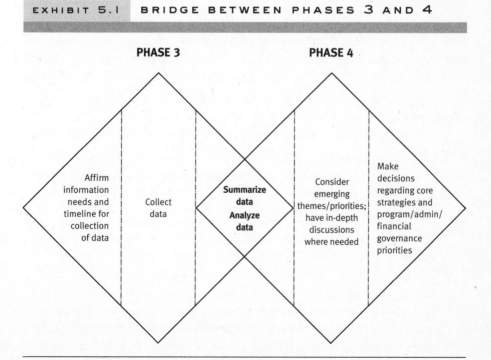

EXHIBIT 5.1   BRIDGE BETWEEN PHASES 3 AND 4

PHASE 3   PHASE 4

Affirm information needs and timeline for collection of data

Collect data

Summarize data
Analyze data

Consider emerging themes/priorities; have in-depth discussions where needed

Make decisions regarding core strategies and program/admin/ financial governance priorities

during the first three phases that changes your understanding of your initial questions?

- The planning committee should stop and reflect on the work it did in developing the mission, vision, and values statements. In addition to the content of the statements, remember the discussions that took place. Are there any additional or reframed questions that need to be addressed in Phase 4?

- Does your plan for planning workplan need to be modified to accommodate the analysis required for coming to decisions that will be supported by your organization? How—and who—should be involved at this point in setting your long-term priorities? Review the workplan and adjust it as necessary.

SWOT Analysis Grid

One way of continuing to make sense of the data you have previously collected is to look at the juxtaposition of strengths, weaknesses, opportunities, and threats through use of a SWOT grid (see Exhibit 5.2). A SWOT analysis grid is a way of looking at the broader implications of the SWOT analysis work done in Phase 3; the grid can help make visible some important dynamics that influence an organization's strategic choices (i.e., the intersection of strengths, weaknesses, opportunities, and threats), and can offer suggestions about action the organization should consider undertaking. In effect, this grid asks a planner to consider the interplay of core competencies with the key forces in the organization's environment.

In an article entitled "From Comparative Advantage to Damage Control: Clarifying Strategic Issues Using SWOT Analysis," Professor Kevin Kearns states that if an organization simply brainstorms strengths, weaknesses, opportunities, and threats:

> SWOT analysis can degenerate into a superficial list-generating exercise that produces four unconnected lists: strengths, weaknesses, opportunities, and threats. Without a systematic effort to relate the lists to each other, they are of limited utility, especially in clarifying fundamental policy choices facing the agency. . . . SWOT analysis requires nonlinear and iterative thinking, which assumes that goals and strategies emerge from the juxtaposition of opportunities and threats in the external environment and strengths and weaknesses in

the internal environment. Dimensions of a critical issue and related responses may emerge that otherwise might not surface. For example, one small community-based counseling center faced two significant threats: a major loss of public support as a result of rumors of embezzlement and increasing demands from funders for more complex financial reporting. These threats intersected with weaknesses in financial management in the "damage control/divest" cell of the SWOT analysis grid. Because the organization believed that its programs were valuable, the initial response was to quell the rumors and build financial management capacity. However, the grid highlighted the fact that these threats were compounded by organizational weaknesses. Thus, instead the organization developed a new strategy that was, in effect, to divest its financial management function by collaborating with a larger organization as its fiscal agent.[3]

In discussing the interplay of strengths, opportunities, weaknesses, and threats, the planning committee may find a much more advantageous way to frame the question. For example, during the mid-1990s, the Public Broadcasting Service (PBS) increasingly needed to look at its loss of government funding, which was a major threat to its survival. PBS's strength was a loyal and relatively affluent audience. A recognized strength from the past (and a lesson from its history) was the use of innovative programming (e.g., Sesame Street). Rather than simply asking, "How can

EXHIBIT 5.2   SWOT ANALYSIS GRID

	Opportunities	Threats
Strengths	INVEST Clear matches of strengths and opportunities lead to competitive advantage	DEFEND Areas of threat matched by areas of strength indicate a need to mobilize resources either alone or with others
Weaknesses	DECIDE Areas of opportunity matched by areas of weakness require a judgment call: invest or divest; collaborate	DAMAGE CONTROL/DIVEST Areas of threat matched by areas of weakness indicate need for damage control

Source: Adapted from Kevin P. Kearns, "Comparative Advantage to Damage Control: Clarifying Strategic Issues Using SWOT Analysis." *Nonprofit Management and Leadership* 3, no. 1 (Fall 1992): 3–22. All rights reserved.

we replace our government funding?" the question was reframed as, "How can PBS leverage or mobilize its strengths to avert or respond to the loss of government funds?" This led to redoubling efforts to provide greater visibility to funders who were willing to sponsor specific programming. We suggest using a SWOT analysis grid in Step 4.1 as a way to see if any major insights can be gleaned before moving to the process of setting priorities.[4]

Professor Kearns developed the SWOT grid partly out of recognition that many organizations that perform SWOT analysis simply come up with a laundry list of strengths, weaknesses, opportunities, and threats. These organizations may prioritize the items listed and decide how to best respond to a particular strength, weakness, opportunity, or threat; however, when one takes that analysis a step further and looks at the juxtaposition of strengths to opportunities and threats and weaknesses to those same external forces, important strategies can emerge:

- If the situation assessment reveals a major opportunity, that opportunity can only be exploited if the organization has complementary strengths. In such cases, the organization should take advantage of its competitive position and invest in the program. If, however, the organization cannot effectively respond to the opportunity because of a significant weakness, the organization needs to decide whether to invest resources and turn the weakness into a strength so it can take advantage of the opportunity or let the opportunity go. For example: A small community clinic was faced with the opportunity of being located in a community that was experiencing a large increased population growth of immigrants from Russia. The planning committee recognized that the clinic did not have the capabilities to respond to that opportunity because it had neither bilingual staff fluent in Russian nor an understanding of the unique needs of that population (weaknesses). The SWOT Grid's recommendation of "collaborate" was taken into consideration, and the clinic approached the Russian Immigration Social Service Center regarding a joint project to meet clients' health needs.

- If the situation assessment reveals a major threat to the organization, that threat can only be successfully responded to if the organization has a complementary strength. In such cases, the organization should mobilize resources either alone or with the help of others. If, however, the organization is faced with a threat and is made more vulnerable because of an identified weakness, the organization needs to, at the very least, do damage control. Example: A consumer protection group was concerned because of increasing legislation that was negatively impacting consumers' rights (threat). They did not have a staff person who was specifically focused on public policy activities, nor a strong member services department (weaknesses). The board recognized that if the organization was going to be able to help consumers that it needed to invest resources into hiring a staff person whose sole focus was on public policy and member education.

Consider Ad Hoc Task Forces for This Phase of the Strategic Planning Process

The strategic planning committee is often the group that not only coordinates the planning process but also leads the discussions that need to occur during Phase 4. As the coordinating body, all of the members of the strategic planning committee may or may not have the in-depth knowledge of operations or sufficient expertise with the program to develop detailed recommendations about future directions. One option in this phase is to assign subgroups to work on answering a specific strategic issue, analyze a particular program, or develop specific goals and objectives for different aspects of the organization. Rather than have the planning committee take on all of this work, the ad hoc task force is assigned the responsibility.

For example, an arts organization established four task forces; three of the task forces focused on a particular program function: education and community outreach, artist support, and exhibitions. The fourth task force addressed issues of marketing. Each task force had a few board members and some staff members on it, and each task force was assigned responsibility for answering the following questions:

- What information do you currently have available to you regarding your strengths, weaknesses, opportunities, and threats (and the interplay of SW and OT) that will impact this program?

- Opportunity map: Who else is doing similar work? (This identifies competitors and collaborators.)

- Do you have any recommendations regarding significant changes in how the program/activity is currently being done? Future growth strategy? What might those recommendations be?

- Are there unanswered questions, or things that need further discussion? Is there additional information that might be useful to have in making a decision regarding this program? If yes, what information is needed and how will you get it?

Each task force completed its work in the two-month time frame allocated and made presentations at an all-day board–management team planning retreat. Based on those presentations, management and board members were able to make decisions regarding the future scope and scale of activities for the organization. The task forces allowed the discussions to get done more efficiently as well as provided a critical opportunity for the people who were most knowledgeable and interested in the topic to have a key role in the decision making, thereby increasing the quality of decisions and the level of buy-in. See Appendix H for more guidelines on using task forces.

Step 4.2: Use Business Planning: Tools for Assessing Your Program Portfolio

We call Step 4.2 business planning because it requires the planning committee to look at the development of programs in a way that is integrated with funding strategies. Often nonprofits have developed their program plans and fundraising plans in parallel, as opposed to jointly. Increasingly, as nonprofits generate multiple funding streams and different program activities have different—and changing—potential for revenue generation, it is important to develop program and funding strategies in concert.

Just as businesses surviving in the for-profit sector have to develop sustainable business models, nonprofit organizations[5] must also have a sustainable business model—one that acknowledges and responds to a nonprofit organization's dual bottom lines: mission accomplishment and financial viability.

During the work on program evaluation that you did in Phase 3, you investigated various ways in which to increase impact and/or add new service offerings to achieve impact. In this phase you are concerned with determining future scope and scale of programs; fundamentally, this is a set of questions about growth. In effect there are only three choices: Is this program (either an existing program or a new program) one you want to grow, to maintain at its current level, or to reduce or eliminate?

Changing the program or combining it with another program is just a more involved way of growing, maintaining, or reducing the original program. The decision about growth needs to be informed by both the potential for impact toward your mission and the potential for funding.

We offer two tools to help in deciding what programs and other activities should make up your program portfolio. The tools are similar in that they produce strategy recommendations for programs, but they differ in the approach to analysis offered. The CompassPoint Dual Bottom-Line Matrix offers an approach to program portfolio building that explicitly takes into account the interplay between mission accomplishment and revenue potential for each program area. The Competitive Strategies Matrix explicitly introduces the concept of alternative coverage and competitive position as a factor for consideration in program planning.

CompassPoint's Dual Bottom-Line Matrix[6]

More and more nonprofit organizations fund their operations with a wide range of revenue sources.[7] No longer can we separate program selection and management from fundraising. A business strategy is a portfolio of business lines that fit together.

When choosing priorities for programs and services, nonprofits can find themselves caught between two undesirable approaches. On one hand, it seems as if programs should be chosen based on which are the most important—which have the most mission impact. On the other hand, financial realities affect program priorities: Some programs bring in money, some break even, and some lose money. Thus, each program or business line should be assessed individually in terms of its financial profitability as well as mission impact. We define high financial viability as a business line that at a minimum pays for all of the costs—both direct and indirect costs—that are required to carry out the related activities.

Adapted from the Growth-Share Matrix developed by the Boston Consulting Group,[8] the Dual Bottom-Line Matrix (see Exhibit 5.3) is a tool to help nonprofits balance these two concerns.

Mission impact refers to the importance of a program or a business activity to the organization's goals. For a health clinic, a program with high mission impact might be the free drop-in clinic that serves hundreds of patients each year. The same health clinic might have a small mental health referral service that, while valuable, changes the world in more modest ways than does the free drop-in clinic.

EXHIBIT 5.3   COMPASSPOINT'S DUAL-BOTTOM
                LINE MATRIX

HIGH

HIGH MISSION IMPACT
LOW VIABILITY

BUSINESS DECISION =
HEART: Keep but contain costs

HIGH MISSION IMPACT
HIGH VIABILITY

BUSINESS DECISION =
STAR: Invest in continuance
and growth

LOW MISSION IMPACT
LOW VIABILITY   **?**

BUSINESS DECISION =
QUESTION MARK: Discontinue
or give away

LOW MISSION IMPACT
HIGH VIABILITY $

BUSINESS DECISION =
MONEY MAKER: Enhance impact

Mission Impact

LOW   ➡   **Financial Viability**   ➡   HIGH

In this example, mission impact varies in part because of scale: a larger program usually has greater mission impact than a small program, but mission impact can also vary by intensity. A tutor-mentor program with middle school students may be viewed by an organization as having higher mission impact than a program in the same school that invites parents for training sessions.

Although quantitative measures and impact studies can be used to think about which programs and activities have the highest mission impact, such studies need not be conducted in order to use the Dual Bottom-Line Matrix. In most cases, consensus can be found fairly easily in determining whether a program has high or low mission impact.

Financial viability, too, lends itself both to consensus-based analysis as well as to quantitative inquiry, and each organization will have to find a balance that is appropriate to the decisions being considered. If broad-stroke strategies are under consideration, broad-stroke analysis may be appropriate, but decisions at a more finely tuned level may require more finely tuned analysis.

Nonetheless, it is clear that some programs and business activities do more or less to contribute to the organization's financial viability. There may be a program—let's say the mental health referral program at the health clinic—that is well funded and that pays for its own direct costs as well as helps with organizational overhead and shared costs. An annual fundraising dinner is a business activity that should be highly profitable: it should pay for its direct costs and also contribute to the organization's financial viability. However, many organizations do activities for which they receive very little or no direct funding. It's easy for organizations to get stuck in a push-pull argument: "This program costs too much!" "But it's really important!"

The overall strategy for an organization is to combine a set of programs and business activities that result in its long-term financial viability as well as high mission impact. We call this a portfolio of programs.

How Do We Use CompassPoint's Dual Bottom-Line Matrix to Help Guide Our Strategic Thinking about the Organization?

Some of the characteristics of programs with high mission impact are tangible results, visible progress toward the achievement of the organization's mission, and high leverage potential—synergy with other programs.

Some of the characteristics of high financial viability are: at the very least covers all costs (both direct and indirect), generates a surplus of revenue (profit), is projected to have financial sustainability for the future, and has a proven financially viable business model.

What Is a Recommended Strategy for Each Quadrant?

Star = High Mission Impact + High Financial Viability
Business Strategy — Invest

A Star program is one we want to keep and grow. To do so, we should invest in it—invest time, attention, and money. Some of the ways to invest include the following:

- Ensure that the staff on this program is top-notch.
- Develop and institutionalize relationships with the federal agency.
- Recruit board members who have the ability to advise the program and/or strengthen relationships with the funding agency.
- Write an article for publication about a special aspect of the program.

The opposite of a Star program is one that has low impact and low viability:

Question Mark = Low Mission Impact + Low Financial Viability
Business Strategy—Discontinue or Give Away

If a program falls within this quadrant, the organization must make a decision: Can this program be changed to have a greater mission impact and/or greater financial viability, or should the program be discontinued or given away?

The recommended strategy for a Question Mark program is to discontinue the program or give it to an organization that can make better use of it. There may not be another organization interested in the program, however, so it may be best to simply let it run out its current funding and then stop.

Money Maker = Low Mission Impact + High Financial Viability
Business Strategy—Enhance Impact and/or Maximize Profits

Some programs or activities bring in money that support the organization but do not do much else to further the organization's mission. Often these are special fundraising events, whose primary purpose is to raise money.

The recommended strategy for a Money Maker is to enhance mission impact. For example, for a special event, an organization might make sure there is an educational component to the event that helps the community of supporters better understand what the organization does. At the very least, any Money Maker programs should be carefully evaluated to see if their profits are maximized so as to support the program's ability to have a higher mission impact.

Heart = High Mission Impact + Low Financial Viability
Business Strategy — Contain Costs

Most organizations have at least one program that has high impact, is deeply associated with the organization, and is underfunded. Perhaps it costs more to deliver than the government funding received for it, or perhaps it is an essential service for low-income people who cannot pay for it. Such a program is too important—in mission impact and in organizational identity—to close down, but at the same time, it's a drain on the organization's unrestricted assets that often cannot be maintained. The strategy for a Heart program is to keep it, but to contain the costs or see if there is any way of increasing revenues (e.g., charging a sliding scale).

Using the Model

Let's look at how CompassPoint's Dual Bottom-Line Matrix might be used in assessing an organization's program portfolio. Let's say a community center is looking at four programs and business activities:

1. Renting the building to community groups such as AA, Girl Scouts, basketball league, and others
2. Home ownership loan and renovation program funded by the federal government
3. Stop smoking program funded by a health foundation
4. Annual fundraising dinner and auction

Each of the programs and business activities were placed in their appropriate quadrant (see Exhibit 5.4):

- *Building rentals.* High mission impact ("this is what we're in business to do—provide space for community efforts"); low financial viability ("these groups can't afford much, and the security, janitorial, and repair costs can get pretty high")

  At the community center, for example, renting rooms to the Girl Scouts, AA, and self-help groups is part of the center's mission and identity, but the fees are low to make it possible for these groups to rent the space. In order to limit the program's drain on the organization's unrestricted funds, the community center could do better financially by raising fees or by leasing rooms for commercial offices. To continue providing this important service without going broke

EXHIBIT 5.4 USING COMPASSPOINT'S DUAL-BOTTOM LINE MATRIX

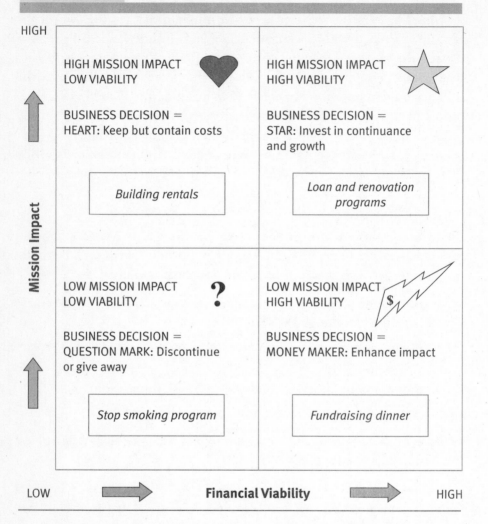

doing so, the center must find a way to limit the net costs of the program. Perhaps the community center can be rented five nights per week, instead of seven. Perhaps the fees can be raised slightly. Perhaps one room—not all—can be leased to a commercial entity. The center could set a limit on janitorial fees for nights and weekends.

• *Loan and renovation program.* High mission impact ("we help people buy and maintain their homes!"); high financial viability ("it pays for two people on staff and its share of the rent, accounting, and other overhead")

As a Star program, the community center should invest resources so that the program has sufficient resources to operate at a maximum potential and at a level of excellence.

- *Stop smoking program.* Low mission impact ("realistically, not that many people really pay attention"); low financial viability ("these foundation grants hardly pay for themselves given how much time it takes to get them and report on them")

  This program is a Question Mark program. It neither helps many people nor brings in significant funding. It takes up physical and mental space. Almost no one really loves the stop smoking program. The organization must make a decision: Can this program be changed to have a greater impact and/or greater financial viability? If neither can be done quickly, the program should be discontinued or given away. For example, a local hospital might be glad to take over the stop smoking program, because they can put their patients right into the program. There may not be another organization interested in the program, however, so it may be best to simply let it run out its current funding and then stop.

- *Fundraising dinner and auction.* Low mission impact ("the wealthier people in the neighborhood bring their wealthy friends and they socialize with each other"); high financial viability ("we make a lot of money on the event")

  The community center might include a short poetry slam at its dinner that would help its wealthier, older donors become more familiar with and sympathetic to the younger people in the community.

CompassPoint's Dual Bottom-Line Matrix is one way of analyzing an organization's current—and potentially new—program portfolio. The matrix provides suggested business strategies regarding the future scope and scale of particular programs.

Another tool that can be used independently of, or in conjunction with, CompassPoint's Dual Bottom-Line Matrix is one that assesses an organization's program portfolio in terms of the organization's competitive position.

Competitive Strategies Matrix

Nonprofits have not traditionally been thought of as organizations that need to be competitively oriented. Unlike for-profit businesses, which compete for customers and whose survival depends on providing services or products to satisfied paying clients, many nonprofit organizations have operated in a nonmarket, or grants, economy—one in which services were not commercially viable. The customer (client) did not decide which provider got funding; government and foundation funders controlled resource allocation to service providers. In fact, because many nonprofits were the only place to get the service, there wasn't any choice in which provider to go to for the client. Until recently, when the funder community and the nonprofits have increased demands for accountability, there were few incentives for nonprofit organizations to limit rather than expand their services, to define or even consider narrowing their niche, or invest in increasing quality, as long as traditional funders were willing to pay the bills.

As a result, nonprofit organizations have traditionally lacked a business incentive to question the status quo, to assess whether client needs were being met, or to examine the cost-effectiveness or quality of available services. (There has always been a moral commitment to these issues within the nonprofit sector.) But while many nonprofit organization's goods and services are still not commercially viable, the competitive environment has changed. Given this situation, it is more difficult to decide whether competition is or isn't good for clients, especially if that competition, along with increased demand by funders for proven effectiveness, motivates organizations to do a better job.

Funders and clients alike are beginning to demand more quality products and accountability; sole-source nonprofits are finding that their success is encouraging others to enter the field and compete for grants; and grant money and contributions are getting more difficult to come by, even as need and demand increase. This last trend — increasing demand for a smaller pool of resources — requires today's nonprofits to rethink how they do business, to assess the implications of duplication of services, to better define or narrow their niche, and to increase collaboration when possible.

As part of the process of deciding what services (or programs) to maintain, cut, eliminate, expand, or start, an organization should ask some of the following pragmatic questions:

- Why is this service needed? What is the current and future market demand for this service?

- For current services: Is this the most effective way for us to meet the needs of our clients? Could we meet those needs by providing the service in a different format?

- Are we the best organization to provide this service? Why? What makes us the best? Do we have the necessary organizational capabilities to provide quality service?

- Is competition good for our clients? By offering this service ourselves, are we meeting a need that is not being effectively done by anyone else?

- Are we spreading ourselves too thin without the capacity to sustain ourselves? Does this current program (or future program) fit well within our organization's niche? Does this program build on our distinct competency? Are we trying to be all things to all people? Can we be all things to all people?

- Should we work cooperatively with another organization to provide some of our services? Could our clients be better served and resources used more effectively if we were to work with another agency?

One tool that can assist you in answering these questions is the Competitive Strategies Matrix (see Exhibit 5.5). In 1983, Professor MacMillan of Columbia University's Graduate School of Business wrote one of the first articles that specifically addressed the issue of competition in the nonprofit sector. In "Competitive Strategies for Not-for-Profit Agencies,"[9] Professor MacMillan developed a matrix to help nonprofits assess their programs within the context of a nonmarket economy and within the reality of decreasing funds to support needs of clients. The matrix was based on the assumption that duplication of existing comparable services (unnecessary competition) among nonprofit organizations can fragment the limited resources available and leave all providers too weak to increase the quality and cost effectiveness of client services. The matrix also assumed that trying to be all things to all people resulted in mediocre or low-quality service and that nonprofits should focus on delivering higher-quality service in a more focused (and perhaps more limited) way.

MacMillian assessed each current (or prospective) program according to four criteria: fit with mission, potential to attract resources, competitive

EXHIBIT 5.5   COMPETITIVE STRATEGIES MATRIX

		Ability to Attract Resources and Enhance Existing Programs YES		Ability to Attract Resources and Enhance Existing Programs NO	
		Alternative Coverage: MANY	Alternative Coverage: FEW	Alternative Coverage: MANY	Alternative Coverage: FEW
GOOD FIT	Strong Competitive Position YES	1) Growth or maintain competitive edge strategy	4) Growth or maintain competitive edge strategy	5) Build up best competitor: assist another organization provide the service	8) Soul of the agency
	Strong Competitive Position NO	2) Develop and implement an exit strategy	3) Invest in program and administrative capacity or Develop and implement an exit strategy	6) Develop and implement an exit strategy	7) Collaboration strategy
	POOR FIT	Divest or do not start to provide this service.			

Source: Adopted from I. C. Macmillan, "Competitive Strategies for Non-for-Profit Agencies," *Advances in Strategic Management* 1 (London: JAI Press Inc., 1983), pp. 61–82.

position, and alternative coverage. The intersection of these four criteria created a matrix, each of which contained a competitive response strategy.[10]

1. *Fit with mission.* The degree to which a program belongs or fits within an organization. Criteria for good fit include:
   - Congruence with the purpose and mission of the organization
   - Ability to draw on existing skills in the organization
   - Ability to share resources and coordinate activities with other programs

2. *Potential to attract resources and enhance existing programs.* The degree to which a program is attractive to the organization from an economic perspective, as an investment of current and future resources, which

primarily has to do with whether the program easily attracts resources or enhances existing resources. Programs that can attract resources are more likely to be economically viable. Conversely, programs that cannot attract resources or have limited resources may not be economically viable. No program should be classified as "Yes: Attracts Resources" unless it is ranked as attractive on a substantial majority of the criteria as follows:

- Complements or enhances existing programs
- Market demand from a large client base
- High appeal to groups capable of providing current and future support
- Stable funding
- Appeal to volunteers
- Measurable, reportable program results
- Able to discontinue relatively easily if necessary (low exit barriers/ ability to discontinue program or abandon past commitment)

3. *Alternative coverage.* The extent to which similar services are provided. If there are no other large, or very few small, comparable programs being provided in the same region, the program is classified as low coverage. Otherwise, the coverage is high.

4. *Competitive position.* The degree to which the organization has a stronger capability and potential to deliver the program than other such agencies—a combination of the organization's effectiveness, quality, credibility, and market share/dominance. Probably no program should be classified as being in a strong competitive position unless it has some clear basis for declaring superiority over all competitors in that program category. Criteria for a strong competitive position include:

- Good location and logistical delivery system
- Large reservoir of client, community, or support group loyalty
- Past success in securing funding; strong potential to raise funds for this program
- Superior track record (or image) of service delivery
- Large market share of the target clientele currently served
- Better-quality service and/or service delivery than competitors

- ○ Superior organizational, management, and technical skills needed for the program
- ○ Most cost-effective delivery of service

The Competitive Strategies Matrix can be used by assessing existing and potential new programs in relation to each of the four criteria: fit, potential to attract resources and enhance existing programs, alternative coverage, and competitive position.

Each of the cells in the matrix has a suggested growth strategy: [11]

- Cell 1: Compete—Growth or maintain competitive edge
- Cell 2: Develop and implement an exit strategy
- Cell 3: Invest in program and administrative capacity or develop and implement an exit strategy
- Cell 4: Compete—Growth or maintain competitive edge
- Cell 5: Build up the best competitor
- Cell 6: Develop and implement an exit strategy
- Cell 7: Collaboration strategy
- Cell 8: Soul of the agency

Perhaps one of the most important concepts contained within the matrix, soul-of-the-agency programs are defined by Professor MacMillan as those programs that are unable to attract sufficient resources to pay for themselves, have low alternative coverage, but offer services that make a special and important contribution in society. The clients who depend on soul-of-the-agency programs have no other place to turn to for help and are therefore reliant on the organization to continue to provide that service. The challenge for organizations that provide soul-of-the-agency services is either to use their scarce, unrestricted resources to subsidize the services or subsidize them from other programs. An organization, however, usually cannot afford to fund unlimited "souls," and as such might have to face some difficult decisions about how to develop a mix of programs that ensure viability of the agency as well as high-quality service to clients. The Competitive Strategies Matrix offers some guidance as to how to choose what programs an organization should offer.

For example, a private art school, based on numerous requests from parents, was considering offering classes for elementary school children. Although the new service was ascertained to be a good fit (within the school's mission), it was deemed not to be able to attract sufficient resources to pay for itself or to enhance existing services; the school was in a strong competitive position because it was well respected as the place to get formal art training in the county, but it was also aware that many other agencies in the city catered to elementary school children. The children's art classes were assessed as fitting in Cell 5. The suggested growth strategy was "build up the best competitor." The art school worked with a small children's museum located in a nearby city to offer art classes at the museum, with faculty from the art school teaching the classes with the assistance of the children's museum's education director.

SIDEBAR

Should We Continue to Support the Children's Theater Program?

In their strategic planning process, the small but successful City Theater Company had an important strategic decision to make about its new multicultural children's theater program. As a pilot program, it was well received by communities of color. The foundation that funded the pilot stipulated that in the second year the funding should be matched. The new program was also partially competitive with a long-established and extremely popular Children's Theater, located in the same city but not targeting a multicultural approach. There were intense pro and con feelings about the program from both board and staff members. Continuing the funding of the children's program could potentially drain resources from the other theater's programming. The SWOT analysis proceeded as follows:

- *Strengths.* Successful first-year pilot with staffing established; actors from adult theater programming intricately involved in the multicultural children's theater program; and good reviews in the local paper.

- *Weaknesses.* Funding not readily available; would need to fund second year with funds from adult theater, creating a moderate risk to an agreed-on expansion; and revenues from ticket sales not sufficient to cover direct costs.

- *Opportunities.* Well received by communities of color, and increased demand for arts programs that specifically address them; remote possibility of funding from a private foundation for funding the program as a national model.

(continues)

- *Threats.* Competitive relationship with established Children's Theater; decreased funding on both a national and state level for the arts.

In the SWOT grid, the multicultural children's program fell into two boxes: First, if the strengths of the successful first year were juxtaposed with the opportunities of client demand, loyalty, and the possibility of alternative funding, then the suggested strategy was to invest resources. If, however, the weakness of the lack of confirmed resources was judged as more significant than the perceived strength and was juxtaposed with the same opportunities, then the suggested strategy was "Decide: Invest or divest; collaborate." The board and staff were split on the invest/divest decision. When using the Competitive Strategies Matrix, the proposed solution became clearer. Although the children's program was successful, it did not seem like it was going to be able to attract resources to cover its costs. The Children's Theater was clearly in the stronger competitive position, even though it did not have a multicultural focus. The planning committee made a recommendation to the board of directors that the Children's Theater be approached as a collaborative partner in the continued development and expansion of multicultural programming for children. The Children's Theater accepted the proposal. This decision helped the board to look at increased partnership as a core strategy in their strategic plan.

Using a Criteria Matrix for Prioritizing Programs

Dual-bottom line factors and competitive position may or may not be the appropriate criteria for your nonprofit organization to use in selecting which products or services to offer. The planning committee might prioritize programs by comparing them against some list of criteria that they have established.

Some of the criteria might include (but would certainly not be limited to):

- Congruence with purpose (fits within our mission)

- Program self-sufficiency (program can pay for itself either through fees for service or contributions or grants)

- Documented need (current and future demands for product or service)

- Increases organization's visibility (improves its public image)
- Increases networking potential (supports collaborative efforts with other organizations)
- Enhances existing programs (complements current programs)
- Fills a need not being met in the community (not duplicating services that are effectively being done by others; we can do it better than others)
- Proven track record (credible service, demonstrated results)
- Supports or is part of a core strategy
- Produces a profit—surplus revenue to support other programs (after paying its share of indirect costs)
- Benefits outweigh or at the very least equal costs (cost-benefit analysis)

The planning committee may choose to assign a weighted number to each of the agreed upon criteria and then rate each program using that criteria. In Exhibit 5.6, given the scores, possible new Programs A and B would be likely programs to consider for the future.

Choosing a Business Assessment Tool

We suggest that you use at least one of the business assessment tools outlined in this chapter in developing your program and funding strategies. ASO/USA used both tools when it filled out Worksheet 13 (see Exhibit 5.7 for process notes).

STEP 4.3: AGREE ON EACH PROGRAM'S FUTURE GROWTH STRATEGY AND DEVELOP YOUR PROGRAM PORTFOLIO

The next step in Phase 4 is to develop your program portfolio (a term borrowed from the financial investment world to describe an investor's holdings). A program portfolio outlines all programs in terms of current and proposed scope and scale.

Remember, during this step we are not looking at the infrastructure needed to support the programs, but rather a description of all the programs (products and services) that an organization intends to offer over

EXHIBIT 5.6   EVALUATION OF FOUR POSSIBLE NEW
PROGRAMS USING A CRITERIA MIX

Criteria	Weight	Program A	Program B	Program C	Program D
Congruence with purpose (fits within our mission)	Required	✔	✔	NO	✔
Leverages strengths to capitalize on an opportunity, mobilizes strengths to avert a perceived threat, prevents a weakness from compounding a threat, or supports the ability of the organization to take advantage of an opportunity that it couldn't do if it continued to demonstrate a specific weakness)	20 points	✔	✔		
Program self-sufficiency (program can pay for itself either through fees for service or contributions or grants)	20 points	✔	✔		
Documented need (current and future demands for product or service)	20 points	✔	✔	✔	
Increases organization's visibility (improves its public image)	15 points		✔	✔	✔
Increases networking potential (supports collaborative efforts with other organizations)	5 points	✔	✔		✔
Produces a profit—surplus revenue to support other programs (after paying its share of indirect costs)	20 points	✔			✔
TOTAL SCORE		100	80	Does not fit within mission	40

the next three to five years. The program portfolio will be the basis for developing specific objectives for each program goal and will be used to define the management and support goals and objectives needed to support all products and services.

EXHIBIT 5.7 WORKSHEET 13: BUSINESS ASSESSMENT TOOLS FOR DEVELOPING A PROGRAM PORTFOLIO

Process Notes

How to do this activity	This worksheet contains two business assessment tools: CompassPoint's Dual Bottom-Line Matrix and Competitive Strategies Matrix. Choose whether you wish to use one or both of these tools for assessing your current (and possible future) programs. Place each of your current and future programs in the appropriate boxes.
Why do this activity	Given a competitive environment and limited resources available to support the work of the nonprofit sector, it is imperative that sound business tools be used to analyze programs—and make hard decisions—regarding what programs the organization will or will not offer.
Who to involve in the process	Program staff should take the lead in filling out these worksheets; the worksheets should then be presented to the planning committee for discussion.
	One caveat: staff may be reluctant to place one of their programs in a box that recommends an exit strategy. The planning committee must be cognizant of this during the discussions; at the same time, this is one of the places in the strategic planning process where hard decisions—what the organization will and will not do in the future—start to be made.

See ASO/USA's example of this worksheet at the end of this chapter. Blank worksheets are provided in Appendix A and on the CD that accompanies this book.

Staff, or a task force, should be assigned the responsibility of recommending a business strategy for each of your current (or proposed future) department/program in terms of:

- *What are you currently doing?* Describe the current level of service (e.g., units of service) and current program activities.

- *What is the suggested future business strategy?* Maintain at existing level, expand, reduce, discontinue, change, invest, enhance impact, maximize profits, contain costs, give away, and so on.

- *Significant changes.* Are there any significant changes in how the department or program is currently operating?

- *Advantages and risks involved in the recommended business strategy.* What are the pros and cons and risks of the suggested future business strategy? What is the justification for the business strategy being proposed?

- *What is the desired future scope and scale of program over the next three to five years?* What might the department/program look in three to five years in terms of scope and scale of operations?

- *Resource implication of business strategy.* What are the potential future revenues sources, and required resources (staff and other major expenses) needed to support the proposed business strategy and scope and scale of operations?

Once these conversations have been completed, a summary of the proposed future program portfolio should be presented using Worksheet 14 (see process notes in Exhibit 5.8). This worksheet provides a way of outlining the entire scope and scale of future programmatic operations on one place.

STEP 4.4: CONFIRM YOUR FUTURE CORE STRATEGIES

The aforementioned analytical tools are used to develop your organization's program portfolio. It is important now to confirm the organization's future core strategies. By this time in the planning process, your future core strategies should be evident, and now is the time to make them explicit.

Core strategies articulate an organization's future direction and communicate how and where an organization will focus its resources in the future. Strategies are means statements, articulated as an overarching method or approach to achieving overarching ends. Strategies should be grounded in a thorough understanding of an organization's external and internal environment (strengths, weaknesses, opportunities, and threats); they describe to external and internal stakeholders what is most important

EXHIBIT 5.8   WORKSHEET 14: SUMMARIZE YOUR FUTURE PROGRAM PORTFOLIO

Process Notes

How to do this activity	List each current and future program (or service) and its current level of activity. Based on your business planning and program evaluation discussions, decide on the overall future growth strategy for each program, and projected future level of activity.
Why do this activity	Provides a simple, visual summary of the scope and scale of programs and services that will be offered in the future, as well as sets the context for developing long-range program objectives. By understanding your proposed future level of program/service delivery, you should be in a better position to be able to articulate staffing and other administrative support needed to provide this level of service.
Who to involve in the process	Staff should take the lead in developing the program portfolio, and presenting it to the Planning Committee for their comments.

See ASO/USA's example of this worksheet at the end of this chapter. Blank worksheets are provided in Appendix A and on the CD that accompanies this book.

for the organization to be paying attention to over the next few years, given the current environment.

Although the statement of strategies will almost certainly be edited as the planning proceeds, the planning committee should attempt to write a draft of what it sees as the handful of important directions the organization will need to pursue over the coming few years.

Strategies can be overarching or they can have a programmatic, financial, administrative, or governance focus. Strategies, if successfully implemented, will have a major impact on how resources get allocated. A strategic plan should include a description of the three to five core strategies the organization will use to best achieve its purpose and vision. Exhibit 5.9 diagrams the relationship of goals and objectives and strategies.

EXHIBIT 5.9   CORE STRATEGIES

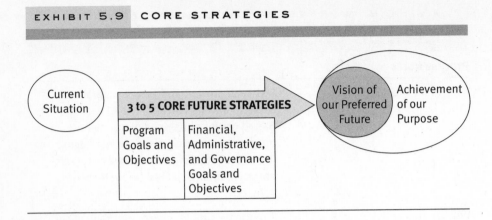

What Does a Strategy Look Like?

In Chapter 1, we gave you samples of strategies. Here are some other examples of strategies:

Multiservice, Multilocation Health Care Organization

- Change our focus from being unit focused to being client focused (overarching strategy).
- Invest in our infrastructure, including increasing the number of staff, improving salaries and benefits, and increasing technology and administrative support (administrative and overarching strategy).
- Change our business model so we are less dependent on government grants (financial strategy).
- Increase collaboration efforts (program strategy).
- Change the nature of the board's role to be less program/hands-on focused and more focused on fundraising—both in their giving and in getting additional resources (finance/governance strategy).

Private School

- Expand from K through 8 to K through 12 (program strategy).
- Continue our efforts to increase minority student enrollment (program strategy).
- Change the composition of our board so it is more representative of the community we serve (governance strategy).
- Buy a building (administrative strategy).

Community Foundation

- Continue to have our programming be local in focus and national in impact (program strategy).

- Increase grant-making efforts in support of women and children's health and reducing homelessness in the region (program strategy).

- Establish a donor advisory board to assist in our grant making to community-based organizations (governance strategy).

It is easy to see how each of the three organizations' core strategies might be translated into specific goals and objectives over a period of several years and for the immediate future. What is not easy to see is how much effort, experimentation, and discussion were required to find these successful strategies. The strategic planning process helps organizations identify various strategic options and make intelligent choices regarding the key priority methods—strategies—that will guide the allocation of resources. Each of these strategies communicates to internal and external stakeholders what the primary focus of the organization's resources (time and money) will be—how the organization will best achieve its purpose.

Although some future core strategies become obvious early on in the planning process (e.g., an assessment of the organization confirms what board and staff had known for a long time: The organization's infrastructure was basically nonexistent, and "investing in our infrastructure" was clearly a core future strategy). Other times, core strategies are not so obvious, and you may need to rely on other tools to help define them.

> *Strategy is not a response to short-term fluctuations in operations or the environment. . . . It is concerned with the longer-term course that the ship is steering, not with the waves.*[12]

Scenario Planning as a Vehicle for Developing Strategies

As stated previously, planning is not about predicting the future but about making better current decisions. No one can predict what the future will bring, but in a planning process you anticipate the future trends and can develop strategies to respond to those trends. Those trends are often fairly evident, and therefore you can develop a plan that responds to the environment that is known and anticipated. But what do you do when the future environment is full of many options? How do you develop strategies based on a few—or many—unknowns or possibilities?

Scenarios can help an organization be more strategic (i.e., be better prepared and proactive and intentional rather than reactive and opportunistic) when such alternative futures become a reality.

In *The Art of the Long View: Planning for the Future in an Uncertain World*, Peter Schwartz describes how alternative scenarios can help an organization to "take a long view in a world of great uncertainty." He defines scenarios as "stories about the way the world might turn out tomorrow" and makes the case that such stories help us "recognize and adapt to changing aspects of our present environment. They form a method for articulating the different pathways that might exist for you tomorrow and for finding your appropriate movements down each of those possible paths. Scenario planning is about making choices today with an understanding of how they might turn out. Such scenarios, therefore, allow an organization to be better prepared for whatever happens by addressing any of the array of possibilities. "Scenarios are not about predicting the future, rather they are about perceiving futures in the present."[13]

Schwartz says that scenarios often seem to fall into three groups: more of the same, but better; worse; and different but better. In fact, reality may turn out to be a combination of all three scenarios. Making the case that scenario thinking is an art, not a science, he encourages his readers to develop an array of scenarios and rehearse possible responses. After developing these scenarios, an organization would identify the possible factors that would influence the scenario, the degree of uncertainty, and the implications if the scenario were to get played out in real life.

Health care organizations that have been better able to respond to the changes in health care delivery are in all likelihood those organizations that were asking the "what if" questions early on. Those organizations that started to think about Medicare and health reform movements long before their competitors did, and that as a result outlined a series of future scenarios, are now probably at a competitive advantage.

Scenario Planning When the Future Is Uncertain

One of the foremost leaders in the field of scenario planning in times of uncertainty is the Global Business Network. The following is a simplified scenario planning process, adopted from the work of the Global Business Network:[14]

- Define a question that would benefit from scenario planning.

- Select two uncertainties, describing both ends of the spectrum.

- Develop a matrix placing each of the two uncertainties on each axis.

- Play out two or more scenarios. Discuss the implications of each scenario for your future.

For example, the board of directors of P.E.A.C.E. was weary of trying to keep the organization from going under. For two years, the organization had been sustaining itself with primarily burned-out volunteers, vendor goodwill, and loans from the board. The organization felt that the only alternative was to stop all of its programs and go out of business. Working with a consultant, the board did some scenario planning in order to determine if there were any other viable strategies than simply going out of business. The two major unknowns were: (1) whether a substantial grant they had been promised would actually materialize, and (2) whether there were any alternatives to going out of business (e.g., merging with another organization). Based on those two unknown variables, they developed the matrix in Exhibit 5.10, with four different scenarios:

1. If they were to get the grant within the next four months and found a partner who was willing and able to take on P.E.A.C.E.'s programs, they would merge.

2. If they were not able to get the grant and therefore were not a very desirable merger candidate, they would try to piecemeal out three of the four programs they offered, assuming that various organizations would be interested in one or two programs that fit within their mission. P.E.A.C.E. would continue in existence but would only operate the one program that had sufficient volunteer energy to operate without many outside resources.

3. If P.E.A.C.E. could not find either partners or resources, it would go out of business.

4. If P.E.A.C.E. did find the resources it needed but not partners, it would continue to operate, but with a new slate of leadership, both on the board and staff.

The organization ended up going with scenario 2—their core future strategy was to give away three of their four programs. The scenario process helped the board and staff members understand that there were more options than simply just stopping all of their programs and closing

EXHIBIT 5.10   SCENARIO PLANNING MATRIX

Major grant/substantial $ received in next four months

	Continue as separate agency with new leadership (board and staff)	*Merge*	
No viable partners			**Many viable partners**
	Go out of business	Piecemeal projects out to various groups and operate as a smaller entity	

$ are not sufficient to sustain organization

their doors. This process also put in place some firm parameters for the future and helped the board and staff develop an alternative strategy from the one they had been considering.

Strategy Development When There Are Many Options: Choosing Among Various Scenario Options

Sometimes the future is somewhat predictable (to the extent that in all likelihood things will work out the way we think they will), and there are multiple choices as to how to move forward. If this is the case, then you might want to develop and assess different scenario options:

- Define a question.
- Brainstorm various options to consider.
- Set the criteria on which to choose the best option.
- Evaluate the options: pluses (advantages, why this makes sense) and minuses (disadvantages, risks), assumptions on which this scenario/option is based.
- Identify what data needs to be collected to be able to inform any decision.
- Choose the best option from among the choices.

For example, a California organization was considering whether it should expand beyond California. Their question was: "What are our potential (alternative) options for expansion?" They brainstormed the various options to consider:

- Operate in California only over the next three to five years.
- For the next two years, primarily focus in California, with one to two regional/national forays; start to ramp up for more significant regional/national work in years three to five.
- Start to ramp up for national work as soon as possible.

They listed criteria: maximize partnerships, funding available, results in increased visibility, meets demonstrated needs; tangible results within a moderate period of time; high impact, staff interest (results in increased satisfaction/decrease burnout). Based on these criteria and as assessment of the advantages and disadvantages of this option, the organization went with Option 2, the strategy of primarily maintaining a focus in California for the next two years, with one or two collaborative endeavors outside of

California. Within one year, they had found a project that met all of the criteria, and by year two the new national project was up and running.

Making Your Core Future Strategies Explicit

Now is the time to make your core future strategies explicit—Worksheet 15 (see process notes in Exhibit 5.11). Some strategies will emerge as a response to a particular strategic issue (e.g., "Should we increase our advocacy efforts?" Answer: "Yes, grow our advocacy program, but in collaboration

EXHIBIT 5.11	WORKSHEET 15: CORE FUTURE STRATEGIES

Process Notes

How to do this activity	Brainstorm a list of possible future strategies. Some strategies may have become apparent as a result of your situation assessment. Other strategies are responses to the strategic issues you identified in Worksheet 1. Narrow your choices to three to five core future strategies. After selecting the best strategy, respond to the rest of the questions on the worksheet: What assumptions, facts, and values support the proposed strategy? What possible obstacles may the organization face in implementing the strategy? And what triggers might encourage the organization to reevaluate the suggested new strategy?
Why do this activity	After all this thinking and brainstorming, it's time to make some decisions!
Who to involve in the process	Planning committee members and selected others develop draft core strategies. Once there is overall agreement, draft strategies should be reviewed by the entire board for sign-off and by the staff (either as a whole or by department) to generate ideas as to how to implement these strategies.

See ASO/USA's example of this worksheet at the end of this chapter. Blank worksheets are provided in Appendix A and on the CD that accompanies this book.

with others."). Other strategies will become apparent after the organization has completed its situation assessment or used some of the business assessment tools described previously (e.g., "Our youth programs have low mission impact and low financial viability. We should give them to the Community Center that already has a successful youth program."). And finally, SWOT analysis may reveal a new way of thinking (e.g., "We need to expand into the north part of our county since there are unmet needs and we are in a strong position to open up and successfully run a satellite office.").

SIDEBAR

Where Do Program Strategies Come From?

An international Catholic religious and social service organization, with headquarters in Brazil, decided to develop a five-year strategic plan. The primary strategic issues on the table were what their primary future goals should be and how they should maximize their resources. In the initial discussions, participants found it easy to describe major goals and objectives, such as increasing membership, expanding the number of churches in Brazil and foreign countries, and building greater awareness of the religion's teachings, both nationally and internationally. However, it was difficult for the participants to define the overall core strategy or strategies through which these goals should be accomplished. Members of the planning group were clear about what they wanted; they simply were unable to describe how this goal could be best accomplished.

In order to overcome this hurdle, the consultant working with the group suggested a simple visioning exercise. The participants were asked to break into small workgroups and to draw on large sheets of paper what the ideal organization would look like at the end of the five-year planning period. The exercise provided an unexpected, yet critical, revelation: Each of the groups included a drawing of telecommunications innovation in some form or another, from satellites to uplink stations to television broadcast stations. Through the visioning process, the participants came to realize that the use of broadcast media and telecommunications technology in order to promote awareness and grow their membership was a pivotal strategy that would support the overall goals and objectives they desired.

When writing up your three to five core future strategies, you need to not only articulate the strategy but also make clear the following points:

- The assumptions, facts, and values that support the proposed strategy
- The possible obstacles that the organization may face in implementing the strategy
- What triggers (warning signs) might encourage the organization to reevaluate the suggested new strategy

Because strategies represent the major agreement about where the organization is going to invest its resources in the future, the planning committee should be sure to get the buy-in of those who will be called on to implement the strategies. To get buy-in, the executive director or designated representative(s) of the planning committee should discuss proposed strategies with the staff and board. Staff and board members should be given an opportunity to voice either support for or concerns about these strategies and make suggestions regarding the long-term and short-term programmatic and management/operations priorities that support the implementation of the core strategies.

STEP 4.5: AGREE ON ADMINISTRATIVE, FINANCIAL, AND GOVERNANCE PRIORITIES

Once core future strategies have been defined and the program portfolio created, the planning committee should turn its attention to the administrative, financial, and governance activities required to support the programs, such as the following:

Finances

- Resource development
- Financial management systems

Administrative Functions

- Staffing and benefits
- Marketing/public relations
- Infrastructure: management information systems, technology, and facilities
- Planning, evaluation, and quality control

Governance Functions

- Board of directors
- Advisory board

The process for selection of the finances, governance, and administrative priorities will depend on the complexity of the organization. If the planning committee's discussions regarding strategic issues and program priorities have not yet provided sufficient guidance for the setting of administrative, governance, and financial priorities, then some questions you may want to consider asking include the following:

Finances

Resource Development

- What resources do we need to support our future vision? Can we invest in this future?
- If we have to raise more money, how much? What is our plan for how to do this?
- Do we have sufficient development staff to succeed in meeting our financial goals?
- What should be our future funding mix?

Financial Management Systems

- What kinds of systems or processes do we need to support (or develop) up-to-date, accurate, and useful financial management and reporting?
- Are we invested wisely, and how can we best maximize the financial return on our investments?
- How well are we recovering costs from funders? Are our overhead cost rates appropriate?
- Are our costs per mission unit competitive?
- Do we have a comfortable unrestricted reserve?

Process note: These questions are best answered by staff with financial management responsibilities, along with the treasurer of the board and/or the finance committee.

Administrative Functions

Staffing and Benefits

- What is our current ability to provide services to our clients/customers?
- What additional staff is needed to meet increased levels of service? (Or, if staff cuts are anticipated, how will these cuts be managed?)
- How can we remain competitive with regard to salary and benefits?
- How do we recruit and retain quality staff?
- How do we orient and provide continuing education for our paid and volunteer staff?
- What other reward and recognition systems can we implement to support staff?
- How do we improve our performance appraisal systems?

Process note: Although the board will ultimately have to approve the budget to support the staffing objectives, staff members should take the lead in answering these questions and coming up with staffing goals and objective recommendations.

Marketing/Public Relations

- How strong is our ability to communicate with intended clients/customers?
- What strategies should we put in place to communicate program/service changes?
- Can additional marketing materials be prepared or alternative methods for communicating our mission be developed?
- What are our short-term and long-term priorities for increasing our visibility in the community?

Process note: If there is no one connected to the organization who has a strong marketing and public relations background, the planning committee might consider asking a public relations firm to donate some time to assist with the responses to marketing-related questions.

Infrastructure: Management Information Systems, Technology, and Facilities

- What information do we need on an ongoing basis to assess efficiency and effectiveness of our services/programs?

- What management information systems do we need to improve or change in order to produce reports to assess our efficiency and effectiveness?
- What other processes need to be developed to support the overall operations of the organization (such as file maintenance systems; materials acquisition and management; equipment maintenance, etc.)?
- What are our short-term and long-term technology needs regarding phones and other communication systems, computers, and so on?
- Are our current facilities adequate for current and future service delivery models? What changes are anticipated, and how do we go about financing them?
- What capital improvements are necessary to maintain our existing facilities?

Process note: Staff should take the lead in answering questions regarding infrastructure.

Planning and Evaluation

- How should we formalize our strategic and operational planning processes so as to be better able to monitor our results and to respond in a timely way to changes in our environment?
- What processes do we need to put in place so that we can, on an ongoing basis, assess customer satisfaction, constituent needs, and our ability to meet those needs in a quality, cost-effective way?

Process note: One of the major by-products of a strategic planning process is ideally the institutionalization of strategic thinking by both the board and the staff. Formalizing the strategic and operational planning processes can lead to a more strategically managed organization, and strategic management keeps an organization adaptive, relevant, and more effective.

Governance Functions

Board of Directors

- Given the future vision of the organization, does the role of the board need to change and, if so, how?
- Does our board composition need to change to effectively govern and support our preferred future and, if so, why and how?

- How do we provide continuing education, support, and recognition for our board?

Process note: The board should devote at least one or two meetings to respond to these board-related questions and develop its own short-term and long-term priorities.

After you have sufficiently answered these questions, summarize your discussions by filling out Worksheet 16 (see process notes in Exhibit 5.12). For each of the functions listed, write one or more goals (broad general results) and objectives (specific, measureable priorities).

EXHIBIT 5.12   WORKSHEET 16: SUMMARY OF ADMINISTRATIVE, FINANCIAL, AND GOVERNANCE PRIORITIES

Process Notes

How to do this activity	For each administrative, financial, and governance function, list the overall goal or goals and any long-term priorities to be included in the strategic plan.
Why do this activity	After all this thinking and brainstorming, it's time to make some decisions!
Who to involve in the process	Planning committee members and selected others develop core strategies to review with board and staff. Board and staff should have some involvement (the level of which will depend on the organization) in the development of the short-term and long-term programmatic and management/operations strategic priorities.

See ASO/USA's example of this worksheet at the end of this chapter. Blank worksheets are provided in Appendix A and on the CD that accompanies this book.

CAUTIONS TO FACILITATORS

- *Paralysis by analysis.* The point of this phase is to make decisions. Because a large amount of information is likely to be gathered, there is a danger that the group will become stuck in an endless loop of sifting the information. The facilitator needs to sense

CAUTIONS TO FACILITATORS *(Continued)*

when enough debate has taken place and help move the group to closure.

- *Pretending to decide.* Phase 4 requires making difficult decisions about what not to do, as well as making decisions about what to do. Sometimes groups resist giving up anything by deciding, in effect, to do everything. This is not making decisions—it is avoidance and pretending.

- *Right people at the table.* Another way groups can find agreement is by having critical discussions when certain people aren't present. If someone's buy-in is necessary for the plan to succeed, get it now or it will surface later as a barrier to implementation.

ENDNOTES

1. Benjamin Tregoe and John Zimmerman, *Vision in Action: Putting a Winning Strategy to Work* (New York: Fireside, 1990), p. 17.
2. W.H. Murray, *The Scottish Himaylayan Expedition* (London: J. M. Dent & Sons, 1951) pp. 6–7.
3. Kevin P. Kearns, "Comparative Advantage to Damage Control: Clarifying Strategic Issues Using SWOT Analysis," *Nonprofit Management and Leadership* 3, no. 1 (Fall 1992): 3–22. The SWOT analysis grid is a widely used approach. Modifications of the grid have been attributed to R. Charistensen et al., *Business Policy: Text and Cases* (Homewood, IL: Irwin, 1983); and J. Freedman and K. Van Ham, "Strategic Planning in Philips," in B. Taylor and D. Hussey (eds.), *The Realities of Planning* (Elmsford, NY: Pergamon Press, 1982).
4. It is also possible to use the SWOT analysis grid during Phase 3 as part of the synthesis process in completing Worksheet 12.
5. Nonprofit organizations are businesses organized for tax-exempt purposes whose profits must be dedicated to furthering their mission as opposed to creating a return on investment for business owners or stockholders.
6. Jan Masaoka, Executive Director of CompassPoint, developed this model and wrote this section.
7. Nationally, the three basic sources of revenues for all U.S. nonprofit corporations are philanthropy 27%, government 27%, and fees and earned revenue 46%, according to Lester Salamon (ed.), *The State of Nonprofit America* (Washington, DC: Brookings Institution Press, 2002).
8. The Boston Consulting Group (BCG) developed the Growth-Share Matrix in the 1970s. This tool, as well as others developed by BCG, is described in Carl

Stern and George Stalk Jr., (eds.), *Perspectives on Strategy from the Boston Consulting Group* (New York: John Wiley & Sons, 1998).

9. I. C. MacMillan, "Competitive Strategies for Not-for-Profit Agencies," *Advances in Strategic Management* 1, (London, JAI Press Inc., 1983): 61–82.

10. This matrix is an adaptation of MacMillan's matrix. In addition to reframing the growth strategies, the authors of this workbook chose to rename one of MacMillan's variables, "program attractiveness," to "Potential to Attract Resources and Enhance Existing Programs." Professor MacMillan defined program attractiveness as the degree to which a program was attractive to the agency as a basis for current and future resource deployment. For many organizations, this term was confusing, and it usually gets interpreted as "it's something that is attractive for us to do." Therefore, the authors of this workbook have changed the wording to "potential to attract resources, emphasizing the financial viability aspect."

11. The authors of this book have changed the wording of the growth strategies as first proposed by Professor MacMillan from: Cell 1) Aggressive competition; Cell 2) Aggressive divestment; Cell 3) Build strength or get out; Cell 4) Aggressive growth; Cell 5) Build up the best competitor; Cell 6) Orderly divestment; Cell 7) Foreign Aid or joint venture; and Cell 8) Soul of the agency.

12. Boris Yavitz and William H. Newman, *Strategy in Action: The Execution, Politics, and Payoff of Business Planning* (New York: The Free Press, 1982), 4.

13. Peter Schwarz, *The Art of the Long View: Planning for the Future in an Uncertain World* (New York: Currency/Doubleday, 1991), p. 23.

14. For more information on scenario planning, see: *What If, The Art of Scenario Thinking for Nonprofits,* by Diana Scarce, Katherine Fulton, and the Global Business Network Community (Emeryville, CA: Global Business Network, 2004).

WORKSHEET 13	Business Assessment Tools for Developing a Program Portfolio

❏ Use one or both of the following business assessment tools to assist in developing your program portfolio

❏ Use the criteria listed for each tool and plot out where each of your programs and other business activities fit within the chart

CompassPoint's Dual Bottom-Line Matrix

HIGH

Mission Impact

HIGH MISSION IMPACT
LOW VIABILITY ♥

BUSINESS DECISION =
HEART: Keep but contain costs

Public Education
Public Policy and Communication

HIGH MISSION IMPACT
HIGH VIABILITY ★

BUSINESS DECISION =
STAR: Invest in continuance and growth

Support Services

LOW MISSION IMPACT
LOW VIABILITY **?**

BUSINESS DECISION =
QUESTION MARK: Discontinue or give away

LOW MISSION IMPACT
HIGH VIABILITY $

BUSINESS DECISION =
MONEY MAKER: Enhance impact

Core Support-Foundations
Fundraising

LOW **Financial Viability** HIGH

• Some of the characteristics of programs with *high impact mission:* tangible results, visible progress toward the achievement of the organization's mission, high leverage potential—synergy with other programs, and high-quality services that distinguish the organization from its competition

(continues)

• Some of the characteristics of *high viability:* At the very least covers all costs (both direct and indirect), generates a surplus of revenue, projected to have financially sustainability for the future, a proven financially viable business model

Competitive Strategies Matrix

		Ability to Attract Resources and Enhance Existing Programs YES		Ability to Attract Resources and Enhance Existing Programs NO	
		Alternative Coverage: **MANY**	Alternative Coverage: **FEW**	Alternative Coverage: **MANY**	Alternative Coverage: **FEW**
GOOD FIT	**Strong Competitive Position YES**	1) Growth or maintain competitive edge strategy *Public Education programs, including outreach to high-risk populations*	4) Growth or maintain competitive edge strategy • *Support services— case management, transportation vouchers, benefits counseling* • *Hotline— prevention information component*	5) Build up best competitor: assist another organization provide the service *Hotline— treatment options component*	8) Soul of the agency *Media advocacy to ensure positive and accurate coverage of HIV/AIDS issues*
	Strong Competitive Position NO	2) Develop and implement an exit strategy *Employment referral services*	3) Invest in program and administrative capacity or Develop and implement an exit strategy *Outreach and case management for immigrant communities*	6) Develop and implement an exit strategy	7) Collaboration strategy *Public policy and advocacy work*
	POOR FIT	Divest or do not start to provide this service.			

- *Program fit.* Is this program congruent with the overall purpose and mission of our organization, and does/could this program draw on existing skills in the organization and share resources/coordinate activities with other programs?

- *Ability to attract resources and enhance existing programs.* Does this program have high market demand from a large client base? Does it have high appeal to groups capable of providing current and future support? Does this program have stable funding? Can you show measurable results? Would you be able to discontinue the program with relative ease if necessary (low exit barriers/ ability to discontinue program or abandon past commitment)?

- *Alternative coverage.* Are there many organizations, or few organizations, providing similar services in the community?

- *Strong competitive position.* Do you have strong client and community support? Do you have a superior track record of service delivery? Do you provide better quality than your competitors? Do you have the administrative capacity to provide this program cost effectively and efficiently?

CASE STUDY—ASO/USA

☐ Develop a detailed program portfolio.

For each of your proposed future programs or services:

- What is the program's current level of activity? (This question, of course, applies only to existing programs. New programs will not yet have a current level of activity.)
- What is its proposed growth strategy (expand, maintain, decrease, eliminate, start new program, modify existing program)?
- What is the program's projected future level of activity?

Note: This is a sample of ASO/USA's program portfolio, rather than the entire portfolio.

Program or service	What is the program's current level of activity? (This question, of course, applies only to existing programs; new programs will not yet have a current level of activity.)	What is its proposed growth strategy (expand, maintain, decrease, eliminate, start new program, modify existing program)?	What is the program's projected future level of activity?
Case management (Subset of case management clients also receive benefits counseling, transportation vouchers, and employment referrals.)	*300 individuals case managed:* • *75% use benefits counseling.* • *20% use transportation vouchers.* • *5% use employment referrals.*	*Moderately increase the level of service, as well as build up the capacity of agencies serving immigrant communities to provide some case management.* *Eliminate employment referrals component—refer clients to Resource Center for Positives.* *Add prevention with positives component.*	*500 individuals case managed:* • *75% use benefits counseling.* • *20% use transportation vouchers.* *Build capacity for other organizations to do case management.* *Incorporate prevention with positives into case management.*

Program or service	What is the program's current level of activity? (This question, of course, applies only to existing programs; new programs will not yet have a current level of activity.)	What is its proposed growth strategy (expand, maintain, decrease, eliminate, start new program, modify existing program)?	What is the program's projected future level of activity?
Support groups for people with HIV/AIDS and caregivers	12 groups	Maintain, but explore reasons for decreased attendance and reduce groups if there truly is a decrease in demand.	12 groups
Hotline	5,000 calls per year (coverage is for 16 hours per day)	Maintain coverage, but limit scope of hotline calls to information about HIV transmission and prevention. Refer HIV care and treatment calls to a national hotline.	5,000 calls per year (coverage is for 16 hours per day)
HIV prevention outreach (collaboration with City Clinic)	2,000 individuals (schools, businesses, street, bars, etc.)	Expand outreach and increase the focus on high-risk populations. Further clarify relationship with City Clinic—do the actual outreach, and they do only HIV testing and referrals to care for HIV-positive people.	3,000 high-risk individuals Reduce work with businesses and schools, increase street and bar outreach with high-risk, vulnerable populations (to be identified).

(continues)

225

Program or service	What is the program's current level of activity? (This question, of course, applies only to existing programs; new programs will not yet have a current level of activity.)	What is its proposed growth strategy (expand, maintain, decrease, eliminate, start new program, modify existing program)?	What is the program's projected future level of activity?
HIV prevention risk reduction/harm reduction	None	Start a new individual risk-reduction counseling program. Use outreach to bring clients into this more intensive one-on-one prevention service.	200 clients participating in 1 to 3 one-hour long sessions
Public policy and advocacy efforts	Not able to quantify level of service	Increase.	Not able to quantify level of service

CASE STUDY—ASO/USA

Core Future Strategies

❑ Identify and assess your core future strategies

Proposed strategy	Assumptions, facts, and values that support this proposed strategy	What possible obstacles do we face in implementing this strategy?	How to respond to possible obstacles: strategies for overcoming obstacles and short-term priorities	What triggers might encourage us to reevaluate this strategy?
Invest in our capacity to support programs, especially in terms of staffing and infrastructure.	Staff continues to be our greatest resource. While we have made progress in recent years in terms of our facilities, administration, technology, and formalizing policies and procedures, there is still a need to invest in our infrastructure to support current and future programs.	Ability to raise resources to support this necessary investment—estimated at about $675,000 above current base funding	• Approach funders for capacity-building grants. • Continue to diversify our funding base.	If we are not able to raise the necessary resources

(continues)

Proposed strategy	Assumptions, facts, and values that support this proposed strategy	What possible obstacles do we face in implementing this strategy?	How to respond to possible obstacles: strategies for overcoming obstacles and short-term priorities	What triggers might encourage us to reevaluate this strategy?
Broaden and diversify our funding base so we are able to adequately support our clients.	In 2003, 82% of our funding came from government sources. While this is typical for many human service agencies, it leaves us very vulnerable to government budget cuts, and limits our ability to provide services not specifically covered by those grants.	Inability to raise significant revenues in an environment where there is increased competition for contributions and an economy that has not yet recovered	• Research corporate and community foundations committed to improving the health of underserved communities. • Develop a plan for an annual fundraiser. • Seek non-HIV/AIDS funds (e.g., substance abuse) to provide services for people living with HIV/AIDS.	Obviously, if we are not able to raise money we will have to make some hard choices about the funding of our strategies.
Focus our resources to serve the highest-risk, most-vulnerable, and disproportionately affected people in our community.	People from marginalized communities—low-income people, people of color, injection drug users, and other disenfranchised people, have the lowest access to prevention and treatment services.	Need for additional staff and partnerships with community-based organizations	• Ensure that our board and staff reflect the populations we want to serve. • Build relationships with community-based organizations, rather than tell them what to do.	Other organizations desire to take the lead in providing these services. We will assist them to do the best job possible/share our expertise

Proposed strategy	Assumptions, facts, and values that support this proposed strategy	What possible obstacles do we face in implementing this strategy?	How to respond to possible obstacles: strategies for overcoming obstacles and short-term priorities	What triggers might encourage us to reevaluate this strategy?
Maximize our collaborative efforts with other agencies and take more of a leadership role in convening meetings focused on public policy and advocacy efforts.	*In order to ensure that government resources continue to be allocated for people with living with HIV/AIDS and that they are protected from discrimination, ASO/USA needs to strengthen its leadership role in the public policy arena.*	*Increased government scrutiny*	• *Consider collaboration with other organizations to set up a separate 501c4 advocacy agency.*	*We cannot take this on by ourselves. If other groups are not willing and able to participate with us on public policy and advocacy efforts, then we may need to reconsider this strategy.*
Do not expand our services beyond HIV/AIDS.	*While there are unmet needs that we could meet, the HIV/AIDS epidemic and its impact on individuals and families has not decreased, and given our current resources, it is not feasible for us to expand beyond HIV/AIDS without seriously undermining the services we are currently offering.*	• *Some staff disagreement with this decision* • *Some community disappointment with this decision*	• *Meet with the agencies most impacted by this decision and figure out if there is any way that we can help them (e.g., provide training to their staff) provide the services they are asking us to provide.* • *Develop talking points that help explain why we have chosen this strategy.*	*If we start to see a reduction in the need for our services and/or we have sufficient staff to meet our clients needs, then we should reevaluate this strategy before the end of the 3-year time period.*

CASE STUDY—ASO/USA

WORKSHEET 16 **Summary of Administrative, Financial, and Governance Priorities**

☐ For each administrative, financial, and governance function, list the overall goal and any long-term priorities to be included in the strategic plan. (These priorities will be the basis for writing objectives.)

Administrative Functions	Goal(s)	Long-Term Priorities (Objectives)
Staffing and benefits	Attract and retain qualified paid and volunteer staff for all services and activities.	• Increase number of paid staff from 25 full-time employees to 34 full-time employees, and increase the number of volunteer hours per year from 5,750 to 9,000. • Assess whether more complex and differing needs of clients require certain jobs that were done by volunteers to be done by paid staff. • Assess overall salary structure and benefits package, develop and implement a plan to increase staff salaries, and offer a competitive benefits package. • Analyze fringe benefits package on an ongoing basis. • Review personnel policies annually. • Establish and maintain a more formalized ongoing training program for all staff and volunteers. • Implement and maintain a new staff-evaluation system that establishes overall objectives for positions and specific objectives for all employees. • Expand our volunteer and paid-staff appreciation program. • Develop and coordinate an agency-wide management-training program. • Update the personnel handbook annually. • Maintain number of volunteers at 80. • Assess current volunteer recruitment, orientation, and training program.

Administrative Functions	Goal(s)	Long-Term Priorities (Objectives)
Public relations and communications	Increase the visibility and community awareness of ASO/USA. Make sure that ASO/USA is properly recognized for its achievements and closely identified as a premier provider to people living with and affected by HIV/AIDS.	• Build public awareness of ASO/USA in the community through increased media coverage and public service announcements. • Produce and distribute a newsletter on a regular basis. • Update brochures regularly and make sure they are available in English, Spanish, and Cantonese.
Infrastructure: information systems, technology, facilities, etc.	Increase the operations and management efficiency and effectiveness of ASO/USA.	• Ensure that timely, accurate, useful information is available and consistently applied in sound decision-making throughout the agency. • Improve and maintain a fully-computerized accounting system. • Develop a system for tracking all necessary information required for funding sources and management. • Continually assess technology needs and update computers and other technology as needed. • Develop and implement a facilities master plan. • Explore the option of getting a building donated — we need to seriously consider moving the central office. • Maintain facilities that are attractive to clients.

(continues)

Administrative Functions	Goal(s)	Long-Term Priorities (Objectives)
Planning, evaluation, quality control	Guarantee that we meet the needs of our constituencies and that all programs provide the highest quality service.	• Establish an ongoing evaluation process for all programs to assess program results, quality of services, and our ability to address the (changing) needs of level of service to our clients and the community. • Hold an annual board/staff retreat to plan for future needs and assess current capabilities. • Review the strategic plan quarterly and make changes as needed. • Ensure that detailed annual operating plans are developed. • Establish and maintain protocols for data collection, data entry, and outcome evaluation.

Financial Functions	Goal(s)	Long-Term Priorities (Objectives)
Financial management	Produce timely, accurate financial reports for the organization as a whole, and for all departments.	• Improve and maintain a fully-computerized accounting system. • Provide executive management and the board with required financial reports, budget comparisons, and cash flow projections. • Assess organization's internal controls annually to ensure adequate safeguard of all resources.

Financial Functions	Goal(s)	Long-Term Priorities (Objectives)
Resource development	*Acquire stable, broad-based, financial and nonfinancial resources to support the programs and growth envisioned in this strategic plan.*	• *Within the next three years, at least 40% of ASO/USA's annual operating budget will be raised through private sector philanthropy. The development of this subsidy is critical for the maintenance and growth of our programs.* • *Explore donations in kind (e.g., printing, equipment, etc.) to help support our services.* • *Increase the money that the organization receives from private individuals to a minimum of 10% each year.* • *Raise a minimum of $50,000 annually from special events/fundraisers.* • *Establish a formal development department.* • *Bring on a new grants writer as soon as budget allows or as funding can be raised.* • *Establish and maintain a computerized donor history file and increase the personal contacts made with donors.* • *Maintain a board-giving policy that requires all board members to contribute financially.* • *Increase the board's participation in all aspects of fundraising.*

(continues)

Governance Functions	Goal(s)	Long-Term Priorities (Objectives)
Board of directors	Develop and maintain an effective, active, and informed board of directors whose governance and support roles help the achievement of AJO/USA's mission.	• Diversify the board to accurately reflect who we serve. • Develop and maintain a community advisory board. • Increase the capability of the board to assist with the following functions: marketing, fundraising, legal matters, public relations, and evaluation. • Develop and maintain an effective board orientation and ongoing training program. • Increase effectiveness of the board by redefining committees and each committee's mandate, and assessing on-going mandates yearly. • Continue yearly evaluation of all aspects of the board. • Implement 100% contribution from all board members. • Increase the board's participation in all aspects of fundraising.
Networking and collaboration	Maintain and develop collaborations and relationships with agencies and funders that benefit our clients, our services, and/or our agency.	• Allocate time to executive director and development director (when hired) to identify potential collaborators and negotiate subcontracts and MOUs as appropriate. • Assess the collaboration with City Clinic. Develop a plan for continuing the collaboration with: (1) more clearly defined roles, responsibilities, and accountability measures, and (2) a shift in program focus to serve higher-risk clients.

CHAPTER 6

Phase 5: Write the Strategic Plan

The end is in sight! The planning process is just about complete: Appropriate stakeholders have had a chance to contribute their ideas, and sufficient data about the organization's operating environment has been gathered. By this time, most of the major decisions have been made, and the big picture should be relatively clear. The organization knows what its strengths and weaknesses are and how to best address them. The planners have articulated the core future strategies that can help the organization succeed. Staff and board members are clear about what programs and services need to be offered in the next three to five years to better achieve the organization's mission. It is now time to develop concrete measures for what the organization wants to specifically achieve and the resources needed. This is the most detailed aspect of the strategic planning process. It is time to commit the ideas to paper by writing goals and objectives and to understand the financial implications of those decisions. Once this work is completed, the strategic planning document can be written.

STEP 5.1: CREATE GOALS AND OBJECTIVES

The actual writing of goals and objectives is one aspect of planning with which most people have experience. Writing goals and objectives should not be a group project. For a large organization, each program and administrative manager should take the lead on drafting his or her unit's objectives. For a smaller organization, one or two individuals should take responsibility for drafting the initial goals and objectives. The drafts of these goals and objectives might go through two or three versions before everyone's feedback has been incorporated and a final document is agreed upon. The planning committee should not shortchange this process of gathering feedback on the proposed outcomes delineated in the goals and objectives. In the course of these discussions, important questions often arise and insights emerge that substantially improve the quality and viability of the entire strategic plan.

Goals are outcome (ends) statements that guide the organization's programs, administrative, financial, and governance functions. For the organization as a whole, for example, the ultimate goal is the purpose spelled out in the mission statement; similarly, the organization's programs, program groups, and management/operations functions need to be guided by their own mini-purposes (i.e., their own goals).

A good place to start the development of program goals is to go back to the organizational profile developed earlier when you completed Worksheet 8; that worksheet identified programs or services and placed them into relevant program groupings. These program groups are the basis for establishing program goals, unless your planning process generated information or decisions that warrant reviewing, and perhaps modifying, certain aspects of the profile (e.g., altering some programs, grouping them differently, or adding a new program). If so, the planning committee must draft a new outline of program goals.

For example, a children's museum initially had grouped all of its programs into two major goal categories: programs offered at the museum and programs offered off-site. As a result of the planning process, the museum reframed its programs to more accurately reflect broadening its activities: environmental education; geography and history; celebrating diversity; and art and culture. Once the appropriate program groupings have been agreed on, revised or new goal statements must then be drafted for each program grouping (goal).

A program grouping is an umbrella or collection of related programs. Larger organizations with many programs may have subgoals. For example, if a new program, Case Management, is added to the Direct Services program group, the program subgoal for Case Management might be "to ensure better coordination of the delivery of direct services to our clients," whereas the overall goal for the Direct Services program group might be more global: "to expand our services continuum to achieve wrap-around support for families with pre-school children."

Goals and Objectives Must Be Written to Support Accountability

Goals and objectives must be written so they can be monitored. "Improve the well-being of the community" is a laudable goal, but it would be difficult to determine whether such a broad goal had been attained. In developing language that will allow goals and objectives to be monitored, important areas of potential ambiguity are likely to arise. Work done now to ensure clearly articulated goals and objectives that can be actively monitored will save hours of frustration later, during implementation of the plan. Clear goals and objectives are also the building blocks of successful program evaluation.

Each goal usually carries with it two or more specific objectives. An objective is a precise, measurable, and time-phased result that supports achievement of the goal.

Write Program Goals and Objectives

The program portfolio that was developed in Phase 4 (Worksheet 4) should contain all of the guiding information necessary to develop specific program objectives for each program. These objectives should typically cover a time frame of three to five years; if the organization's environment is particularly turbulent, the time frame may be shorter. In any case, the objectives must identify the measurable numbers that will support the fulfillment of the goal and/or strategy and support the achievement of the organization's purpose. The standard form for an objective is:

(verb noting direction of change) + (area of change) +
(target population) + (degree of change) + time frame

For example:

Direction of change	To reduce
Area of change	Unemployment status
Target population	For our graduating students
Degree of change	So that 75 percent gain full-time employment
Time frame	Within six months of graduation

Method for collecting data	Pre/post training questionnaires
Objective	To reduce the unemployment status of our graduating students so that 75 percent are fully employed within six months of graduation.

All objectives should be precise, measurable, and time-phased. However, in developing objectives to support program goals, it is important to distinguish between process and outcome objectives.

- *Process objectives* typically begin with phrases such as "to develop, to implement, to establish, to conduct." These phrases all describe activities that will be undertaken by the organization.

- *Outcome objectives* describe outcomes that will be made by the end users of the organization's services, changes that are a result of process activities. Outcome objectives typically begin with phrases such as "to increase, to decrease, to improve."

Remember that if the objective describes something a staff person or volunteer is going to do, it is almost certainly an activity or process objective. If the objective describes a change in behavior, skills, awareness, health status, and so on, by a client or consumer of your services, it is almost certainly an outcome objective. Both types of objectives are useful as long as the writer is clear that they refer to different things: One is an ends statement and the other is a means statement.

The section on the language of strategic planning in Chapter 1 makes it clear that the distinction between activities and outcomes is exactly the same as between mission and purpose in the mission statement. It is the difference between means and ends. Activities (or process objectives) and mission descriptions are means selected to achieve the ends of outcome objectives and the purpose statement.

Exhibit 6.1 shows examples of both process and outcome objectives in support of program goals.

Write Administrative, Financial, and Governance Goals and Objectives

Each financial, administrative, and governance function should have its own goal statement. For example, a goal statement for Staffing and Benefits might read, "To attract and retain qualified, competent staff, volunteers, and interns to carry out programs of the Community Counseling Center."

EXHIBIT 6.1   SAMPLE GOALS, OBJECTIVES,
AND TASKS

Examples of Program Goals	Examples of Related Program Objectives (Process/Outcome)
Family Workshop Program To increase coping skills of families in stress (Martha's Shelter offers workshops to family members who need to acquire healthy coping skills.)	• Present two workshops for 20 families in July (process objective). • Increase performance on self-administered test in coping strategies by 50% on average for all participants as a result of the two workshops (outcome objective).
Volunteer/Victim Advocate Program To decrease the immediate trauma of victims of crime (This program of the Victim's Assistance Fund provides victims of crime with volunteers who will accompany them and speak for them at police and legal proceedings.)	• To match 200 victims of crime with 200 volunteers to provide support during police interviews in 1997 (process objective). • Using provider-administered surveys, achieve a significant decrease in the immediate trauma reported by victims as a result of this program; "significant" to be defined once a baseline is established in 2004 (outcome objective).
Traveling Exhibition Program To increase the public's awareness of neon art (This program of the Museum of Neon Art makes the collection of world-class neon art pieces available to the finest museums in the world.)	• To sponsor one showing per quarter in 2004 (process objective). • Using attendance as a measure of cultural awareness, double the number of people attending the exhibit in 2004 compared to previous year (outcome objective).

A long-range objective for this staffing goal might then read, "Community Counseling Center anticipates a staff of 13 full-time employees in the next three to five years to fully staff the program and its projects as outlined in the organizational chart attached to this plan."

It is important that these objectives be as specific and measurable as possible. For example, "increase board involvement in fundraising this year" is too vague; a more effective objective would be "to achieve 100 percent board contributions to our agency in each fiscal year of the strategic plan" or "the board will lead a major donor fund drive to raise \$25,000 by the end of year two," which are both measurable and specific objectives.

The selection of the administrative, finance, and governance goals will depend on the complexity of the organization. Small organizations may have only two management goals: fundraising and administration. Larger organizations may have many more goals. The final administrative, finance, and governance goals and objectives directly come out of the decisions you made in Phase 4, Worksheet 16. Review and affirm the goals and your tentative list of long-term priorities. Make any adjustments to the wording of your priorities so they become specific and measurable process or outcome objectives.

Step 5.2: Understand the Financial Implications of Your Decisions

Now that the scope and scale of programs and services have been decided on and the organization is clear on which administrative, finance, and governance objectives will be needed to support those programs and services, the planning committee is ready to work with staff to develop long-range financial projections. The planning committee will need to work with the people who are most involved with finances in estimating the overall costs of implementing the plan and ask those involved in fundraising to develop a fundraising plan to support the future vision. Obviously, revenue and cost considerations have been involved from the beginning. Now is the time to finalize projections.

Is it okay to complete a strategic plan without long-range financial projections? Yes, in that even without detailed financial projections, the overall directions set in the strategic plan will still guide the allocation of resources to support your program, fundraising, administrative, and governance functions. This directional clarity is absolutely essential for a strategic plan.

It is better, however, to have some sense of your long-range financial projections. Financial projections can not only serve as a reality check about the cost of implementing the strategic plan and where that money will come from, but they are also essential if you desire to create a detailed long-term fundraising plan that can be used by your board and development staff to raise those resources.

Be reasonable. The capacity to develop these forecasts in a meaningful way depends on the financial management skills and financial systems infrastructure present at the time of the planning process. It isn't possible to develop long-range financial forecasting competency during the strategic planning process.

Develop Long-Range Financial Projections

The long-range financial projections are not precise forecasts, and the focus of developing long-range financial projections should not be on budgets that are incredibly detailed. From a development point of view, however, it would be useful to know whether the additional staffing needed to support the strategic plan will cost in the neighborhood of $100,000 or $1 million, or whether the total budget to support the plan is closer to $1.5 million or $3 million.

Strategic Budgeting: How Much Is All of This Going to Cost?

Just as strategic planning is different from planning, strategic budgeting is different from regular, year-to-year budgeting. For example, one decision in a strategic plan might be to open a new clinic in a neighboring town. The strategic plan may not include details such as which specific services to offer at the new clinic and probably will not discuss how much space will be needed, which section of town is preferable, how to publicize the new location, or other similar details. But such a decision reflects a strategic choice to expand geographically: More detailed operational planning and operational budgeting will take place later.

As authors Peters and Schaffer state: "A budgeting process that is motivated by quality programming and mission impact should start with expense forecasting not income forecasting."[1] If at this point you limit your planning to what income you are currently receiving, you are missing an important planning opportunity. Strategic budgeting focuses on a broad-stroke plan that reflects the programmatic and organizational strategic plan. Strategic budgeting focuses on the anticipated scale of each of the programs, the infrastructure needed to support that level of programming, and a realistic assessment of how the organization might be able to support this vision.

Estimate Expenses

A budget, simply stated, is a plan expressed in dollars. To estimate future expenditures, therefore, an organization's financial staff will have to review the goals and objectives with an eye to identifying what major resources are going to be needed to achieve those end results. This can be an extremely difficult task. The authors of the premier text on accounting, *Financial and Accounting Guide for Not-for-Profit Organizations,* aptly summed it up when they wrote: "Estimating the costs involved in reaching each of these goals can be difficult because there are always many unknowns and uncertainties as to the details of how each goal will be accomplished."[2]

The expense side of the strategic budget is most easily derived by looking at the big-ticket items that make up the organization's budget (e.g., staffing and benefits, overhead expenses, supplies, and capital improvements). Because much of the nonprofit sector is service-oriented, these expenses will typically make up the majority of expense items.

Program managers or department managers who have responsibility for the development of annual operating budgets should be involved in the development of projected expenditures to support any long-range goals and objectives that have been articulated in the strategic plan. Remember that the planning committee is not looking for detailed expense projections, but rather an overall vision of how big an organization you are projecting to have and the costs associated with achieving that vision. These numbers can then be compared to the future revenue potential of the organization.

Estimate Program and Other Costs

The first step in developing a long-term budget is to conduct a cost analysis of your proposed future program portfolio. Whether you are developing an annual operating budget or estimating how much it will cost for you to support the goals and objectives articulated in your strategic plan, you will need to be able to estimate direct program costs.

Program (direct) costs are easily identified with one or more programs or projects. If you can take the receipt or invoice for an expense and easily identify to which program it belongs, it is a program direct cost. Types of program costs include:

- Salaries for staff members who spend time specifically on the project (e.g., workshop coordinator)
- Materials and supplies for project activities
- Rent for project-specific space
- Travel for program staff
- Equipment used exclusively for project activities

Other costs such as common (indirect) costs and overhead costs are usually not so easy to identify.[3] Common (indirect) costs benefit more than one program and tare not easily identifiable with *one* program. Types of common costs include:

- Salaries for staff members who benefit more than one program or the entire agency (e.g., program director, office manager, receptionist)
- Staff benefits that are difficult to identify with individual staff members
- Rent, maintenance, and utilities for common office space
- Supplies, postage, and telephone expense for shared office facilities
- Lease expense for common office equipment
- Insurance for the site and professional liability coverage

Overhead costs are associated with administration, fundraising, and membership development. Types of overhead costs include:

- Salaries for administrative and development personnel (e.g., the accountant, executive director, and grant writer)
- Auditing, accounting, and legal fees
- Board travel and meeting expenses
- Contract and revenue management expenses
- All fundraising expenses
- Membership solicitation and support

Although it is important that you have the ability to track in great detail and allocate these types of costs during your regular annual budgeting process and when writing proposals, it is not really important for you to be able to do that level of financial analysis during this phase of the planning process. What you are really trying to accomplish is to get a *broad-stroke estimate* of how much it will cost to implement your strategic plan.

The Long-Range Fundraising Plan: How Much Do We Need to Raise?

Once you have a general sense of how much your strategic plan is going to cost, you are ready to develop your fundraising plan. A long-term fundraising plan is critical for ensuring that you will have the necessary resources to support the vision you have just articulated in your plan.

The plan can also serve as a reality check for your plan. Given the three- to five-year programmatic and administrative goals and objectives that you have set, is it realistic to secure the resources needed, or is it possible you will need to modify the time horizon for achieving those goals given the resources you are likely to be able to raise? This does not mean that your plan is wrong, but it does mean that you may need to scale down what you are hoping to achieve over the strategic planning time frame, while communicating in your vision statements the ideal scope and scale of your operations.

Most organizations undertaking strategic planning already have some plan for how to currently support their organization and have some sense of which areas have the most potential for growth. The strategic planning process provides the opportunity to consider the role of fundraising in the organization's future and to plan for what will be needed to implement the plan. A detailed strategic fundraising plan is usually developed as a companion piece to the strategic plan. This plan can be integrated into the final strategic planning document, or it can be a stand-alone document.

Forecast Revenues and Develop the Fundraising Plan

When estimating revenues, many people simply use intuitive judgment and make an educated guess. Sometimes the educated guess is made by a group or is based on the opinions of several informed people.

In the for-profit sector, forecasting techniques are used (e.g., to predict sales income, costs of parts and materials, investment performance, and the effects of capital purchases). In the nonprofit sector, forecasting is usually used to project revenue, such as sales or fees. Forecasting techniques can also be used to predict the number of hospital admissions, enrollment in various college classes, and other statistics necessary for planning.

For small or new organizations—and for simple decisions in all kinds of organizations—making an educated guess may be the best forecasting method. More formal forecasting involves applying statistical and mathematical techniques to historical data to make projections for the future. All forecasting and predicting—from "seat of the pants" guesses to highly complex modeling—is based on the premise that future events can be predicted based on patterns discovered through reviewing historical information. This point might seem obvious, but future events may not follow the patterns of the past.

Hank Rosso of the Fundraising School was famous for his maxim: "There are five parts to successful fundraising: Planning, Planning, Planning, Planning, and Asking." Strategic planning for successful fundraising is an important component for long-term success; the agencies with strategic fundraising plans may not have more money the next year or even the year after that, but they will be successful 10 years from now.

Seven Steps to the Development of a Fund Development Plan[4]

1. *Review your fundraising performance from the previous two to three years.*
   When reviewing your fundraising performance from the previous two to three years, note any trends in previous support. What do the trends (declining or increasing) in individual donations, institutional gifts, and grants tell you? Has your donor base increased? Are you receiving funding from more funding sources? What has changed in your capacity to raise funds (staffing, systems, board development)? Make some educated guesses about the key factors that influenced the revenue from a certain activity, and determine how these factors affected your revenue generation and the implications for the future.

2. *Gather and analyze stakeholder information: Interview current donors and funders.* If you have not already interviewed current donors and funders during Phase 3, this is a good time to involve your current and potential external stakeholders or go back to the ones with whom you have already talked to discuss your future vision. In your

discussions, you want to test donor and funder receptiveness to any new organizational strategies and focus in your strategic plan (you hopefully have already tested the feasibility of new strategies earlier in strategic planning). Staff members, board members, volunteers, or a consultant can conduct these interviews. Use the interviews as opportunities to educate, cultivate, and further your network of supporters, and use the information to validate your funding projections.

3. *Review your current and potential fundraising vehicles.* Next you want to assess which of your current fundraising vehicles you want—and can maintain or increase—and what future funding is available, or is potentially available, to support the priorities articulated in your draft plan. Here are some common vehicles to consider:

- Unrestricted foundation grants
- Restricted foundation grants
- Corporate contributions
- Individual contributions
- Special events
- Bequests
- Planned gifts: life income funds

For example, a community theater may identify contributed funds at the annual dinner as comprising about half of the funds needed for each season, with box office funds making up the remainder of the budget. A public-interest law firm that has relied predominantly on attorney fees from class-action settlements may see fundraising growth in major donor gifts supplanting attorney fees over time.

Once the anchor fundraising vehicles have been selected, then the following questions should be applied against each of the vehicles:

- Which of the vehicles represent increasing opportunities? Declining opportunities?
- Which have the highest return on investment (including cash, staff time, volunteer time)?
- Which have the most nonfinancial benefits? What are those benefits?
- Which have the most positive impact on other fundraising components?

- ○ Which are the most popular among volunteers? Board members? Least popular?

4. *Select primary revenue sources.* After assessing the full potential of each revenue source, decide on strategies to realize the full potential of each vehicle (e.g., "Increase gifts from current individual donors with more personal approach," "Cultivate relationships with statewide and national grantmakers"). As part of assessing your future fundraising goals, you want to consider how many vehicles you can possible manage in a year, while planning for "fundraising diversity"[5] (i.e., your plan for organizational sustainability). Determine how staff, board, volunteers, and systems will need to support the plan's implementation.

   Whoever is developing the strategic fundraising plan might also link the vehicles in order to maximize the connections. For example, one homeless shelter conducts an annual mail campaign for contributions, mailing to existing donors and volunteers, and tries to expand the list each year by about ten percent. This mail campaign makes a modest amount of money, but its bigger purpose is to identify more significant donors, who are then invited to an annual open house during the holiday season. Following the open house, volunteers make personal visits to all donors who attended the open house, seeking more substantial contributions. During those visits, names are solicited for next year's mailing as well. If any of these activities (i.e., mail campaign, open house, major donor visits) were considered in isolation of the others, each would be far less successful.

   Once the key components are selected and linked into a plan and calendar, the organization must identify what is needed to make the fundraising plan work. For example, if major gifts are identified as key for fundraising growth, such a decision will affect board recruitment and composition. Board training in asking for contributions may also be appropriate. If corporate contributions are targeted for growth, more efforts may be invested in recruiting volunteers from selected corporations. If contributed funds have not been a significant factor up to now, but the organization wishes to grow in this area, a multiyear investment in a development officer may be appropriate.

5. *Set fundraising targets.* Based on the previous analysis, you can start to set long-term and short-term financial targets for each funding

source, validated by historical performance with defendable ratio-
nales. If some of your estimates are somewhat questionable, you
might want to discount fundraising targets by the probability of
their attainment before placing numbers into the long-term and
short-term fundraising plans. If, however, your fundraising targets
are substantially less than the funds needed to support your strategic plan, you may need to revisit some of the objectives outlined
in the plan and either limit the three- to five-year scope and scale
of your vision or prioritize which of the objectives you may want
to put on hold if you are not able to raise the money necessary to
support the plan.

6. *Write the development plan.* Summarize your targets in a long-term
   fundraising plan, with an annual fundraising plan for the first year
   of the strategic plan's implementation. Remember to have the plan
   be simple enough so everyone can refer to it but specific and realistic so it can successfully be put into action.

7. *Adopt the development plan.* After the strategic plan and supporting
   developing plan have been adopted, ask the board to take the first
   step in implementing the fund development plan—making their
   gift!

Worksheet 17 (see process notes in Exhibit 6.2) will help you develop
the broad-stroke, long-range financial projections that you need if you
want to have a better idea of the costs of supporting your strategic plan
and how you might be able to support the plan. Remember, you are trying to get a sense of whether in five years you are striving to grow from
being a $500,000 organization to one that needs $800,000 of support.
You are not trying to figure out if that $800,000 is $783,000 or $821,500.

One organization came up with a projection of how much it would
cost to support its strategic plan in one hour. After the program portfolio
and administrative, financial, and governance priorities were completed,
the controller asked the management team to estimate how many full-
time staff or equivalent (FTEs) were needed to run the organization and
operate the programs at the level that was projected. The management
team estimated that in five years the organization needed to grow from a
current staff level of 24 individuals to 36 individuals—a 50 percent
growth in staff. Assuming that the proportion of direct salaries and benefits
to total expenses remained relatively the same, the controller estimated

EXHIBIT 6.2   WORKSHEET 17: LONG-RANGE
FINANCIAL PROJECTIONS

Process Notes

How to do this activity	This worksheet has two parts. Part 1 asks you to draft out an estimate of how much it might cost to operate at the proposed scope and scale of programs with the necessary infrastructure supported needed. Use Worksheets 14 and 16 to help guide your thinking about possible costs. Part 2 of this worksheet asks you to identify the revenue sources for each program and administrative group of expenditures.
Why do this activity	The information from this worksheet can serve as a reality test—Can we really support the plan as currently articulated?—as well as used to develop a detailed long-range fundraising plan.
Who to involve in the process	Program staff and financial staff need to be working together to complete this worksheet.

See ASO/USA's example of this worksheet at the end of this chapter. Blank worksheets are provided in Appendix A and on the CD that accompanies this book.

that in five years the organization would grow from a $2 million to a $3 million organization. At the end of the five years, the organization's annual budget was approximately $2,750,000. Although the estimate was off considerably, it was close enough for the development staff to write and implement a long-term development plan.

STEP 5.3: WRITE THE STRATEGIC PLANNING DOCUMENT

Identify the Writer of the Plan

Who should write the plan? This question was first raised in Phase 1: Step 1.4. If the appropriate writer was designated at the beginning of the process, that writer will be able to begin work sooner rather than later in starting to write up the decisions made during the planning process. If the question of who should write the plan needs to be revisited, a few thoughts should be kept in mind. It is useful to remember that one or two individuals, not a whole group, are able to write most efficiently. The writer simply crafts the presentation of the group's ideas. Often an executive director will draft the plan, or the task may be delegated to a staff person, board member, or a consultant who has been working with the planning committee. In the end, it really doesn't matter who writes the strategic plan; what matters is that it accurately documents the decisions made by the planning committee, that it represents a shared vision, and that it has the support of those who will be responsible for carrying it out. (In all likelihood, and ideally, the decision about who will write the plan will have been made early on in the process.)

Develop a Review Process for the Document

The process of review and approval is one of the most important considerations in this phase because this is where you accomplish quality control and have your last opportunity for building commitment before approval. The planning committee should decide in advance who will review and respond to the draft plan. Obviously, strategic planning committee members will participate in the review process, but should the full board and the full staff also contribute? The guiding principle of participation in the strategic planning process is that everyone who will help execute the plan should have some input in shaping it. Whether this includes review of the final drafts of the plan is a judgment call that depends on the particular circumstances of an organization.

Ideally, the big ideas have been debated and resolved, so that revisions amount to only small matters of adding detail, revising format, or changing wording in a particular section. Some text editing can be helpful, but reviewers should be looking at how the whole plan holds together and whether it is appropriately ambitious. If reviewers get bogged down in too many specific proofreading details, the plan could linger in draft form forever. The planning committee must exercise leadership in setting a realistic time frame and in bringing the review process to a timely close. The committee needs to choose the level of review appropriate for the organization, provide copies for review to the selected individuals, and set a deadline for submitting feedback (usually allowing one to two weeks is sufficient). Upon receiving all feedback, the committee must agree on which suggested revisions to accept, incorporate these changes into the document, and submit the strategic plan to the full board of directors for approval.

Choose What to Include in the Strategic Plan and Its Format

A strategic plan is simply a document that summarizes why an organization exists, what it is trying to accomplish, and how it will go about doing so. Its audience is anyone who wants to know the organization's most important ideas, issues, and priorities: board members, staff, volunteers, clients, funders, peers at other organizations, the press, and the public. It is a document that should make clear in which direction the organization is headed and provide enough rationale for this direction to be compelling. So, the more concise and ordered the document, the greater the likelihood that it will be used and that it will be helpful in guiding the operations of the organization.

Depending on the intensity of the strategic planning process used—abbreviated, moderate, or extensive—strategic plans will have slightly different formats containing various levels of specificity and length. The written plan should reflect the nature and extent of the planning discussions and the level of detail that needs to be communicated to the reader. Whatever the format, remember that the point of the document is to allow the best possible explanation of the organization's plan for the future—the format should serve the message.

For an abbreviated strategic planning process, the strategic planning document will probably be no more than three to eight pages long and will include mission and vision statements, a summary of core strategies, and a list of long-term and short-term program and management/operations priorities. The edited notes from the retreat may serve as the appendix.

For a moderate planning process, the strategic planning document will probably be 8 to 12 pages long and will include the following elements:

- Introduction by the president of the board (one page)
- Mission, vision, and values statements (one page)
- Summary of core strategies (one page)
- List of long-term and short-term program and management/operations goals and objectives (four to six pages)

- Optional appendices: summary of situation assessment, summary of client surveys, summary of any other stakeholder surveys or interviews (one to three pages)

For an extensive strategic planning process and/or a multidepartment organization, a document that is 15 to 50 pages will most likely be needed. Exhibit 6.3 includes a table of contents for such a strategic planning document. Brief descriptions of each component are listed in the next section. Such a table of contents should help writers as they begin to organize their thoughts and their material.

A Detailed Explanation of Each Section of the Strategic Plan

I. Introduction by the President of the Board

A one-page cover letter from the president of the organization's board of directors introduces the plan to readers; it gives a stamp of approval to the

---

EXHIBIT 6.3   SAMPLE TABLE OF CONTENTS FOR A STRATEGIC PLANNING PROCESS

1. Introduction by the President of the Board

2. Executive Summary

3. Mission, Vision, and Values Statements

4. Organization History and Profile

5. Summary of Core Strategies

6. Program Goals and Objectives

7. Financial, Administrative, and Governance Goals and Objectives

8. [Possible] Appendices:

   - Summary of environmental assessment: strengths, weaknesses, opportunities, and threats

   - Summary of client surveys, community interviews, etc.

   - Membership of board and planning committee

   - Long-range budget projections

   - Long-range development plan is implemented

---

plan and demonstrates that the organization has achieved a critical level of internal agreement. (This introduction is often combined with the executive summary.)

II. Executive Summary

In one to two pages, this section should summarize the strategic plan. The executive summary should reference the mission and vision, high-light the core future strategies and major program and administrative pri-orities (what the organization is seeking to accomplish), and perhaps note the process for developing the plan, as well as thank participants in the process. From this summary, readers should understand what is most important about the organization's plan: What is the story line you are planning to pursue? (*Note:* This executive summary might be published in the organization's newsletter or special mailing to supporters and par-ticipants in the planning process.)

III. Mission, Vision, and Values Statements

These statements can stand alone without any introductory text, because essentially they introduce and define themselves.

IV. Organization Profile and History

(*Note:* This section may be included as an appendix instead of as a part of the main strategic planning document.)

In one or two pages, readers should learn the story of the organiza-tion—key events, triumphs, and changes over time—so they can under-stand its historical context (just as the planning committee needed to do so during the information-gathering phase of the planning process). Major accomplishments for the past year should be highlighted in this section as well. Depending on how well the readers of your strategic plan know the organization's history, this section may be as detailed or as short as you need it to be.

V. Summary of Core Strategies

This section makes explicit the strategic thinking behind the plan and tells readers where the organization will be primarily focusing its resources over the next few years. The section might be presented as a brief listing of the organization's three to five core future strategies. After each strategy there may be an explanation of that strategy so that the outside reader has a better understanding of the "why" of that strategy.

VI. Program Goals and Objectives

In many ways, the program goals and objectives are the heart of the strategic plan. The mission statement answers the big questions about why the organization exists and how it seeks to benefit society, but the goals and longer-term objectives are the plan of action—what the organization intends to do over the next few years. As such, this section should serve as a useful guide to annual operational planning and a reference for evaluation. Depending on the complexity of the organization, this section may be 3 to 15 pages long, but multidepartmental institutions and large organizations often exceed that number of pages. (See Appendix K for a sample of the ASO/USA's Program Goals and Objectives.)

VII. Financial, Administrative, and Governance Goals and Objectives

The financial, administrative, and governance functions are separated from the program functions here to emphasize the distinction between service goals and organization development goals; this section gives the reader a clearer understanding of the difference and the relationship between the two. This section directly addresses what resources are needed to support the service goals. Goals typically include staffing and benefits, resource development, board of directors, planning and evaluation; public relations/marketing; infrastructure (includes technology, financial and information reporting, and facilities), and networking and collaboration. Depending on the complexity of the organization, this section usually is 3 to 12 pages long but may be longer.

VIII. Appendices

The reason to include any appendices is to provide needed documentation for interested readers. Perhaps no appendices are necessary (many organizations opt for brevity); they should be included only if they will truly enhance readers' understanding of the plan, not just burden them with more data. Most organizations will at least summarize strengths, weaknesses, opportunities, and threats here, and paraphrase the results of any client/customer surveys. Appendices can be from one to five pages, but they could be considerably longer.

SIDEBAR

Sometimes goals and objectives can be organized under each core strategy. For example: One organization had the following four strategies:

1. Invest in our capacity to support programs in terms of staffing, infra-structure, and governance.

2. Broaden and diversify our funding base so we are less dependent on government sources.

3. Expand our services so that we provide a continuum of services that meet the needs of our clients.

4. Improve our visibility and broaden the understanding of what we do and the impact we have on our client's lives.

Each of the core strategies had a series of related goals and long-term objectives. For example: Broaden and diversity our funding base so we are less dependent on government sources:

- Goal: Increase support received from individuals, foundations, and corporations. (A sample objective: Each year, increase our private revenue fundraising goal by at least 10% over previous year's actual.)

- Goal: Increase the Board's role in and capacity to do fundraising. (A sample objective: Maintain 100% board giving.)

- Goal: Improve our marketing and visibility as a vehicle for increased funds. (A sample objective: Improve our ability to track clients and state outcomes.)

- Goal: Improve our capacity to maintain appropriate public funding. (A sample objective: Develop and implement best practices for identifying and securing public funding and addressing ongoing reporting requirements associated with public funding.)

Write the Plan

If there will be multiple writers, create a plan for completing the strategic plan (see Exhibit 6.4). For each section of the plan, include a brief description of purpose, the name of the person responsible for completing the section, a target length (e.g., one page, two pages, etc.), and status.

For an abbreviated strategic planning process, the writer(s) of the plan simply needs to use the notes from the planning retreat and summarize

EXHIBIT 6.4 EXAMPLE OF A PLAN FOR COMPLETING THE STRATEGIC PLAN WHEN THERE ARE MULTIPLE WRITERS

Section	Purpose of Section	Prime Mover	Suggested Length	Status
Introduction	About the process, summary of what the plan contains, excitement about the future	Juan	1 page	June 15 when sent out to the board
Mission Statement	Let the reader know what is our purpose and what we do	Sue	1 page	Completed
Vision Statement	Inspire the reader about what we hope to achieve—our dream of the possible	Kathleen	1 page	Completed
Statement of Values, Beliefs, and Guiding Principles	Lets the reader know what are the values, beliefs, and assumptions on which we do our work	Juan	1 page	Completed
History of the Organization, Who We Currently Serve, and Priority Clients for Future	Lets the reader understand our roots, why we serve the people we serve, and who are our	Juan	2 pages	Completed
Context for Our Decisions: What We Learned from Our Shareholders	Provides the reader with a context for our decisions: a summary of our SWOT	Kathleen	1 page	Due by May 14
Where Does Our Organization Fit in the Provision of Services to Our Clients?	Helps the reader understand who else serves our clients and our unique competitive position	Sue	1 page	First draft circulating

Section	Purpose of Section	Prime Mover	Suggested Length	Status
Summary of Core Strategies	Summarizes our primary focus of resources for the next three to five years	Michael	2 pages	Completed
Detailed Core Strategies with Key Directions/Goals and Objectives	Detailed description of each of the core strategies, including the background about why we are doing so. Overall goals and specific objectives to accomplish in the next five years	Each section has designated writer. Juan is coordinator.	15 pages	Due by May 14
Appendix	Includes: List of who we spoke with during external stakeholder assessment Detailed long-range development plan More detailed description of client needs and what we learned from external stakeholders			Due by June 1

the key ideas on paper. If the group decided at the retreat to rewrite its mission statement, two or three individuals might collect each participant's Worksheet 5 and ideas generated during the retreat discussion, and craft a revised statement. The newly drafted mission statement would be given to the strategic plan writer to include in the final document. The key to writing the plan is to keep it simple and short, circulate it among internal stakeholders for their comments, and then submit the final version to the board of directors for approval.

For a moderate planning process, the writer(s) of the plan should use the notes from any retreats and all planning committee meetings. These notes, plus copies of the following worksheets if used as the basis of discussion, would probably be most helpful for developing the moderate strategic plan:

- Worksheet 5: Create a Mission Statement
- Worksheet 6: Create a Vision Statement
- Worksheet 7: Articulate Your Organization's Values, Beliefs, and Guiding Principles (optional)
- Worksheet 14: Program Portfolio
- Worksheet 15: Core Future Strategies
- Worksheet 16: Summary of Administrative, Financial, and Governance Priorities
- Worksheet 17: Long-Range Financial Projections
- The appendices to the moderate strategic plan might include data from Worksheet 12: Summary of Data Analysis

After the board president or planning committee chair has written the introduction to the strategic plan, the document should be circulated among key stakeholders for their input and then a final version submitted to the board of directors for their approval.

For an extensive strategic planning process and multidepartment organizations, the strategic planning document has, for the most part, already been written if most of the worksheets have been completed. The writer(s) of the strategic plan could simply cut and paste the supporting worksheet data into the strategic planning document. For example, the mission statement and vision and values statement data will be found on Worksheets 5, 6, and 7, respectively, and the core strategies were reviewed in Worksheet 15. Even if organizations have not completed every worksheet (this is the case for most organizations), the worksheets would have framed the discussions, and therefore the notes from the meetings simply need to be summarized in the strategic plan.

The rule of thumb for writing the extensive strategic plan is the same rule for writing the abbreviated strategic plan: Keep it simple and keep it as short as you can and still provide enough guidance to develop an annual operating plan. The heart of the strategic planning document is the core strategies and program and administrative priorities/goals and objectives sections. The supporting data should all be contained in the strategic plan's appendices.

For multidepartment organizations, overall strategies and overarching program and management/support goals and objectives for the entire organization should be developed first. Then, each department manager or director would be responsible for developing goals and objectives for his or her department, making sure that the departmental plan was consistent with the overall organization plan. The prime writer or writers of the extensive strategic plan would then incorporate those department plans into the overall strategic planning document.

The strategic plan for ASO/USA is located at the end of this chapter.

Alternative Formats for Strategic Plans

As stated previously, strategic plans usually have all of the following components: introduction by the president of the board; executive summary; mission statement (and vision and values statements); organization history and profile; and core strategies. In addition, most strategic plans also have a section that includes a detailed narrative of program goals and long-term objectives, and administrative, finance, and governance goals and long-term objectives. There is no rule, however, that says you have to follow any one format.

Some organizations use a columnar format to describe their goals and long-term objectives, rather than an outline narrative (see Exhibit 6.5). The columnar format allows the reader of the plan to easily see the connection between goals, subgoals, and objectives. The inclusion of the commentary column allows the reader of the strategic plan to have a greater understanding of why the goal is important. The inclusion of either background, historical data, or a summary of the future emphasis or focus of the goal helps the reader put the goal in some context.

EXHIBIT 6.5   EXAMPLE: USING COLUMNAR FORMAT

Support Services—Goal: Ensure that families have a safe place to express their feelings and to lessen their sense of isolation.

	Goal	Commentary	Objectives
Support Groups	Ensure a structured yet informal support group process that encourages families to seek support and offer support.	Support groups are the heart of SFCD. Support groups are the primary places where families meet and connect. Support groups continue to receive the highest rating from parents/caregivers who have used them. We have also found that although all families who have children with different disabilities have much to share, some disabilities or issues are so prevalent that it is critical to provide a group focusing on that specific disability or that issue. In addition to parents/caregivers, children with disabilities, as well as their siblings, benefit from having a safe place to share their feelings/experiences. In response to these needs, we offer support groups such as the sibling group. We want to continue the support groups that we have and also be flexible and expand to meet new needs in San Francisco. We are trying to create as much accessibility as possible by providing groups in different communities, in different languages and with child care.	1. By the end of year 2 of this plan, develop and implement a program to provide support and professional development to group leaders, and maintain an infrastructure to ensure the support groups' success. 2. Increase the average number of support group participants from five to eight members. 3. Ensure that we have at least one support group in each of the major neighborhoods in the city. 4. Improve the linkage of support group members to our other services.

EXHIBIT 6.5 EXAMPLE: USING COLUMNAR FORMAT (Continued)

	Goal	Commentary	Objectives
Peer Mentor Program	Provide opportunities for families/family members to gain support from another individual, who has had personal experience with the disability world, is culturally/linguistically a good match, has been trained by SFCD, and will ensure follow-up.	Parent-to-Parent offers families support from an individual who has shared a similar experience. Individual peer support is important because not everyone benefits from the group experience. Many families are private about their experience, and being a part of a group may be overwhelming and sometimes even threatening. Also, by offering individual support, an individual can connect with a family when it is convenient for them or when the need arises, as opposed to group attendance, which has a preset schedule. We have developed a model that works really well and would like to expand this model to include siblings and children with disabilities as mentors.	1. Maintain the cultural diversity of trained mentors. 2. Develop and implement our mentor training in Chinese and Spanish. 3. Increase the numbers of mentor matches to an average of 10 per month. 4. Increase the annual participation of the mentor support group to 20 participants. 5. Explore the possibility of expanding the model to include youth.

One choice planners face is whether to include detailed year-by-year objectives. Some strategic plans outline in great detail what the organization wants to achieve each year for the next three (or five) years. For example, "In year one we want to increase from 100 to 150 clients, in year two we want to increase to 200 clients, in year three to 225 clients, in year four to 250 clients, and by year five we want to have 300 clients." The challenge with this approach is that is assumes that you can predict—and control—the level of activity each year. But more important, it assumes that there is sufficient value to be gained in outlining in such detail the outcomes you want to achieve for the time frame for the plan.

The authors feel that the amount of effort—and skill needed to predict that level of detail—is neither necessary nor effective. The strategic plan should articulate the scope and scale that you wish to achieve ("Within five years we want to triple the number of clients being served"), but the strategic plan does not need to have detailed year-by-year forecasting. A detailed first year's operating plan and supporting budget is sufficient to successfully start to implement your strategic plan. (See Phase 6 for more information on the annual operating plan.) If the board and staff prefer a plan that includes year-by-year objectives, the format might look like Exhibit 6.6.

Another option is to write each goal with both long-range and short-range objectives. This helps tie the strategic plan directly to the annual operating plan (see Exhibit 6.7).

Another option, one that more and more organizations are favoring, is to eliminate the long-term program and administrative goals sections and instead focus on a detailed list of priorities for each of the core strategies (see Exhibit 6.8).

The bottom line for the strategic planning document format is that you should use whatever format will easily communicate to internal and external stakeholders what you intend to accomplish and how you will accomplish it.

Dealing with Uncertainty in Your Planning Decisions: Time for a Reality Check?

After you have completed costing out your vision and drafted a plan for how to pay for the vision, it's time to collectively step back and take a deep breath for a reality check.

EXHIBIT 6.6 EXAMPLE: GOALS WITH THREE-YEAR OBJECTIVES

Goal: Increase the graduation rate of girls in high school

Year 1 Objectives	Year 2 Objectives	Year 3 Objectives
Complete study of current services available in the city for high school girls. Develop a program to offer enhanced support to girls from ABC High School.	Implement a pilot project for at least 10 girls from grade 9.	Continue pilot project. By year-end, evaluate progress and decide whether to continue.
Continue to offer after-school tutoring program for 20 girls from grade 9 to 12.	Ongoing	Ongoing
	Initiate job training program for at least five girls, in collaboration with Jobs Training Institute.	Increase number of girls served to at least 15.
	Update tutorial materials for all grades.	
		Research possibility of starting for-profit arm for employment training of high school seniors.
Corporate Mentor Program: Match at least 60% of participating girls with a mentor.	Ongoing	Ongoing
Sponsor "Bring Your Daughter to Work" program.	Ongoing	Ongoing

EXHIBIT 6.7 EXAMPLE: TYING STRATEGIC PLAN ADMINISTRATIVE GOAL DIRECTLY WITH AN ANNUAL OPERATING PLAN

Staffing and benefits: To attract and retain qualified paid and volunteer staff for all services and activities

Background/commentary: Our staff are our most valuable resource. Over the past two years, the demand for our services has increased dramatically, without our having been able to increase the number of staff to manage such growth. Low salaries and increased expectations of staff have resulted in high stress levels and increasing turnover, especially among line staff. We need to focus our resources on bringing our staffing capacity in line with our service levels, and make sure we have the administrative support to provide for the efficient and effective delivery of services. In addition, to remain competitive, we need to increase our entire compensation package over the next three to five years.

	What do we want to have accomplished in the next five years?	Intermediate milestones	What do we want to accomplish this upcoming year?	Measures of success; feedback and evaluation mechanisms	Who responsible	By when?
Staffing	Increase number of paid staff from 8 FTE employees to 15 FTE to support our ability to provide needed services	Hire staff for new program that will begin in next 18 months	Increase number of staff from 8 FTE (full-time equivalent) employees to 11 FTE employees to support our ability to provide needed services	Hire a new Client Services Director and Client Services Specialist; Hire PT Technology Specialist and PT Clerical Worker	Jan Doe	By mid-year
			Develop revised job descriptions for all staff	All job descriptions be revised by end of fiscal year	Clare Wilson	By beginning of new fiscal year

	What do we want to have accomplished in the next five years?	Intermediate milestones	What do we want to accomplish this upcoming year?	Measures of success; feedback and evaluation mechanisms	Who responsible	By when?
Salaries and Benefits	Bring salaries up to par with similar agencies and offer health, vision, and dental to all	Offer new medical benefits package within 2 years	Assess overall salary structure and benefits package; develop and implement a plan to increase staff salaries and offer a competitive benefit package	Revised salary range schedule and personnel policies approved by the Board	Board personnel Task Force with consultant	By year-end
	Review personnel policies annually to make sure they are in legal compliance		Revise personnel policies			
	Offer a retirement plan with matching employer contribution	Start retirement program (nonemployer match) by year 2				

Resources Required (Optional):

15 FTE in terms of current dollars	$675,000	
Benefits	$135,000	

Resources Required (Optional):

11 FTE in terms of current dollars	$495,000	
Benefits	$ 79,200	
Consultant:	$ 5,000	

EXHIBIT 6.8   EXAMPLE: DETAIL OF PLAN
THAT FOCUSES ON CORE FUTURE
STRAGEGIES AND PRIORITIES

Strategy: Broaden and diversify our funding base so we are less dependent on government funds.

Background/commentary: Currently, 68% of our revenue is from government grants and contracts, with 5% from individuals, 2% from foundation and corporation grants, and 25% program. While this is very typical for many social service organizations, especially those that provide services to disenfranchised populations, there are certain limitations that are caused by reliance on government grants. Among those challenges are that government grants are restricted for specific activities that fit within a specific grant's requirements and government grants do not usually pay for their full share of indirect costs. In addition, the federal government is about to significantly reduce its funding in the subsidized housing arena. Both internal and external stakeholders have stated that we should expand our foundation and individual donors. Especially with individual donor solicitation, additional staff and board time is necessary to make such support a reality.

Key directions/overall goals:

1. Increase support received from individuals and foundations: decrease reliance on government sources.
2. Expand major donor program.
3. Increase the allure and profitability of the annual fundraising event.
4. Increase the board's role in and capacity to do fundraising.

Five-year objectives:

Goal	Related Long-Term Objectives
Increase support received from individuals and foundations: decrease reliance on government sources.	• Research and apply for operating grants and capacity-building grants to support the core administrative priorities: Raise $300,000 to 400,000 new dollars for capacity support and increase support from foundations to offset ongoing operating needs.
	• Increase support from foundations for restricted purposes.
	• Increase fundraising goal by at least 10% over previous year's actual.
	• Elevate the direct mail materials and lists to achieve fundraising goals.

EXHIBIT 6.8	EXAMPLE: DETAIL OF PLAN THAT FOCUSES ON CORE FUTURE STRAGEGIES AND PRIORITIES *(Continued)*

Goal	Related Long-Term Objectives
Expand major donor program.	• Increase cultivation events from two to three in year 1, from three to four in year 2. Increase attendance at cultivation events in years 3 to 5. • Increase number of major donor prospects 10% to 20% each year. • Increase number of one-on-one solicitations to 20 in year 1; 30 in year 2, etc. • Upgrade major donors to higher gift levels in years 4 and 5.
Increase the allure and profitability of the annual fundraising event.	• Increase sponsorship and attendance at annual fundraising event.
Increase the Board's role in and capacity to do fundraising.	• Obtain 100% participation in annual fund, in addition to any event support.

Are many of your decisions based on a high degree of optimism? Do many of the assumptions on which your goals and objectives are based have a high degree of uncertainty? What should you do then? We have emphasized that planning is not about predicting the future but about making better current decisions. Although no one can predict what the future will bring, in a planning process you can anticipate times of turbulence or uncertainty and respond accordingly.

Planning in Turbulent Times

Because nonprofit organizations—like for-profit companies—are operating in turbulent and constantly changing and difficult environments, it is sometimes worth the time and effort to anticipate these uncertainties and/or more financially challenging times and develop responses to such factors.

The economic cycle at the turn of the twenty-first century required dramatic and sometimes drastic changes in assumptions. In the mid- to late 1990s, most organizations were thinking: "We believe that, in this current financial environment, we will be receiving more funding." They developed ambitious plans based on that assumption. By 2002, that assumption—for many nonprofit organizations—had changed to: "We believe and hope that our current financial support will at least stay at its current level." Strategic plans were made with this new assumption, but as the worst of the economic recession continued, many organizations recognized that their worst-case scenario was not "remain the same" but actually "revenues will significantly decline."

Should you put such thinking in your plans? The answer is: maybe. If, after your data collection is completed, you are aware that revenues may decline even more than you feared or that economically difficult times will continue for longer than initially thought, you have a few choices:

- You can make your overall plan less ambitious. Go back and adjust those objectives that are highly unlikely, paring back the plan as necessary or prioritizing the areas of growth to ensure that the organization does not fail by spreading itself too thin.

- You can develop an ambitious plan and acknowledge in your introduction that it is ambitious and may not be able to be reached in the strategic plan's time frame, but nonetheless communicates to the reader the scope and scale that is necessary for the organization to have the impact it wants.

- You can develop contingency plans if certain assumptions do not play out the way you had hoped.

Develop Contingency Plans

To develop a contingency plan, you will need to:

- List the most important factor(s) that might impact the success of a program.

- Develop a contingency plan of action to respond to each potential factor, including trigger points that would indicate when the potential contingency plan should be put into place.

> If _____ (factor) occurs, we should consider _____ (contingency plan of action). This contingency plan should be put in place when _____ (trigger point) happens.

Examples:

- Our proposed plan suggests moderate growth in our housing and legal services departments. Such growth depends on our receiving funding to support our infrastructure in terms of staffing, management information systems, and facilities. If we are not able to secure such funding, we will hold off on increasing services until our infrastructure has been stabilized.

- One of our future core strategies is to expand our services into neighboring Harris County. To date we have received a favorable response to our doing so from other service providers and have documented the need for our services in Harris County. If we secure sufficient financial support from government and foundation sources to fully cover the cost of such expansion, we will move forward with this expansion.

STEP 5.4: ADOPT THE STRATEGIC PLAN AND NEXT STEPS

Finally, the planning process is completed and a document has been produced. Make certain to have the plan formally adopted by the board of directors as the official strategic plan of the organization. This is a moment of closure on the process, and it is necessary for getting all stakeholders energized to put the plan in action.

Share the Plan

Once the plan has been approved, at the very least, the executive summary or a condensed version of the plan should be prepared and sent out to the members, funders, and other individuals whose knowledge of the organization's future is key to their support. Most external stakeholders do not need a copy of the full strategic plan, although they do need to know the hopes and aspirations and priorities of the organization. Some detailed strategies and priorities (e.g., those that talk about beating out the competition) are best kept within the knowledge of internal stakeholders. A typical executive summary of the plan might include:

- Introduction to the Plan and the Planning Process
- Mission Statement

- Vision Statements
- History of the Organization
- Values, Beliefs, and Guiding Principles
- Core Future Strategies and a one- or two-paragraph description of why the strategy is important

You might want to write a one- to three-page summary of the executive summary and include it in your monthly newsletter if you have one. Copies of the strategic plan should be made available to all staff and board, and the key components should be presented at staff or management meetings.

Thank Participants

Along with the executive copy of the strategic plan, any stakeholder whose input was sought from surveys, interviews, or focus groups should be sent a thank you. Have a party to thank the strategic planning committee; in short, celebrate the accomplishment and choose an appropriate way to convey the message that this plan represents an important consensus about where you are going together for the future of the organization.

Prepare to Execute the Plan

The journey, however, is not yet complete. We need some way to make sure that the plan is implemented. The organization needs to develop an annual operating plan—the first step toward the actual implementation of the plan.

COMMON OBSTACLES ENCOUNTERED IN PHASE 5

No One Wants to Write the Plan

It is not uncommon that no one has the time or interest in writing the strategic plan. A useful strategic plan doesn't have to be long, it doesn't have to be polished, it doesn't have to be pretty, but it does need to be written. If you are working with a consultant, ask the consultant to craft the first draft of a plan, and then have someone—usually the executive director or development director—take responsibility for the second draft. Because a consultant can rarely write about your organization with the degree of passion and understanding that staff members are able to

do, it is important that the next version reflect more of the organization's voice. If you are not working with a consultant, remember that it is much better to complete a brief strategic plan with a summary of long-term and short-term priorities than to let someone with writer's block— who is intent on producing a beautiful and complete document— prevent you and your organization from finishing the job.

Some Issues Are Still Unresolved

There will always be more discussions that need to happen. If the organization can't move forward without resolution, go back to the planning table. An alternative is to identify the resolution of an issue as a goal. In other words, move the issue into the action plan. For example: "Continue discussions, and develop and implement a plan within the next year that addresses the issue of whether we should expand our programs to serve students beyond ninth grade."

People Are Still Working on the Mission Statement

They don't want the strategic plan to be adopted until the final wording has been agreed on. It is not uncommon for an organization to spend two or more months writing the definitive mission statement. In the World Forestry Center's annual report, the chairs of the board wrote: "We educate and inform people about the world's forests and trees, and their importance to all life, in order to promote a balanced and sustainable future." This simple phase, crafted in plain-spoken language, took a team of 10 people more than two months to formulate. Each word was painstakingly deconstructed, analyzed, and considered before being approved, but it was worth the effort. Together, these 26 little words form that organization's mission statement, giving them purpose and guiding everything they do.

If you find yourself facing this challenge, write the strategic plan with one of the drafts of the mission statement. Because strategic plans are not cast in stone, they can be modified and changed, including the change to the mission statement.

CAUTIONS TO FACILITATORS

There is only one caution to facilitators for this phase: Make sure you produce a document! All kinds of situations mysteriously arise when it comes time to write the final plan. Committees fail to convene, writers don't return messages, files get lost, and so on. Without the actual and symbolic closure of completing and then adopting the plan, the strategic planning process cannot end. Although value may be gained through the conversations about strategic planning, the sense of completion and energy that can be released through finishing the process will be lost without taking this last step.

ENDNOTES

1. Jeanne Peters and Liz Schaffer, *Financial Strategies for Nonprofit Leaders* (St. Paul, MN: Amherst H. Wilder Foundation, 2005), p. 17.

2. Malvern J. Gross Jr., Richard F. Larkin, Roger S. Bruttomesso, and John J. McNally, *Financial and Accounting Guide to Not-for-Profit Organizations,* 6th ed. (New York: John Wiley & Sons, Inc., 2000), p. 442.

3. For a more detailed explanation of these costs and assistance in developing detailed annual budgets, see the reference cited in note 1.

4. It is beyond the scope of this strategic planning book to discuss in great depth all that goes into the creation of fund development plans. Numerous books focus on the art and science of fund development plans and raising money.

5. A definition of fundraising diversity from Kim Klein (colleague of the authors) states: "Your organization has the money it needs coming from as many sources as it can manage, raised by as many people as you can coordinate.

CASE STUDY—ASO/USA

☐ Transfer data from Worksheet 14: name of program and desired scope and scale in the next three to five years

☐ For each program, estimate FTEs and salaries and benefits costs, and any other significant direct costs to operate at the desired scope and scale (e.g., materials and supplies, rent for program-specific space, travel, equipment used exclusively by program, etc.).

☐ Identify nondirect expenses—in-common costs that benefit more than one program and overhead costs.

☐ Total all expenses to come up with a rough estimate of the cost of supporting the strategic plan.

Part 1: Estimate Future Costs

	Program A *Support services*	Program B *Public Education*	Program C *Public Policy and Communications*	In-Common Costs (shared indirect and administrative costs)	Total
Desired future scope and scale in the next three years	*See Worksheet 14 for a list of future scope and scale*				
Estimated FTEs	17	10	3	5	35
Estimated salaries and benefits costs	$650,000	$475,000	$140,000	$195,000	$1,460,000

(continues)

Part 1: Estimate Future Costs

	Program A *Support Services*	Program B *Public Education*	Program C *Public Policy and Communications*	In-Common Costs (shared indirect and administrative costs)	Total
Other significant costs: • Materials and supplies • Rent • Travel • Equipment	Other direct costs = $325,000: • Rent for satellite offices • Travel • Client incentives • Transportation vouchers	Other direct costs = $65,000: • Printed materials • Travel • Condoms	Other direct costs = $40,000: • Travel • Meetings • Designer for developing media kits	Indirect and administrative costs = $165,000	$ 595,000
Total Estimated Costs	$975,000	$540,000	$180,000	Salaries and indirect costs = $360,000	$2,055,000*

*Estimate costs by year 3 of the plan as opposed to current budget of $1,600,000.

Part 2: Estimate Future Revenues

	Program A	Program B	Program C	Unrestricted Revenues	Total Revenues
Government contracts	$ 775,000	$240,000	0	0	$ 1,015,000
Earned fees/revenues		$ 40,000			$ 40,000
Unrestricted foundation grants				$ 155,000	$ 155,000
Restricted foundation grants	$ 200,000	$175,000	$125,000		$ 500,000
Corporate contributions		$ 75,000		$ 90,000	$ 165,000
Individual contributions				$ 90,000	$ 90,000
Special events				$ 90,000	$ 90,000
Bequests/Planned gifts: life income funds					0

Total Estimated Revenues	$ 975,000	$530,000	$125,000	$425,000	$2,055,000
Total Estimated Costs (from Part 1)	$ 975,000	$540,000	$180,000	$360,000	$2,055,000
Total Net	0	($10,000)	($55,000)	$ 65,000	0

CASE STUDY—ASO/USA

ASO/USA STRATEGIC PLAN

Introduction by the President of the Board

On behalf of the board, staff, and volunteers of AIDS Service Organization, U.S.A., it is my honor to introduce the strategic planning document that is enclosed in the following pages.

This plan is the culmination of nine months of intensive work by staff, Board members, and volunteers. During that period, we have conducted focus groups, one-on-one interviews, held management and staff meetings and retreats, made numerous presentations to our board of directors, and poured over research and evaluation data. Our board/staff strategic planning committee, charged by our board of directors to conduct this plan, has devoted a great deal of time and effort to this process. Our discussions have been at times serious, comical, frustrating, contentious, and engaging, but have always centered upon one critical focus: how best to reduce the impact of HIV and AIDS in our community.

We have looked closely at our strengths as well as our vulnerabilities and have learned from our experiences. As a result, over the next three years, we have decided to focus our programmatic efforts on three areas of organizational competence: providing comprehensive support services (including case management) for people living with HIV/AIDS, conducting HIV Prevention and Education programs and public policy and advocacy work. In particular, we are increasing our efforts to reach disenfranchised high-risk populations— those who are the most vulnerable to acquiring HIV/AIDS. We also recognize that, to be effective in these three areas, we must not only continue our collaborative efforts with other community based organizations but increase such collaborations

The plan also recognizes that if we are to continue to provide quality services to the community, we must ensure that we have a strong enough infrastructure to sustain our current and future programs as well as invest in our most valuable resource—our staff.

This plan is firmly rooted in our values and in our commitment to stay at the forefront of the fight against AIDS.

Thank you for your interest in ASO/USA.

Sincerely,

Sam Green, President of the Board, ASO/USA

Mission Statement

AIDS Service Organization/USA (ASO/USA) is a community based nonprofit organization dedicated to improving the quality of life for people living with

HIV/AIDS and preventing the spread of HIV in our community. We strive to achieve our mission by providing support services to people living with HIV/AIDS, education and information on preventing HIV, and advocating for responsible public policies. We envision a world in which HIV/AIDS has been eradicated and people living with HIV/AIDS are able to lead quality productive lives.

Vision Statement

Our vision is that all people with HIV get the appropriate care they need in a comfortable, accessible setting and that we see the day soon when HIV and AIDS no longer devastate our community.

Organizational History and Profile

AIDS Service Organization/United States of America (ASO/USA) is an organization in a midsize Eastern city founded in 1988 to meet the needs of the growing number of people infected with and affected by HIV/AIDS. Ken Brown, the founding executive director, led the organization for 12 years and was succeeded by Joseph Chin in 2000. The organization started out operating a hotline and doing prevention work and won a federal grant to continue its work in the second year of operation. Since its inception, ASO/USA has gained a reputation as a reliable community agency serving low-income men and women of all racial/ethnic backgrounds.

In 1993, the agency received its first federal grant to provide care services in addition to prevention services. Under the direction of program manager Delores Molina, the Support Services Division was established. This division now provides case management services, support groups for people living with HIV/AIDS (PLWHA) and their caregivers transportation vouchers, benefits counseling, and employment referral. The agency also continues its prevention work through community outreach, a program under the Public Education Division. ASO/USA also continues to operate the hotline (currently housed in the Support Services Division), which provides information on prevention and transmission, as well as information on treatment and care. ASO/USA also has a Public Policy and Communications Division, which does a limited amount of policy work and media advocacy, supported by local foundations.

The organization's budget in 2003 was $1.6 million, with 25 FTE staff (20 FTE program staff and 5 FTE administrative staff) and a core team of 80 volunteers. In 2003 our revenue was generated from four principal sources: $900,000 came from federal sources, $400,000 came from the city health department and general fund, $200,000 came from foundations, and another $85,000 was raised from special events, individual donors, and other fund-raising.

Core Strategies

The following five overarching strategies will inform ASO/USA's goals for the next three years.

1. *Focus our resources so we are able to serve the highest risk, most vulnerable and disproportionately affected people in our community.* People from marginalized communities—low-income people, people of color, injection drug users, and other disenfranchised people—have the lowest access to prevention and treatment services. While continuing our commitment to serve all those at need, we must allocate maximum resources to these communities if we are to really assist in reducing the spread of HIV/AIDS and helping those with the least access to health services get the assistance they need.

2. *Maximize our collaborative efforts with other agencies and take more of a leadership role in convening meetings focused on public policy and advocacy efforts.* In order to ensure that government resources continue to be allocated for people with living with HIV/AIDS and they are protected from discrimination, ASO/USA needs to strengthen its leadership role in the public policy arena. Recognizing that this leadership cannot be done in isolation, we will work in collaboration with a broad spectrum of private, nonprofit, and public sector agencies.

3. *Do not expand our services beyond HIV/AIDS.* In recent years we have been approached by other causes with requests that we expand our services to include other life-threatening illnesses. While certainly there are unmet needs that we could meet, the HIV/AIDS epidemic and its impact on individuals and families has not decreased, and given our current resources, it is not feasible for us to expand beyond HIV/AIDS without seriously undermining the services we are currently offering. We would like to revisit this question in three years, but for now, ASO/USA can best be of service to the community by not expanding our services beyond AIDS.

4. *Invest in our capacity to support programs, especially in terms of staffing and infrastructure.* Staff continues to be our greatest resource. In countless interviews, clients as well as community partners affirmed the dedication and knowledge of our staff. The strategic plan reflects an investment in our most valuable resource through our commitment to improving staff salaries and benefits and ensuring sufficient staffing levels. In addition, our capacity to grow programs and maintain quality services is limited by the extent to which we have invested in our infrastructure.

While we have made progress in recent years in terms of our facilities, administration, technology, and formalizing policies and procedures, there is still a need to invest in our infrastructure to support current and future programs.

5. *Broaden and diversify our funding base so we are able to adequately support our clients.* In 2003, 82 percent of our funding came from government sources. While this is typical for many human service agencies, it leaves us very vulnerable to government budget cuts and limits our ability to provide services not specifically covered by those grants. In addition, most government contracts do not sufficiently pay for their full share of indirect costs. Over the next three years we hope to increase the support from other sources, in particular individuals. Our board has made this a high priority and is committed to being a role model for individual supporters.

Program Goals and Objectives: Support Services*

Goal: To improve the quality of life and health for people living with HIV/AIDS and their caregivers through the delivery of a comprehensive set of support services

Case Management

Subgoal

Improve access to health care and social services for disenfranchised people living with HIV/AIDS.

Objectives

- Expand our case management services to serve 500 clients within the next three years, from current base of 300 clients.
- Increase number of referrals we receive from other providers in the city who serve marginalized populations.
- Develop and implement new quality control procedures to ensure that our case management services remain of highest quality.
- Survey all clients regarding access to primary health care. After baseline is established, set objective for level of increase in access to be sought over the next three years.
- Provide ongoing training for case managers on new treatments.
- Evaluate the possibility of forming a collaboration with Immigrant Services to better meet the needs of immigrant populations.

Other Support Services (Benefits Counseling, Transportation Vouchers, Employment Referral)

Subgoal

Ensure that our clients get the support they need to access to health care and home support services.

Objectives

- Provide ongoing training to benefits counselors on latest resources and eligibility criteria.
- Provide transportation vouchers to individuals who would otherwise not be able to make their medical appointments.
- Eliminate our employment referral program by end of fiscal year, and develop a referral relationship with Resource Center for Positives to provide this service to our clients.

Support Groups

Subgoal

Improve the mental well-being of individuals or their caregivers impacted by HIV disease while decrease their feeling of isolation.

Objectives

- Conduct ongoing client satisfaction activities to monitor support group attendance, identify reasons for decreasing attendance, and identify incentives to improve attendance.
- Continue to offer 12 support groups for people with HIV/AIDS and their caregivers and adjust number and/or composition of groups based on findings from ongoing client satisfaction activities.

AIDS Hotline

Subgoal

Improve community-wide knowledge about HIV prevention and transmission in a safe, anonymous environment.

Objectives

- Change the purview of the hotline to focus only on HIV prevention and transmission information.
- Develop a relationship with a national HIV/AIDS hotline that can provide treatment and care information and create a process for transferring such calls to this hotline.

- Move the hotline out of the support services division and into the public education division, since it will be focused solely on prevention information.

- Provide hotline services in Chinese, in addition to having full coverage from volunteer and paid staff who speak Spanish.

- On an ongoing basis, update the database of resources so as to ensure accurate information and referral.

Financial, Administrative, and Governance Goals and Objectives

Staffing and Benefits

Goal: Attract and retain qualified paid and volunteer staff for all services and activities.

Staffing

- Sufficiently meet needs of clients and prevent burnout, increase number of paid staff from 25 full-time employees to 34 full-time employees to support our ability to provide needed services, and increase the number of volunteer hours per year from 5,750 to 9,000.

- Assess whether more complex and differing needs of clients require certain jobs that were done by volunteers to be done by paid staff.

Salaries and Benefits

- By end of year one of the plan, assess overall salary structure and benefits package; by end of year two, develop and implement a plan to increase staff salaries and offer a competitive benefit package.

- Analyze fringe benefits package on an ongoing basis and identify ways of meeting employee needs (e.g., pension plan, cafeteria approach to benefits, etc.)

- Review personnel policies annually to make sure they are in legal compliance.

Training, Evaluation, and Other Support

- By end of year one of the plan, establish and maintain a more formalized ongoing training program for all staff and volunteers.

- By end of year one of the plan, implement and maintain a new staff-evaluation system that establishes overall objectives for positions and specific objectives for all employees.

- Expand our volunteer and paid-staff appreciation program.

- Develop and coordinate an agency-wide management-training program to help staff build skills needs to perform their duties and interface with other departments, including a cross-training program.

- Update the personnel handbook annually.

Volunteers

- Maintain number of volunteers at 80.

- Assess current volunteer recruitment, orientation, training program, and make modifications as necessary.

Resource Development

Goal: Acquire stable, broad-based, financial and nonfinancial resources to support the programs and growth envisioned in this strategic plan.

Diversification of Funding

- Within the next three years, at least 40 percent of ASO/USA's annual operating budget will be raised through private sector philanthropy. The development of this subsidy is critical for the maintenance and growth of our programs.

- Explore donations in kind (e.g., printing, equipment, etc.) to help support our services. Within the next three years, to have similar donations to support all educational brochures and our annual report.

- Increase the money the organization receives from private individuals to a minimum of 10 percent each year.

- Raise a minimum of $50,000 annually from special events/fundraisers.

Infrastructure Support for Resource Development Function

- Establish a formal development department within the management structure of the organization, staffed by a full-time professional development officer to supervise overall fundraising functions and work closely with board and management staff to develop and implement a successful development program.

- Bring on a new grants writer as soon as budget allows or as funding can be raised.

- Establish and maintain a computerized donor history file and increase the personal contacts made with donors.

Board of Directors Role in Fundraising

- Maintain a board-giving policy that requires all board members to contribute financially to the organization.
- Increase the board's participation in all aspects of fundraising.

Board of Directors

Goal: Develop and maintain an effective, active, and informed Board of Directors whose governance and support roles help the achievement of ASO/USA's mission.

Board Membership

- Diversify the board so it more accurately reflects who we serve.
- In year two of this plan, develop and maintain an advisory board to help supplement the board's expertise and contribution.

Board Effectiveness

- Increase the capability of the board to assist with the following functions: marketing, fundraising, legal matters, public relations, and evaluation.
- Develop and maintain an effective board orientation and ongoing training program.
- Increase effectiveness of the board by redefining committees and each committee's mandate, assessing ongoing mandates yearly, holding an annual board retreat to set overall objectives for the board and each committee, and requiring each committee to submit detailed work plans to support accomplishing agreed-upon goals and objectives.
- Continue yearly evaluation of all aspects of the board.
- Implement 100 percent contribution from all board members.
- Increase the board's participation in all aspects of fundraising.

Planning, Evaluation and Quality Control

Goal: Guarantee that we meet the needs of our constituencies and that all programs provide the highest-quality service.

Long-term objectives:

- Establish an ongoing evaluation process for all programs to assess program results, quality of services, and our ability to address the (changing) needs of level of service to our clients and the community.
- Hold an annual board/staff retreat to plan for future needs and assess current capabilities.
- Review the strategic plan quarterly and make changes as needed.
- Ensure that detailed annual operating plans are developed for all programs and internal management functions.
- Establish and maintain protocols for data collection, data entry, and outcome evaluation.

Public Relations and Communications

Goal: Increase the visibility and community awareness of ASO/USA, and to make sure that ASO/USA is properly recognized for its achievements and closely identified as a premier provider to people living with and affected by HIV/AIDS

Long-term objectives:

- Build public awareness of ASO/USA in the community through increased media coverage and public service announcements.
- Produce and distribute a newsletter on a regular basis.
- Update our brochures regularly and make sure they are available in English, Spanish, and Cantonese.

Infrastructure and Technology

Goal: Increase the operational and management efficiency and effectiveness of ASO/USA.

Long-term objectives:

- Ensure timely, accurate, useful information is available and consistently applied in sound decision making throughout the agency.
- Produce timely, accurate financial reports for the organization as a whole, and for all departments.
- Improve and maintain a fully computerized accounting system.
- Provide executive management and the Board with required financial reports, budget comparisons, and cash flow projections.
- Annually assess organization's internal controls to ensure adequate safeguard of all resources.
- Develop a system for tracking all necessary management information and train all staff to use the MIS systems and proper documentation of services.
- Continually assess technology needs and update computers and other technology, as needed, to have available the technology and equipment necessary to provide quality, efficient, and effective service
- Provide adequate and accessible space in a pleasant, comfortable environment for all ASO/USA clients and paid and volunteer staff.
- Develop and implement a facilities master plan to locate programs and services in facilities that provide comfort and ease of access to clients and staff.
- Explore option of getting a building donated or at least explore options of moving the central office to a safer location.
- Maintain facilities that are attractive to clients.

Networking and Collaboration

Goal: Maintain and develop collaborations and relationships with agencies and funders that benefit our clients, our services, and/or our agency.

Long-term objectives:

- Allocate time to executive director and development director (when hired) to identify potential collaborators and negotiate subcontracts and MOUs, as appropriate
- Assess the collaboration with City Clinic and develop a plan for continuing the collaboration with (1) more clearly defined roles, responsibilities, and accountability measures, and (2) a shift in program focus to serve higher-risk clients.

CHAPTER 7

Phase 6: Implement the Strategic Plan

A vision without a plan is a hallucination.

Congratulations! You have completed your strategic plan. Your long-term direction is clear; program and administrative priorities have been set. Ideally, at this point, two important things have been accomplished. First, through the many ways that various stakeholders have been engaged in the process, the major decisions have a high level of commitment within the stakeholder communities. Second, through the work of the committee, various authors and reviewers, the written document presents the direction and priorities in organized and compelling language.

Still, while the process of planning has hopefully energized and focused organization members, the full value of the planning effort will only be realized through its implementation. There are two major barriers to effective implementation: (1) the difficulty of translating big ideas into specific operational steps, and (2) the difficulty of maintaining the focus that was achieved through the planning process. Phase 6 addresses the first difficulty through the development of annual operating plans. Phase 7 addresses the second difficulty through evaluating the plan and setting up regular monitoring of the plan.

STEP 6.1: PLAN TO MANAGE CHANGE

The starting place for the implementation of the strategic plan should be on identifying the changes—the skills needs, systems and structures, and organization culture changes—that bridge the gap between the old way of doing things and the new ways things need to be done.

There are three levels of changes that need to be looked at:

1. What new skills will board and staff members need to successfully implement the strategic plan?

   Example: One organization's core strategy focused on becoming less dependent on government funding. Both the board and staff members needed to increase their skills in such areas as individual solicitation and grant writing.

2. How might the current structures and systems (such as accounting decision making, and communication systems and structures) need to change in order to support the new vision?

   Example: One agency set as a major priority greater delegation of authority to departmental and program managers. However, the accounting system that was in place was not designed to produce user-friendly reports that monitored budgeted-to-actual expenses for programs; the outdated system monitored expenses and revenue by funding source. The financial staff needed to make the accounting system meet the needs of the agency, not simply the funder.

3. How might the organization's culture (mindset) need to change to support new core strategies. Organization culture is "the behaviors that mirror the practiced values and beliefs of the organization and its members."

   Example: One of the core future strategies for a multisite social-service agency focused on ensuring that the strategic direction set for the organization was supported by the appropriate organizational infrastructure. Infrastructure changes included optimizing operational processes and patient service delivery methodologies to provide integrated and seamless delivery of service. It also included improving facilities and information technology systems to meet the expected increase in demand for the organization's services. In order to successfully implement this strategy, management needed to work with staff to change from a site-centered mindset to a client-centered mindset.

Sometimes, by identifying the changes required to support the strategic plan, board and staff resistance (fears of loss of control, lack of confidence, or vulnerability) can be identified. By taking the time to manage the changes needed, fears can be alleviated and the framework is in place for the successful implementation of the plan (see process notes in Exhibit 7.1).

EXHIBIT 7.1	WORKSHEET 18: MANAGE THE TRANSITION—THE CHANGES REQUIRED FOR SUCCESS

Process Notes

How to do this activity	• Identify the changes that are inherent in the strategic plan: changes in focus, changes in ways of doing things, etc.
	• For each of the changes, list any new skills that may be needed, any structures that need to be modified or introduced, and changes in culture—behaviors and beliefs of staff and board—that are needed to support the changes articulated in the strategic plan.

(continues)

EXHIBIT 7.1   WORKSHEET 18: MANAGE THE TRANSITION—THE CHANGES REQUIRED FOR SUCCESS *(Continued)*

Process Notes

Why do this activity	• Supporting actions to implementation of the strategic plan can be identified through this activity, and thereby overcome obstacles and/or resistance.
Who to involve in the process	• Both the staff and board should separately do this activity, because both will be responsible for, and affected by, the decisions reflected in the strategic plan.

See ASO/USA's example of this worksheet at the end of this chapter. Blank worksheets are provided in Appendix A and on the CD that accompanies this book.

Step 6.2: Develop a Detailed Annual Operation Plan

The next step in implementing the strategic plan is to develop a first-year operating plan based on the strategic plan. This is an important step to ensure that the strategic plan is implemented in a coordinated and effective manner, it must be translated into specifics: The strategic plan must be converted into an annual operating plan, with a supporting annual budget.

The annual operating plan provides a detailed plan for the upcoming year, in the language of objectives, action steps, timelines, and responsibilities. The budget provides a detailed plan in the language of dollars, organized by types of revenue and types of expenses. The operating plan describes what services will be provided, what types of action will be conducted to provide these services, and who is responsible for taking the actions. The budget describes how much it will cost to carry out the plan.

What Level of Detail Is Necessary in an Operating Plan?

Imagine you are driving a car going on vacation. It is important to have a destination in mind, your long-range goal. The destination alone, however, is not enough to get you there successfully. You need to have detailed information about which roads are most likely to get you there, estimates about the distance to be covered and the time it will take, estimates of how much money will be needed for meals and gas for the car, and warning systems to tell you if the engine gets overheated or other systems fail.

Now imagine that you are not driving the car alone. Instead, you have 20 people doing different jobs simultaneously: Your organization's executive director is at the steering wheel with a couple of board members looking over her shoulder, staff members are stationed at each tire making them spin, other people are pooling their money for gas, and someone else is in the back making sandwiches. It is going to take an impressive plan to move this crew in the same direction efficiently!

This is the stuff of annual operating plans and annual budgets: Which programs and management/operations functions are going to be implemented for the upcoming year, by whom, by when, and how much "gas" (money and person power) will they require? This level of detail is unnecessary in a strategic plan. In fact, it would clutter up the presentation of the long-range vision. The strategic plan focuses on the destination you are going to, not which gas station to stop at along the way (see Exhibit 7.2 for a summary of the characteristics of a useful annual operating plan). The annual operating plan needs to provide enough guidance for the travelers to move ahead at full speed, so there is no need to constantly discuss where to go next or why the driver took the last turn.

What If You Don't Have All of the Information You Think You Need?

Organizations typically have more developed routines around the annual budgeting process than they do around annual program planning. It is a rare board that approves a budget with vague information about planned

---

EXHIBIT 7.2 CHARACTERISTICS OF A USEFUL ANNUAL OPERATING PLAN

There are three important characteristics of a useful annual operating plan:

1. An appropriate level of detail—enough to guide the work, but not so much detail that it becomes overwhelming, confusing, or unnecessarily constrains flexibility

2. A format that allows for periodic reports on progress toward the specific goals and objectives

3. A structure that allows a user to easily see that it is consistent with the priorities in the strategic plan

expenses and little detail about projected revenue. (For this reason, and because there are many useful resources already available, this workbook does not go into detail about the mechanics of the annual budgeting process.)

However, the process of developing detailed operating plans is much less precise than budgeting. Perhaps for this reason, some organizations have fairly informal planning processes that are not tied into their strategic plan. Program planning is often not as coordinated on an agency-wide basis as the budgeting process nearly always is. The potential for staff to waste effort, or worse, to work at cross-purposes, is much greater when program planning is not coordinated and detailed enough to ensure that objectives get met in a timely manner.

The purpose of the operating plan is to provide enough detail to keep everyone moving in the same direction with a common understanding of when and how far and how fast to move. This does not mean every detail. To go back to the vacation metaphor, the operating plan probably does not need to include instructions on how to make sandwiches, but it does need to mention that someone is in charge of feeding the travelers. What if you do not know who is in charge of feeding the travelers, or what the travelers' dietary needs are, or what route to take that will get you to your destination on time? The operating plan mentions the fact that these jobs have to be done or the information gathered, and assigns responsibility for figuring them out.

For example, organizations doing strategic planning for the first time may never have conducted in-depth program evaluation. If there isn't time to do this work before the strategic plan is to be completed (and often there isn't), doing program evaluation work can become an objective of the operating plan. "We think our programs are doing a good job, but we do not know as much as we'd like, so our objective this year is to conduct a thorough program evaluation. When we get new information, we will adjust our strategic plans accordingly."

The appropriate level of detail depends on how much authority or latitude staff members have to use their judgment in pursuing objectives. Jack Welch, CEO at General Electric for many years, said he didn't even want to know about any decisions that cost less than $25 million to implement. Below this expenditure level, his staff had the authority to use their own judgment in pursuing corporate objectives. Few nonprofit staffs will have quite this much authority! Typically, more detail is useful when a program is new, staff members are inexperienced, or actions in one program area have extensive implications for the operation of other programs. In general, the more concise the operating plan, the easier it is to implement and to monitor. So, provide only as much detail as is appropriate.

The format of an annual operating plan is important. A confusing format implies confused thought and inevitably leads to confused implementation. There are two questions to ask yourself about your annual operating plan format:

1. Can everyone who needs to use the plan make sense of what it says?
2. Are the objectives and action steps written and organized in a way that makes it easy to monitor?

Developing a User-Friendly Annual (Work) Plan

Because the operating plan should be the beginning of the implementation of the strategic plan, the structure of the operating plan must be congruent with the priorities outlined in the strategic plan. As the year unfolds, choices will arise about whether and how to modify the original objectives. All of the work that goes into the strategic planning process will be more useful to decision makers if choices in the middle of the year can be easily placed in the context of the long-term priorities of the organization.

Just as monthly financial statements often present a budget for revenue and expenses and compare the budget with actual figures for a given time period, so should operating plans allow for the same type of comparison: The plan declares the work in terms of goals and objectives for each program, area, and management/operations function and reports the actual progress on a monthly or perhaps quarterly basis. This operating plan budget-to-actual report, along with the financial budget-to-actual report, gives a clear reading of how the year is going.

Two sample-operating plans are included at the end of this chapter. The first is for a program goal at an economic development agency, and the second is for a development effort at a museum. Both examples meet all three characteristics of an effective operating plan: They state the strategic goal to be addressed, clearly break out the activities or action steps required to accomplish the goal, establish time frames and who is responsible, and note the progress thus far (obviously, the information in this last column would change with each report).

These are the requisites for the operating plan. Many organizations already have some tracking system in place that might be adapted for the purposes of the operating plan, or perhaps will want to customize the suggested format to best suit their purposes. The point is to develop a format that keeps the organization on the right track. Blank templates for a strategic plan and annual operating plan are included in Appendix I.

What If We Already Have Program Operating Plans Written for Specific Grants?

No problem. In an organization with more than one program, it makes sense to have two levels of operating plans. The level of detail required in a program plan by many funders is often specific. It may not be practical or useful to compile several of these plans into one large operating plan. In the first place, they are usually too long to be useful to individuals who are not directly involved with the particular program. In the second place, the funding cycles are often different from the organization's fiscal year.

For both of these reasons, the answer is to create a less detailed organization-wide annual operating plan, which serves as the one-year implementation version of the strategic plan and as the umbrella plan for more detailed program plans. The organization-wide plan is useful to the board and to all staff members who are interested in gaining a better understanding of the work of a program in the context of the work of the entire organization. This concept is illustrated in Exhibit 7.3.

EXHIBIT 7.3   PROGRAM WITHIN CONTEXT
OF ORGANIZATION'S WORK

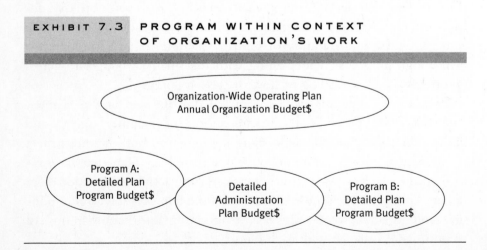

Organization-Wide Operating Plan
Annual Organization Budget$

Program A:
Detailed Plan
Program Budget$

Detailed
Administration
Plan Budget$

Program B:
Detailed Plan
Program Budget$

Sample (Annual) Operating Plan: Program Goal for an Economic Development Agency

Overall agency goal. Increase economic development capacity to foster job creation and business investment in our city.

Enterprise zone unit goal. Enhance the application of the tax incentive programs by:

- Completing the designation process for approval of new zones
- Offering suggestions for the improvement of the programs of those previously approved.

Task	Measure	Staff	Date	9/03
1. Select and train scoring team for final enterprise zone application	Select two sets of five scoreres	AB/PM	Dec 2002	Done
2. Print and distribute scoring materials and final applications	Distribute materials to scorers	AB/PM	Sept 02 – Dec 02	Done
3. Conduct technical review	Complete six technical reviews	AB/PM	Sept 02 – Jan 03	Done
4. Conduct substantive review	Complete six substantive reviews	PGN and scorers	Oct 02 – Feb 03	Done
5. Tabulate results of scoring team	Compile two sets of results	PGN	Oct 02 – Feb 03	In process
6. Announce winners of competition	Two press releases and two e-mails	JW and PM	Feb 02	In process

Fund Development Goal for Museum (from Annual Operating Plan)

Annual goal (the same as the strategic plan goal). Acquire a stable, broad base of financial and nonfinancial resources to support our museums' programs.

Long-term objective (the same as the strategic plan objective). Double the amount of foundation or corporate support that we receive.

Annual operating plan objectives (what needs to be accomplished this year to support the long-term objective):

- Secure $25,000 for the new children's art program by the end of the calendar year.
- Maintain foundation and corporate contribution levels at least at the current level.
- Raise at least a total of $150,000 in unrestricted revenue from new foundation and corporate sources.

Feedback mechanisms (check-in mechanisms to ensure that the work is being accomplished). Director of development will provide a monthly status report of all proposals pending, accepted, or declined.

Resources required. One-half FTE Development Associate; $5,000 to produce annual report

Detailed action plan (what activities need to happen, who is responsible for making sure they happen, and by when; status report updated quarterly):

Action Steps for Securing $25,000 for New Children's Art Program	Responsible Personnel	Time Frame or by When	Status as of 3/31/03
1. Develop proposal to describe program	Selena Garcia, Program Director	January 1–February 1	Done: It looks beautiful!
2. Research possible funders and develop list of at least ten prospective funders	Susan Seeker and Pam Proposal* (*designated prime mover)	February 1	Completed 1/25/03
3. Arrange interviews with each prospect	Pam Proposal	February 15	3/1/03
4. Submit at least three proposals	Pam Proposal	April 15	Three proposals submitted as of 3/31
5. Follow up on proposals	Pam Proposal	Two weeks after submission	
6. Cash the checks!	Pam Proposal	As soon as the money arrives!	

CAUTIONS TO FACILITATORS

Ideally, an organization will have ongoing discussions about the implementation of the strategic plan. The strategic plan and the organization's annual planning cycle should be intricately connected.

- *Unit plans aren't detailed enough.* Phase 6 is all about implementation. The level of detail in the unit-level plans needs to be sufficient to provide meaningful guidance.

- *Not learning from the past.* Failure to create an opportunity of monitoring the implementation of the plan prevents explicit and shared learning from taking place. If the facilitator of the process is an outside consultant, then it is important to set up mechanisms for the leadership to ensure that monitoring takes place.

- *Managing change.* The impact on staff and others of implementing new strategies may be dramatic. The bigger the changes, the more attention should be given to the process of leading and managing the change process.

- *Not making adjustments when needed.* Even if a group does monitor the plan, if people don't seriously consider making adjustments, then the monitoring becomes an empty exercise instead of an important part of the ongoing strategic discussion.

CASE STUDY—ASO/USA

WORKSHEET 18 Manage the Transition: The Changes Required for Success

☐ List the major changes that may need to happen as a result of the decisions reached in the strategic planning process.

☐ Identify skills needed, system structures, and organization culture changes that need to happen to ensure these changes are successful:

- Changes that will impact staff and the skills they may need in the future
- Changes that will impact the structures and systems that may need to be modified to support the changes
- Changes that will impact how the organization's culture (mindset) may need to be modified to support the changes

List the major changes that may need to happen/will happen as a result of the strategic plan:

- *We need to increase our emphasis on accountability and formalizing financial and data-tracking systems, which will require staff to allocate increased time to documentation.*
- *We need to improve capacity to identify and reach high-risk disenfranchised populations.*
- *We need to aggressively go after new and diverse funding.*

New skills that may be needed	Modified or new structures and systems that may be needed	New culture/mindset that may be needed
Staff who are fluent in Chinese and Spanish	*New accounting systems*	*Less of a versus mentality between board and the staff*
Data gathering and interpretation skills to identify and ensure we are reaching high-risk groups	*Better ability to track clients and have a seamless intake system no matter where our clients enter the system*	*Change from "We can get by with whatever we do" to "We provide client-centered, high-quality services"*
Board needs increased skills in fundraising		*Staff deserve living wages and good benefits (as opposed to mindset that low wages are normal and acceptable for people working in the nonprofit sector)*

CHAPTER 8

Phase 7: Evaluate and Monitor the Strategic Plan

Aren't we finished yet? Well, yes and no. A strategic plan is written and annual operating plans are in place. The last step is to reflect on the planning process and put in place monitoring processes.

STEP 7.1: EVALUATE THE STRATEGIC PLAN AND THE STRATEGIC PLANNING PROCESS

The planning committee should plan a meeting to celebrate its accomplishments and evaluate its work. This meeting is an opportunity to reflect on the process to set the stage for future successful plans. Therefore, at this celebration, the committee should evaluate both the planning process and the planning documents that have been developed. The committee might simply ask the questions: What worked about the planning process? What did we learn that could help improve future planning endeavors?

In a slightly more formal evaluation process, the planning committee might evaluate both the planning documents and the planning process. The strategic plan should be assessed in terms of whether it accomplishes the following:

- Provides guidance to both short-term and long-term priorities
- Helps the organization to allocate resources
- Is understandable by people who have not participated in the development of the plan
- Is responsive to the organization's best understanding of its internal and external environments

- Is the product of a consensus and commitment–building process
- Has been formally adopted by the board of directors
- The annual operational plan(s) meets these measures of success:
  - Developed by staff who are responsible for the implementation of the goals and objectives
  - Provides an easy implementation, monitoring, and reference tool
  - Operationalizes the strategic plan
  - Realistic

Process notes for Worksheet 19 are provided in Exhibit 8.1. See ASO/USA's Worksheet 19 (at the end of this chapter) for an illustration. This celebration and evaluating meeting should represent the formal end of the present cycle of the strategic planning process.

EXHIBIT 8.1	WORKSHEET 19: EVALUATE THE STRATEGIC PLANNING PROCESS

Process Notes

How to do this activity	Use the evaluation of plans and the strategic planning process worksheet to:
	• Evaluate the strategic plan
	• Evaluate the annual operational plan(s)
	• Make suggestions for how future planning endeavors may be improved
Why do this activity	You want to build on your successes and ensure successful future planning efforts.
Who to involve in the process	The planning committee. Feedback may be sought from other stakeholders regarding how they felt about the process and the products of the strategic planning process.

See ASO/USA's example of this worksheet at the end of this chapter. Blank worksheets are provided in Appendix A and on the CD that accompanies this book.

STEP 7.2: MONITOR THE STRATEGIC PLAN AND UPDATE AS NEEDED

Are we finally finished now? Not quite! Because strategic planning is designed to help the organization do a better job, the organization will need to put processes into practice to find out if it is doing a better job. Therefore, the organization will need to monitor and affirm/update/revise the plan at least once a year after it is implemented.

Strategic planning is a dynamic process; therefore, it is really never completed. However, a rhythm needs to be established, for by necessity the intensity of information gathering, analysis, and decision making has ebbs and flows. Each organization needs to decide the rhythm of its planning efforts. For every organization there should be time set aside to do strategic planning, develop annual operational plans and budgets, and then to implement these plans. Implementation is going on all the time. The development of annual operational plans happens once a year. A formal strategic planning process should happen every three to five years, but the strategic plan should be monitored at least yearly, to assess progress toward the achievement of the goals, and to modify if necessary to reflect the usually ever-changing environment. A typical three-year planning cycle might follow a pattern similar to the one in Exhibit 8.2.

EXHIBIT 8.2   THREE-YEAR PLANNING CYCLE

January 1	April	July 1	October 1	December 31
Year 0			❏ Develop three-year strategic plan	
			❏ Annual operating plan and budget	
Launch plan Year 1	*		❏ Monitor strategic plan, adjust if necessary**	
			❏ Develop annual operating plan and budget	
Continue plan Year 2			❏ Monitor strategic plan, adjust if necessary	

(continues)

EXHIBIT 8.2   THREE-YEAR PLANNING CYCLE (Continued)

January 1	April	July 1	October 1	December 31
Continue plan Year 2				❏ Develop annual operating plan and budget
Finish plan Year 3				❏ Develop NEW three-year strategic plan ❏ Annual operating plan and budget

 * Quarterly check-in on annual operational plan and budget
** Monitor Strategic Plan = assess progress toward achievement of goals in three-year strategic plan

Many organizations already gather information necessary to assess implementation. Once a planning cycle has been agreed on, the parties responsible for implementation need to know how to track and report on the objectives included in the plans and to make adjustments as necessary.

Establish Intermediate Checkpoints

At this point, the planning committee may want to establish intermediate checkpoints that will be used to measure progress toward the achievement of the strategic plan. For example, in its strategic plan, a museum may want to increase its membership from 500 fee-paying members to 1,000 members. The planning committee might set two targets or milestones to assess progress: The first checkpoint might be an increase in membership to 750; the second milestone might be 850. The final, or ideal, target would be to reach 1,000.

Monitoring the Strategic Plan

A good way to monitor the implementation of the strategic plan on an ongoing basis is to assign one individual to be a prime mover for each overall strategy and/or overall goal contained in the strategic plan. Each prime mover would then be responsible for monitoring progress the strategy or goal that he or she was assigned to monitor: for example, the board's goals should be the responsibility of the board president; infrastructure goals might be assigned to the executive director or an administrative director; the director of development would be the prime mover for any fundraising strategy or goals.

Then, on a regular basis, no less than once a year, the "prime movers" would develop and submit a report the strategic planning committee on progress toward the completion of the plan. The planning committee would then assess whether any major or minor adjustments should be made to the strategic plan.

LIFE AFTER THE STRATEGIC PLAN IS DONE

Rather than go out of business after the completion of its strategic plan, the planning committee of Community Action changed its title and mandate to reflect new responsibilities, that if being the Planning and Evaluation Committee. Made up of board and staff, the committee assigned responsibility for monitoring each of the organization's five core strategies to an individual who was willing to monitor progress and follow-through to make sure that annual operating plans for each strategy were developed and implemented. On a quarterly basis, the Planning and Evaluation Committee convened, along with prime movers for each core strategy. In addition, on an ad hoc basis, the Planning and Evaluation Committee met to review senior management's proposals for adding, modifying, or dropping programs.

As part of this monitoring process, the planning committee should organize and plan a yearly retreat that would focus on these questions:

- Is the current strategic plan on target? What has or has not been accomplished?

- Are the assumptions of the internal and external environment still valid?

- What are the current issues facing the organization, and, after discussing these issues, do any changing or new priorities need to be added to the strategic plan?

- Are there new performance targets and/or modified intermediate checkpoints that need to be looked at?

If the organization is relatively small, all staff and board members might be invited. If there are more than 40 or 50 board and staff members, then smaller meetings of all internal stakeholders should be held before the annual retreat. The board would then meet with senior managers and program directors to discuss these questions and agree on overall priorities. The planning committee may also choose to gather information in advance of the retreat from external stakeholders (e.g., client surveys, interviews, feedback) and present that information at the retreat.

As a result of the retreat, the executive director would work with senior managers and program directors to develop the next year's annual operating plan. A written record of the decisions made at the planning retreat should be summarized on Worksheet 20: Monitor and Update the Strategic Plan (see process notes in Exhibit 8.3).

EXHIBIT 8.3   WORKSHEET 20: MONITOR AND UPDATE THE STRATEGIC PLAN

Process Notes

How to do this activity	The worksheet should be filled out after a series of meetings that assess the current strategic plan and set new priorities for the upcoming year and beyond. The worksheet should:
	• Summarize overall accomplishments and the status of the implementation of the core strategies as articulated in the strategic plan
	• Summarize status of the implementation of long-term and short-term objectives/priorities
	• Briefly explain the reasons for not implementing the core strategies of nonaccomplishment of objectives/priorities
	• List the changes in the environment since the last meeting
	• Record any changes in core strategies and long-term and short-term priorities
Why do this activity	Plans are road maps from which you should consciously choose to deviate.

EXHIBIT 8.4   WORKSHEET 20: MONITOR AND UPDATE
THE STRATEGIC PLAN (*Continued*)

Process Notes

Who to involve in the process	Planning committee has responsibility to coordinate the monitoring efforts and plan the necessary retreat(s) that involve board, staff, and other key stakeholders in revisiting the strategic plan and either affirming or modifying the overall direction and priorities

See ASO/USA's example of this worksheet at the end of this chapter. Blank worksheets are provided in Appendix A and on the CD that accompanies this book.

CONCLUSION: A WORD TO LEADERS

If we had reliable crystal balls, strategic planning would be a snap. Because there is uncertainty about the future, however, strategic plans are more like roadmaps to a new land drawn up before the journey has been made. No one has been to where we want to go; it is in the future. We can ask many people their advice about how best to make the journey. We can do extensive analysis to forecast the conditions we will encounter and to assess our capabilities to handle various situations. We can dream about how we would like the journey to go. All of this work can be discussed and written down in the form of a strategic plan. Once the journey begins, a strategic plan will remind us where we want to go as well as where we don't want to go.

The Cheshire Cat says to Alice, "If you don't know where you are going, any road will take you there." The strategic planning process helps the leaders of an organization to articulate their vision about where they are going and to choose the best road to take the organization there.

Still, things change. In the external environment, the economy is better, or worse, than expected, and this has a ripple effect on your clients or your environment. Science finds a new way to deal with an issue you have long worked on. A new organization begins offering services that compete with one of your programs. A long-time funder changes its priorities. Any of the many assumptions you have made as part of the planning process turns out to be wrong. Internally, the executive director might

move or become ill, a case of embezzlement might surface, or staff members may either do much more or much less than they thought possible.

There is no way to foresee these changes. They must be responded to as they arise. Ultimately, the end sought is to be effective in pursuing your mission, not to correctly predict the future. The strategic planning process is a means to that end. As the future unfolds, because the organization knows where it wants to go, it will be much easier to see if the road is taking you there, and if not, to select a better road.

It is the responsibility of the leadership of every organization to ensure that a strategic plan is in place and that appropriate adjustments are made in the implementation of that plan as circumstances change. The strategic plan is a reference document, a map to assist with these responsibilities.

We hope this workbook will make it a little easier to put the process of strategic planning to good use in your organizations. Good luck. We are counting on you to succeed, because our world will be better for it.

CASE STUDY—ASO/USA

❑ Evaluate your strategic plan, your annual operating plans, and the strategic planning process

❑ Make any suggestions for improving future planning endeavors

Strategic plan	Yes	No
Provides guidance to both short-term and long-term priorities?	X	
Helps the organization to allocate resources?	X	
Is understandable by people who have not participated in the development of the plan?	X	
Responds to the organization's best understanding of its internal and external environments?		
Was developed from a consensus and commitment-building process?	X	
Has been formally adopted by the board of directors?	X	
Comments and suggestions for future strategic plans: *The goals and priorities may need further explanation—perhaps we should add a "commentary/background" section to each goal to explain why we have made the decisions regarding specific objectives.*		
Annual operating plan(s)	**Yes**	**No**
Has both process and outcome objectives specified?	X	
Has been developed by staff members who are responsible for the implementation of the goals and objectives?	X	
Provides an easy implementation, monitoring, and reference tool?	X	
Operationalizes the strategic plan—helps ensure that the strategic plan will be implemented?	X	
Has a realistic budget to support the operational plan?	X	
Comments and suggestions for future annual operational plans: *The budget may need to be refined as we get further into the fiscal year. We need to get better at articulating outcome objectives.*		

(continues)

Planning process met the following criteria	Yes	No
The process was consensus building: It offered a way to surface the needs and interests of all stakeholders and allowed sufficient time to reach agreement on what is best for the long-term and short-term interests of the client/customer?	X	
The process allowed sufficient time to assess programs, and the strengths, weaknesses, opportunities, and threats?	X	
The process supported the achievement of the outcomes that were initially identified in Worksheet 1?	X	
Comments and suggestions for future planning processes: *The plan took 9 months to complete due to unforeseen operational issues that surfaced and a longer amount of time to get internal and external stakeholder feedback. It would be nice to try to complete it in 6 months next planning cycle. We did not do as good a job as we could have in terms of using the findings from program evaluation to inform the strategic plan. Perhaps next time we should consider hiring an outsider evaluator to help us summarize our program evaluation findings in a way that can be useful for strategic planning.*		

CASE STUDY—ASO/USA

❏ Review your strategic plan, noting accomplishments and disappointments. Assess any changes in the environment since the last strategic planning meeting. If necessary, make changes in strategies and long-term and short-term priorities.

(*Note:* As an alternative to reviewing the plan as a whole, this worksheet can also be used to assess each of your plan's strategies or goals. Each strategy or goal would have its own page, and you would answer the same questions for each strategy or goal.)

Update—Evaluation of:

✔ *Plan as a whole*

❏ Specific strategy _____

❏ Specific goal _____

What have we accomplished to date?

Programmatically we have accomplished much—we have phased out the employment referral program and now refer people to Resource Center for Positives. We have collaborated with a national hotline that now provides the treatment and care information, and we continue to operate a prevention-focused hotline that is now under the management of the public education division. We have hired 5 new staff (3 are case managers), and we have increased our caseload to 400 clients (previously 300, with a goal of 500). Finally, we have a new MOU with City Clinic that is much clearer, our collaboration is working better, and we are reaching higher-risk clients, as evidenced by a higher HIV-positive rate among the individuals who are referred through our outreach program to City Clinic for testing. This means we are finding more people who have become infected, getting them into care, and helping them lead healthy lives.

Regarding funding, we have received a new prevention grant from a corporate foundation to do prevention with positives for $200,000 annually, as a result of intensified networking by the executive director and board.

What have we not yet accomplished?

We still have not hired a development director. We have not assessed our staff salaries and benefits package, which is a concern given how high a priority we placed on valuing our staff in the strategic plan.

(continues)

---

[1]*Source:* Adapted from I. C. Macmillan, "Competitive Strategies for Non-for-Profit Agencies," *Advances in Strategic Management* 1 (London: JAI Press, Inc., 1983), pp. 61–82.

Reasons for nonaccomplishments?

We have not been able to hire a development director because we have not taken the time to carve out money in the budget for this staff position. We have not assessed staff salaries and benefits because the ED and board have chosen to focus on fundraising, which has left little time for this activity.

Are we still on track?

For the most part, we are on track with our goals and have done especially well with programs and fundraising. However, we are off track with our personnel goals. We still recognize our staff as our greatest resource and, as such, we must make personnel goals and objectives the primary focus of year 2.

How has the environment changed since we last revised our plan/developed this goal or strategy?

Description of previous assessment of the organization's situation	Description of current assessment of the organization's situation
Previous strengths: • *Strong track record of results in direct services* • *Good reputation in the community* • *Solid volunteer program* • *Dedicated, talented, experienced staff* • *Well-respected and highly-developed case management program* • *Good relationship with the city and state government officials* • *Successful transition from a founder to a new executive director*	What are our organization's current strengths? • *Programs are more responsive to client needs, and we can serve more clients.* • *Our fundraising ability is stronger.* • *We do the things we do best, and have stopped doing the things other organizations do better.* • *Our collaborations are working. They are benefiting our clients and our agency.*
Previous weaknesses: • *Our financial and information management and reporting systems are not giving us the information we need.*	What are our organization's current weaknesses? • *We need to put our "money where our mouth is" in terms of showing that we value staff.*

Description of previous assessment of the organization's situation	Description of current assessment of the organization's situation
Previous weaknesses: • *We are not able to document impact on prevention.* • *Our board is not as active as it could be.* • *Recent program data are showing that our educational programs are not having significant effect on behavior.* • *Our staff can't keep up with new treatment options.* • *People with AIDS are not integrated with our HIV prevention efforts.* • *We do not have sufficient bilingual staff.* • *We have high staff turnover: Staff feel overwhelmed and line staff salaries have kept up with the cost of living in our city.* • *We do not have sufficient ethnic diversity in staff.* • *Our prevention outreach and education programs are unfocused. We are supposed to be reaching high-risk groups, but in reality we mostly reach the general public.*	What are our organization's current weaknesses? • *Our administrative capacity is insufficient to support the implementation of the strategic plan.*
Previous opportunities: • *We have been approached by other community organizations that work with homebound populations about expanding our scope of service to people other than AIDS and HIV.*	What are the main opportunities for our organization in the current landscape? • *Other cities have inquired about our collaborative model with City Clinic and want to adapt/replicate it, which is evidence of our strong leadership in the field.*

(continues)

Description of previous assessment of the organization's situation	Description of current assessment of the organization's situation
Previous opportunities: • *Increased need for housing (not that we could really respond to this)* • *Increased volume of calls on our hotline looking for information on treatment options* • *New drugs allowing people to go back to work and need less direct service — other people with terminal illnesses (e.g. cancer) could benefit from our services*	What are the main opportunities for our organization in the current landscape? • *Our research uncovered a group called Funders Concerned About AIDS, who is helping us with forming our fund development strategies.*
Previous threats: • *Increased monitoring of some of our more controversial education programs* • *The economy* • *The complexity of new AIDS treatments and our ability to help our clients understand their choices* • *Issues of homophobia and perceptions that AIDS is still primarily a gay problem* • *Continued evidence of new HIV infections among men and women in the African-American community and immigrants from Southeast Asia* • *Increasing demand from funding community to document success* • *Changing policies and funding priorities at the federal level*	What threats is the organization currently facing in the current landscape? • *The future of federal HIV/AIDS funding continues to be uncertain.* • *The city is facing a financial crisis and deep cuts to health and social services are expected in the next fiscal year.* • *Qualified bilingual people are in high demand throughout the human services sector and have been hard to find and retain on staff.*

Given all of the above, what changes should we make to the current plan/goal/strategy? New or changed priorities?

Our main priority in year 2 needs to be our personnel goals, especially regarding reviewing the salary and benefits packages. We also need to prioritize hiring a development director, so that the ED and Board can spend less time on fundraising and more time on the staff issues.

Issues that need further discussion? Who, how, and when?

Given that we now have a successful collaboration with City Clinic, and others are interested in replicating it, we may need to design training on this model that we can do in other cities. This will be discussed at the next board meeting, and if we decide to move forward, the public education division will lead the effort.

Blank Worksheets

| WORKSHEET 1 | Identify Planning Process Issues and Outcomes |

❏ What would success look like at the completion of the planning process? What does your organization wish to achieve from a planning process?

❏ What issues or choices do you think need to be addressed during the planning process?

❏ Are there any non-negotiables that need to be articulated up front? Any constraints regarding the planning process?

What would success look like at the completion of the planning process? What do you wish to achieve from a planning process?

Many of the strategic issues discussed during a strategic planning process address some or all of the following four questions:

1. *Mission.* How well are we achieving our mission and how could we have a greater impact?

2. *Financial.* Are our operations financially viable, and how can we ensure the long-term financial stability of our organization? Do we have effective financial management systems in place to monitor our finances?

3. *Administrative capacity.* Do we have the administrative capacity to effectively and efficiently support our programs and services? What would it take to maximize our organizational capabilities in terms of planning, human resources and leadership, organization culture and communication, and our technology and facilities infrastructure?

4. *Governance.* How effective is the board at protecting the public's interest, ensuring that charitable dollars are used effectively and efficiently and that the organization is fulfilling its mission? What can we do to ensure that our board is able to fulfill its governance role now and for the future?

What specific strategic questions or choices does your organization need to address during the planning process? (Note: Not every strategic issue will have a short-term focus question).

Strategic (longer-term) issues to be addressed—framed as a question:	Short-term focus? Are there some operational questions that need to be in the near future? If yes, list below:

Are there any issues that are non-negotiable (not open for discussion)?
Any constraints regarding the planning process?

WORKSHEET 2   Set Up Your Planning Process for Success

❏ Are the conditions and criteria for successful planning in place at the current time? Can certain pitfalls be avoided?

❏ Is this the appropriate time for your organization to initiate a planning process? Yes or no? If no, where do you go from here?

The following conditions for successful planning are in place:	Yes	No	Unsure or N/A
1. Commitment, support, and involvement from top leadership, especially the executive director and board president, throughout the entire process			
2. Commitment to clarifying roles and expectations for all participants in the planning process, including clarity as to who will have input into the plan and who will be decision makers			
3. Willingness to gather information regarding the organization's strengths, weaknesses, opportunities, and threats; the effectiveness of current programs; needs in the community, both current and future; and information regarding competitors and (potential) collaborators			
4. The right mix of individuals on the planning committee—strategic thinkers and actionaries (individuals who are in a position to see things through to completion), as well as big-picture (conceptual) thinkers and detail-oriented (perceptual) thinkers			
5. Willingness to be inclusive and encourage broad participation, so that people feel ownership of and are energized by the process			

WORKSHEET 2 *(Continued)*

The following conditions for successful planning are in place:	Yes	No	Unsure or N/A
6. An adequate commitment of organizational resources to complete the planning process as designed (e.g., staff time, board time, dollars spent on the process for market research, consultants, etc.)			
7. A board and staff that understand the purpose of planning, recognize what it is and is not able to accomplish, and have clarity about the desired outcomes of the process and issues to be addressed			
8. A willingness to question the status quo, to look at new ways of doing things; a willingness to ask the hard questions, face difficult choices, and make decisions that are best for the organization's current and future constituencies as well as a willingness to support organizational change as a result of the planning efforts			
9. The organization has the "financial capacity" to sustain itself for the immediate future without a financial "crisis" appearing to detract from strategic planning.			
10. Top management's commitment to carefully considering recommendations made during the planning process rather than disregarding decisions in favor of his or her intuitive decisions			
11. There is no serious conflict between key players within the organization (although a healthy dosage of disagreement and perhaps some heated discussions can be expected during a strategic planning process).			

(continues)

The following conditions for successful planning are in place:	Yes	No	Unsure or N/A
12. There are no high-impact decisions to be made in the next six months by an external source.			
13. No merger or other major strategic partnership effort is under way (separate strategic planning conversations are not taking place while strategic restructuring negotiations are taking place).			
14. Board and top management are willing to articulate constraints and non-negotiables upfront.			
15. A commitment to tie the strategic planning process to the organization's annual planning and budgeting process—to create a detailed annual operating plan for the upcoming year, and monitor/revise the strategic plan as needed			
16. A commitment to allocating sufficient resources to support the implementation of core strategies			

Comments to explain—and/or suggestions on how to respond—to "No" or "Unsure or N/A" answers

Go or no go/other issues/concerns?

Is this the appropriate time for your organization to initiate a planning process? Yes or No? If no, what steps need to be put in place to ensure a successful planning process—where do you go from here? Or, should the organization consider doing something other than a formal strategic planning process?

☐ Using the strategic issues you identified in Worksheet 1, develop a plan for gathering information—from internal and external sources—to inform those questions.

Data Collection from Internal Stakeholders—Board and Staff

Internal Stakeholders	Outcome of contact with them? Questions they can answer? What information do you want to gather from this stakeholder?	How best to involve them (such as: surveys, discussions at regularly scheduled meetings, retreats, in-depth program evaluation worksheets, etc.)	Details (may be filled out when starting to implement data collection phase: time frame and who is responsible for implementation)
Staff—do you want to engage: • All of the staff • Management team • Some staff (list individuals)			
Board of directors			

(continues)

Data Collection from Internal Stakeholders—Board and Staff

Internal Stakeholders	Outcome of contact with them? Questions they can answer? What information do you want to gather from this stakeholder?	How best to involve them (such as: surveys, discussions at regularly scheduled meetings, retreats, in-depth program evaluation worksheets, etc.)	Details (may be filled out when starting to implement data collection phase: time frame and who is responsible for implementation)
Others—do you want to engage others (such as advisory board members, volunteer staff, etc.)			
Departments/program units			
Specific individuals to be interviewed (such as director of finance, development director)			

Data Collection from External Stakeholders—How to Involve External Stakeholders

(List specific names if possible)	Why talk with them? Relationship building or information gathering, or both?	Outcome of contact with them? Questions to answer? What information do you want to gather from this stakeholder?	How best to involve stakeholder (i.e., questionnaires, interviews [face-to-face or phone], focus groups, meetings, etc.)	Details (may be filled out when starting to implement data collection phase: time frame and who is responsible for implementation)
Constituents/ clients (current, past)				
Institutional funders (foundations, corporations, government agencies)				
Government officials				

(continues)

Data Collection from External Stakeholders—How to Involve External Stakeholders

(List specific names if possible)	Why talk with them? Relationship building or information gathering, or both?	Outcome of contact with them? Questions to answer? What information do you want to gather from this stakeholder?	How best to involve stakeholder (i.e., questionnaires, interviews [face-to-face or phone], focus groups, meetings, etc.)	Details (may be filled out when starting to implement data collection phase: time frame and who is responsible for implementation)
Organizations we partner with				
Individual donors				
Ex-staff, ex-board members				
Other:				

Which of the following documents would help provide important background information and/or inform your strategic issue decisions? (Check appropriate documents to assemble)

Mission-related documents

☐ Program descriptions/workplans

☐ Needs assessments

☐ Client satisfaction surveys

☐ Previous evaluation findings

☐ Evidence of innovation/reputation in the field

☐ Other data (such as government reports, etc.)

Administrative capacity documents

☐ Mission, vision, values statements; strategic plan; annual plans.

☐ Program descriptions/workplans

☐ Organizational chart

☐ Internal newsletters or other communication vehicles

☐ Personnel policies and performance appraisal forms

☐ Previous organizational effectiveness surveys and/or "climate surveys" (or other formal review of culture and staff satisfaction)

☐ Volunteer management plan

☐ Information technology plan

☐ Visual survey of facilities and equipment

Financial-related documents

☐ Fundraising materials

☐ Fundraising plans

☐ Budget reports

☐ Audit

☐ Sample financial reports

☐ Internal controls procedures manuals

Governance documents

☐ Board minutes

☐ Board roster and committee structure

☐ Previous board self-evaluations

☐ Board manual

WORKSHEET 4   **Design a Strategic Planning Process to Meet Your Organizational Needs**

❑ What has been your previous experience with strategic planning?

❑ Consider some of the choices to be made when designing your strategic planning process

❑ Other considerations for the strategic planning process

What has been your previous experience with strategic planning—what has worked or not worked in the past that might inform the design of your strategic planning process?

The following is a list of some of the choices to be made when designing a strategic planning process:

• Who makes what decisions—who decides the strategic direction for the organization, and what degree of input is sought from the board and the staff

• Whether to involve external stakeholders in addition to internal stakeholders (board and staff)

• How long a process to have (abbreviated, moderate, or extensive)

• Whether to use an existing committee or a strategic planning committee for such activities as coordinating the work and assisting with some of the planning activities (such as external stakeholder interviews, research, etc.)

- Whether to have a strategic planning committee—and/or ad hoc issue-focused task forces—charged with the responsibility for discussing future program or administrative options and making recommendations to the board

- If using a strategic planning committee, deciding who should be on that committee. If using ad hoc task forces, deciding membership on those committees (including the decision as to whether nonboard members might be on those committees)

- Who will lead the process

- Who will be the primary writer of the plan (with guidance from a consultant if necessary)

- The sequencing of discussions (i.e., "do data collection first and then have a retreat" or "kick off the planning process with a board/staff retreat and then create issue focused board/staff task forces to collect and analyze data and make recommendations to the board of directors")

- Whether to use a consultant and if yes, how best to use a consultant/ expectations regarding the consultant's role

(continues)

WORKSHEET 4   *(Continued)*

Other considerations for the strategic planning process:

Planning committee membership:

Name	Representing what key stakeholder

Milestones and deadlines:

Planning principles and values (e.g., we are committed to being inclusive of all key stakeholders; we are willing to look at new and different ways of doing things and face the hard choices regarding how to best use our resources):

Meeting agreements (e.g., when offering a dissenting opinion, be willing to offer a solution that meets your needs and the needs of others; show up at meetings and be prepared; seek first to understand, then to be understood; respect differences):

How board and staff will be kept informed about the strategic planning discussions:

> **WORKSHEET 5   Create a Mission Statement**
>
> ❑ Draft a mission statement for your organization (please write legibly if
>   filling out by hand).

What is the focus problem(s) that our organization exists to solve?
(In considering the focus problem or need, you might want to consider the
following questions: What need or opportunity does our organization exist to
resolve? Who is affected by the problem? How are they affected? If we were
successful, what impact would we have regarding this problem?)

What are the assumptions upon which our organization does its work?

What is the purpose of our organization?
(A purpose sentence answers the question of why an organization exists; it does
not describe what an organization does. The sentence should be a short succinct
statement that describes the ultimate result an organization is hoping to
achieve. When writing a purpose sentence, make sure to indicate outcomes and
results [e.g., to eliminate homelessness], not the methods of achieving those
results, which is what you do [e.g., by constructing houses].)

What are the methods that our organization uses to accomplish its purpose?
Describe our business or businesses—our primary services or activities:

Combine your purpose sentence and description of primary services/activities in
a compelling mission statement:

Develop a powerful tag line or slogan:

WORKSHEET 6   Create a Vision Statement

❑ Dare to dream the possible. What is your organization's realistic but challenging guiding vision of success? (please write legibly if filling out by hand)

External vision: Describe how the world would be improved, changed, or different if our organization was successful in achieving its purpose.

Internal vision: Envisioning our organization's future

Programmatic vision:

Administrative vision:

WORKSHEET 7   Articulate Your Organization's Values, Beliefs, and Guiding Principles

❏ Clarify your organization's belief systems: What are some of the values, beliefs, and/or guiding principles that do (or should) guide your board and staff's interactions with each other and with constituencies?

❏ Practical impact: What behaviors should you commit to doing in everyday practice to support your values and beliefs?

Clarify your organization's belief systems: What are some of the values, beliefs, and/or guiding principles that do (or should) guide your board and staff's interactions with each other and with constituencies?	Practical impact: What are the behaviors you should commit to doing in everyday practice in support of our values, beliefs, and guiding principles

☐ Summarize your organization's history, listing the appropriate span of years such as 1-year, 5-year, or 10-year increments, depending on the organization's age. Identify lessons from your history.

☐ Summarize what has or has not been accomplished since your last strategic planning process. Optional: Describe your programs, staffing levels, and financial capacity (or attach a document that describes what you do and how it is supported).

Presentation of Organization's History

Timeline	19	19	19	19	19	20	20	20	20	20

List key organizational events and shifts in priorities (use the timeline to place events in chronological order)

(continues)

Presentation of Organization's History

Timeline	19	19	19	19	19	19	20	20	20	20
List external events impacting the organization (use the timeline to place events in chronological order)										

Lessons from history: Keys to stability and growth	Lessons from history: Recurring themes that show causes for instability
What have we accomplished since our last strategic planning process?	What have we not accomplished since our last strategic planning process?

Summary of Programs

Name of program/department:

Program/department purpose:

Description of current scope and scale of activities:

Name of program/department:

Program/department purpose:

Description of current scope and scale of activities:

Name of program/department:

Program/department purpose:

Description of current scope and scale of activities:

(continues)

Summary of Operations

Number of staff and board:

Financial data: (sources of revenue, budget, etc.)

WORKSHEET 9   Articulate Previous and Current Strategies

❏ Identify and assess your organization's previous and current strategies.

Previous and current strategy	Was or is the strategy effective? Why or why not? Should it be considered as the strategy for the future? Why or why not?

WORKSHEET 10   Staff and Board Perceptions of Organization's SWOT

❏ List our organization's primary (program and administrative) strengths and weaknesses—internal forces working for and against our organization achieving its mission.

❏ List our organization's key opportunities and threats—political, economic, social, technological, demographic, or legal trends that are or may impact our organization's ability to achieve its mission.

❏ (Optional) Indicate any possible connection between an opportunity or threat and a strength or weakness? (Are there any opportunities we can take advantage of because of a particular strength? Are there any threats that are compounded by a weakness?)

Internal Forces	**External Forces**
Strengths:	Opportunities:
Weaknesses:	Threats:

WORKSHEET II   Evaluate Current Programs

❏ Evaluate each of your programs in terms of community needs, results, competitive position, and potential for increased efficiency.

Note: If you are filling this out by hand, please write legibly.

Program/service name:

Name of person(s) filling out this assessment:

Date:

Description of program service:

Units of service/number of people served including demographic information (if applicable)

Total Annual Expenses: Total Annual Revenue:

What is the need in the community that this program exists to meet?

Who is the target audience(s) that this program serves to reach?

What impact does this program currently have, or intend to have, on addressing the need articulated above? What is the outcome(s) of this program's work?

(continues)

Measures of success: What evidence do you have to show that this program is having the impact you want it to have? How do we know we are being successful? What do this program's customers/clients consider value? How do we currently measure success: What are the indicators of success (benchmarks) we currently use to measure success?

How should we measure success? Are there other indicators of success we should use in measuring success? How should we measure results/impact/outcomes of this program in improving the quality of constituents' lives and making a difference in the world?

What are the greatest strengths of this program?

What are the greatest weaknesses of this program?

What are the trends in the environment—political, social, economic, technological, demographic, legal forces—that are or will be impacting this program in the future: trends either potentially moving the program forward (opportunities) or holding it back (threats)?

How could we improve the cost-effectiveness of this program?

WORKSHEET 11 *(Continued)*

How could we improve the quality of this program? How could we improve our ability to deliver this product/provide this service? If we were to reinvent this program, what changes would we make in how the service/product is delivered?

How might we better market this program (i.e., increase the public's awareness of this program)?

Is there potential for (starting/increasing/improving) collaboration?

Within the organization? How? With whom?

Outside of the organization? In what ways? With whom? Why?

If the budget for this program were suddenly cut, what would you recommend we do?

If the budget for this program was suddenly increased, what would you recommend we do?

(continues)

WORKSHEET 11   *(Continued)*

Competitive Analysis of This Program

Program fit:

How is this program congruent with the overall purpose and mission of our organization?

How does/could this program draw on existing skills in the organization and share resources/coordinate activities with other programs?

Ability to Attract Resources:

(*Note:* The ability to attract resources deals with issues of market demand; stable funding or ability to provide current and future support; appeals to volunteers; measurable, reportable program results; complements other programs; low exit barriers—ability to discontinue program or abandon past commitment without alienating supporters.)

Does this program have the potential to attract resources and enhance existing programs?

_____ Yes   _____ No

Competitive Position:

(*Note:* A program with a strong competitive position is one that meets the following criteria: good logistical delivery system; large reservoir of client, community, or support group loyalty; past success in securing funding; strong potential to raise funds; superior track record/image of service delivery; large market share of the target clientele; better-quality service/product/service delivery than competitors; superior organization, management, and technical skills; cost-effective delivery of service.)

Are there many groups, or few groups, providing similar services in the community? Who else is doing the same or similar work to address this need in our geographic area?

_____ Few Groups   _____ Many Groups

List names of groups here:

Do you think your program is in a strong competitive position in relation to the above groups?

_____ Yes, strong competitive position   _____ No, not a competitive position

Why do you think it is important for our organization to address this need (as opposed to another organization)? What is your program's competitive advantage? What makes your program unique in comparison to the competition?

Suggested future growth strategy for this program:

_____ Increase   _____ Maintain   _____ Decrease   _____ Eliminate

Why this strategy? Include the implications if we were to ignore this strategy.

What impact would this growth strategy have on our resources (staff time and other expenditures) and revenues?

(continues)

Analysis of Competitive Position (fill this in only if applicable)

Name of organization	Ability to provide service			Quality of service			Why did you rate the ability to provide service the way you did? Why did you give the rating on quality of service
Our program:	4 Excellent	3 Good	2 Fair	1 Poor	4 Excellent	3 Good	2 Fair	1 Poor	
Competitor:	4 Excellent	3 Good	2 Fair	1 Poor	4 Excellent	3 Good	2 Fair	1 Poor	
Competitor:	4 Excellent	3 Good	2 Fair	1 Poor	4 Excellent	3 Good	2 Fair	1 Poor	
Competitor:	4 Excellent	3 Good	2 Fair	1 Poor	4 Excellent	3 Good	2 Fair	1 Poor	

Other competitors not assessed:

WORKSHEET 12   Summary of Data and Analysis of Possible Considerations for the Future

❑ Summarize the data you have collected during your strategic planning process; summarize your findings. You can summarize your data either by the categories of mission, money, administration, and governance, or, if you gathered data according to your strategic issues, use the issue summary page to summarize your findings.

❑ You may wish to compile a summary of all of your findings regarding your organization's strengths, weaknesses, opportunities, and threats on the last page.

Summary of Findings—Mission: How well are we achieving our mission and how could we have a greater impact?

What did you find out regarding current and future needs of your constituencies? How well is the organization meeting the needs in the community?

Who else is providing similar products/services—potential and real competitors/collaborators? What distinguishes our organization from others doing similar work?

Is the organization providing services/products effectively and efficiently? Is the organization valued for offering high quality, innovative and effective services/products? Is the organization well known and respected in the community? What evidence do you have to support your answer?

(continues)

Possible Considerations for the Future—Program: How well are we achieving our mission and how could we have a greater impact?

Emerging themes and/or priorities:

Based on the information gathered, are there things that the organization should consider doing differently, more of, less of, the same? Are there things that the organization should consider starting/stopping? Does the mission or vision need to be revisited? How or why? What is the unique niche that the organization fills? How does or should the organization distinguish itself from the competition?

What discussions pertaining to program still need to happen? How and when will those discussions happen?

WORKSHEET 12   *(Continued)*

Summary of Findings—Finances

Are our operations financially viable, and how can we ensure the long-term financial stability of our organization?

Do we have effective financial management systems in place to use our resources effectively, monitor our finances, and ensure accountability?

What are the emerging themes/priorities regarding our financial capacity?

Ensuring our long-term financial viability (resource development):

Ensuring effective financial management:

What discussions still need to happen regarding our finances? How and when will those discussions happen?

(continues)

Primary Strengths— organizational strengths that support the organization's long-term financial viability and financial accountability	Primary Weaknesses— organizational weaknesses that work against the organization's long-term financial viability and accountability	Primary Opportunities— trends that the organization could take advantage of so as to better ensure its long-term financial viability and financial accountability	Primary Threats—trends in the external environment that are working against the organization's long-term financial viability and accountability)

Summary of Findings—Administrative Capacity

Do we have the administrative capacity to effectively and efficiently support our programs and services?

Summary of Primary Administrative Strengths—organizational strengths that indicate a strong administrative capacity	Summary of Primary Administrative Weaknesses—organizational weaknesses that indicate a vulnerability in administrative capacity

What are the themes that are emerging from our data collection regarding our administrative capacity?

What discussions still need to happen regarding administrative capacity? How and when will those discussions happen?

(continues)

Summary of Findings—Goverance

How effectively is the board protecting the public's interest—ensuring that
charitable dollars are used effectively and efficiently and that the organization
is fulfilling its mission?

Primary Board Strengths—indicators of a strong and effective board	Weaknesses—indicators of a vulnerability in the board's ability to govern and support the organization

How might the board's composition, responsibilities, and processes need to
change to support the long-term goals and objectives of the organization?

What discussions still need to happen regarding board governance? How and
when will those discussions happen?

WORKSHEET 12   *(Continued)*

(Optional) Summary of Data Collection by Strategic Issue

Strategic issue:

Summary of findings—issue:

Possible considerations for the future:

What discussions still need to happen? How and when will those discussions happen?

(continues)

| WORKSHEET 13 | Business Assessment Tools for Developing a Program Portfolio |

❏ Use one or both of the following business assessment tools to assist in developing your program portfolio

❏ Use the criteria listed for each tool and plot out where each of your programs and other business activities fit within the chart

CompassPoint's Dual Bottom-Line Matrix

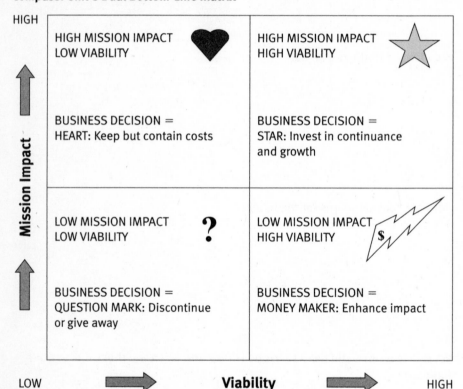

* Some of the characteristics of programs with *high impact mission:* tangible results, visible progress toward the achievement of the organization's mission, high leverage potential—synergy with other programs, and high-quality services that distinguish the organization from its competition

* Some of the characteristics of *high viability:* At the very least covers all costs (both direct and indirect), generates a surplus of revenue, projected to have financially sustainability for the future, a proven financially viable business model

WORKSHEET 13   *(Continued)*

Competitive Strategies Matrix

		Ability to Attract Resources and Enhance Existing Programs YES		Ability to Attract Resources and Enhance Existing Programs NO	
		Alternative Coverage: **MANY**	Alternative Coverage: **FEW**	Alternative Coverage: **MANY**	Alternative Coverage: **FEW**
GOOD FIT	**Strong Competitive Position YES**	1) Growth or maintain competitive edge strategy	4) Growth or maintain competitive edge strategy	5) Build up best competitor: assist another organization provide the service	8) Soul of the agency
	Strong Competitive Position NO	2) Develop and implement an exit strategy	3) Invest in program and administrative capacity or Develop and implement an exit strategy	6) Develop and implement an exit strategy	7) Collaboration strategy
	POOR FIT	Divest or do not start to provide this service.			

(continues)

- *Program fit.* Is this program congruent with the overall purpose and mission of our organization, and does/could this program draw on existing skills in the organization and share resources/coordinate activities with other programs?

- *Ability to attract resources and enhance existing programs.* Does this program have high market demand from a large client base? Does it have high appeal to groups capable of providing current and future support? Does this program have stable funding? Can you show measurable results? Would you be able to discontinue the program with relative ease if necessary (low exit barriers/ ability to discontinue program or abandon past commitment)?

- *Alternative coverage.* Are there many organizations, or few organizations, providing similar services in the community?

- *Strong competitive position.* Do you have strong client and community support? Do you have a superior track record of service delivery? Do you provide better quality than your competitors? Do you have the administrative capacity to provide this program cost effectively and efficiently?

Summarize Your Future Program Portfolio

☐ Develop a detailed program portfolio.

For each of your proposed future programs or services:

- What is the program's current level of activity? (This question, of course, applies only to existing programs. New programs will not yet have a current level of activity.)
- What is its proposed growth strategy (expand, maintain, decrease, eliminate, start new program, modify existing program)?
- What is the program's projected future level of activity?

Program or service	What is the program's current level of activity? (This question, of course, applies only to existing programs; new programs will not yet have a current level of activity.)	What is its proposed growth strategy (expand, maintain, decrease, eliminate, start new program, modify existing program)?	What is the program's projected future level of activity?

(continues)

Program or service	What is the program's current level of activity? (This question, of course, applies only to existing programs; new programs will not yet have a current level of activity.)	What is its proposed growth strategy (expand, maintain, decrease, eliminate, start new program, modify existing program)?	What is the program's projected future level of activity?

Program or service	What is the program's current level of activity? (This question, of course, applies only to existing programs; new programs will not yet have a current level of activity.)	What is its proposed growth strategy (expand, maintain, decrease, eliminate, start new program, modify existing program)?	What is the program's projected future level of activity?

☐ Identify and assess your core future strategies

Proposed strategy	Assumptions, facts, and values that support this proposed strategy	What possible obstacles do we face in implementing this strategy?	How to respond to possible obstacles: strategies for overcoming obstacles and short-term priorities	What triggers might encourage us to reevaluate this strategy?

Proposed strategy	Assumptions, facts, and values that support this proposed strategy	What possible obstacles do we face in implementing this strategy?	How to respond to possible obstacles: strategies for overcoming obstacles and short-term priorities	What triggers might encourage us to reevaluate this strategy?

☐ For each administrative, financial, and governance function, list the overall goal or objectives and any long-term objective/priorities to be included in the strategic plan. (These priorities will be the basis for writing objectives.)

Administrative Functions	Goal(s)	Priorities (Objectives)
Staffing and benefits		
Public relations and communications		

Administrative Functions	Goal(s)	Priorities (Objectives)
Infrastructure: information systems, technology, facilities, etc.		
Planning, evaluation, quality control		

(continues)

Financial Functions	Goal(s)	Priorities (Objectives)
Financial management		
Resource development		

Governance Functions	Goal(s)	Priorities (Objectives)
Board of directors		
Networking and collaboration		

WORKSHEET 17 **Long-Range Financial Projections**

☐ Transfer data from Worksheet 14: name of program and desired scope and scale in the next three to five years

☐ For each program, estimate FTEs and salaries and benefits costs, and any other significant direct costs to operate at the desired scope and scale (e.g., materials and supplies, rent for program-specific space, travel, equipment used exclusively by program, etc.).

☐ Identify nondirect expenses—in-common costs that benefit more than one program and overhead costs.

☐ Total all expenses to come up with a rough estimate of the cost of supporting the strategic plan.

Part 1: Estimate Future Costs

	Program A	Program B	Program C	In-Common Costs (shared indirect and administrative costs)	Total
Desired future scope and scale in the next three years					
Estimated FTEs					
Estimated salaries and benefits costs					

Part 1: Estimate Future Costs

	Program A	Program B	Program C	In-Common Costs (shared indirect and administrative costs)	Total
Other significant costs: • Materials and supplies • Rent • Travel • Equipment					
Total Estimated Costs					

(continues)

Part 2: Estimate Future Revenues

	Program A	Program B	Program C	Unrestricted Revenues	Total Revenues
Government contracts					
Earned fees/revenues					
Unrestricted foundation grants					
Restricted foundation grants					
Corporate contributions					
Individual contributions					
Special events					
Bequests/Planned gifts: life income funds					

Total Estimated Revenues			
Total Estimated Costs (from Part 1)			
Total Net			

Manage the Transition: The Changes Required for Success

☐ List the major changes that may need to happen as a result of the decisions reached in the strategic planning process.

☐ Identify skills needed, system structures, and organization culture changes that need to happen to ensure these changes are successful:

- Changes that will impact staff and the skills they may need in the future
- Changes that will impact the structures and systems that may need to be modified to support the changes
- Changes that will impact how the organization's culture (mindset) may need to be modified to support the changes

List the major changes that may need to happen/will happen as a result of the strategic plan:

New skills that may be needed	Modified or new structures and systems that may be needed	New culture/mindset that may be needed

WORKSHEET 19	Evaluate the Strategic Planning Process

❑ Evaluate your strategic plan, your annual operating plans, and the strategic planning process

❑ Make any suggestions for improving future planning endeavors

Strategic plan	Yes	No
Provides guidance to both short-term and long-term priorities?		
Helps the organization to allocate resources?		
Is understandable by people who have not participated in the development of the plan?		
Responds to the organization's best understanding of its internal and external environments?		
Was developed from a consensus and commitment-building process?		
Has been formally adopted by the board of directors?		
Comments and suggestions for future strategic plans:		
Annual operating plan(s)	**Yes**	**No**
Has both process and outcome objectives specified?		
Has been developed by staff members who are responsible for the implementation of the goals and objectives?		
Provides an easy implementation, monitoring, and reference tool?		
Operationalizes the strategic plan—helps ensure that the strategic plan will be implemented?		
Has a realistic budget to support the operational plan?		
Comments and suggestions for future annual operational plans:		

Planning process met the following criteria	Yes	No
The process was consensus building: It offered a way to surface the needs and interests of all stakeholders and allowed sufficient time to reach agreement on what is best for the long-term and short-term interests of the client/customer?		
The process allowed sufficient time to assess programs, and the strengths, weaknesses, opportunities, and threats?		
The process supported the achievement of the outcomes that were initially identified in Worksheet 1?		
Comments and suggestions for future planning processes:		

WORKSHEET 20   Monitor and Update the Strategic Plan

❏ Review your strategic plan, noting accomplishments and disappointments. Assess any changes in the environment since the last strategic planning meeting. If necessary, make changes in strategies and long-term and short-term priorities.

(*Note:* As an alternative to reviewing the plan as a whole, this worksheet can also be used to assess each of your plan's strategies or goals. Each strategy or goal would have its own page, and you would answer the same questions for each strategy or goal.)

Update — Evaluation of:

❏ Strategic plan as a whole _____

❏ Specific strategy _____

❏ Specific goal _____

What have we accomplished to date?

What have we not yet accomplished?

Reasons for nonaccomplishments?

Are we still on track?

WORKSHEET 20   *(Continued)*

How has the environment changed since we last revised our plan/developed this goal or strategy?

Description of previous assessment of the organization's situation	Description of current assessment of the organization's situation
Previous strengths:	What are our organization's current strengths?
Previous weaknesses:	What are our organization's current weaknesses?

(continues)

WORKSHEET 20   *(Continued)*

Description of previous assessment of the organization's situation	Description of current assessment of the organization's situation
Previous opportunities:	What are the main opportunities for our organization in the current landscape?
Previous threats:	What threats is the organization currently facing in the current landscape?

Given all of the above, what changes should we make to the current plan/goal/strategy? New or changed priorities?

Issues that need further discussion? Who, how, and when?

Sample Workplans for Abbreviated, Moderate, and Extensive Planning Processes

How to Use the Workplan Templates

There are three workplan templates for each of the three planning processes: abbreviated, moderate, and extensive. Once the planning committee has chosen which process they are going to use, the workplan should be modified to reflect the specific needs of the organization. Changes will probably need to be made on the format or activity that will be undertaken, who should be involved, and which worksheets and templates the planning committee wishes to use. Finally, times will vary, and should be adjusted accordingly, with specific dates or time frames added to the time commitment section.

Abbreviated Planning Process Workplan: One-Day[1] Retreat Agenda

Participants: Entire board, executive director, and all staff

Proposed Agenda Topics	Process and Personnel Responsible	Time Frame
Introductions, meeting agreements, and agenda review	Facilitator	9:00–9:15 A.M.
• State of the organization and update on the external forces impacting the organization (presentation on trends, funding environment, competitor situation, statistics on client needs)	Presentation by exexutive director	9:15–10:15 A.M.
• Organizational history[2]	Either presentation by designated individual or entire group recreate on wall chart	
• Program services currently being offered • Future needs of clients and future challenges	Staff presentations	
Mission statement[3] • Purpose • Values, beliefs, and assumptions • Business	Discussion of each component by all attendees	10:15–10:50 A.M. Break 10:50–11:05 A.M.
Vision the possible: Our preferred external and internal vision	Brainstorming session by board and staff; summary of agreements and disagreements	11:05–11:30 A.M.
Program and management/operations: SWOT (strengths and weaknesses, opportunities and threats)	Brainstorming session by board and staff; if time, identify priority items	11:30 A.M.–noon

[1] Because of the number of programs or number of issues to discuss, a second day may need to be scheduled.

[2] If a presentation of the organization's history was done recently, an alternative presentation might include: Where we are in relation to our prior strategic plan (accomplishments, disappointments, effectiveness of prior strategies).

[3] If there is already a mission statement, then the mission statement should either be reaffirmed or modified.

Abbreviated Planning Process Workplan: One-Day Retreat Agenda *(Continued)*

Proposed Agenda Topics	Process and Personnel Responsible	Time Frame
Identification of key issues/challenges facing the organization	Discussion by all	noon–12:30 P.M.
Lunch		12:30–1:30 P.M.
Discussion of key issues. Agreement on overall core strategies and short-term and long-term program and management/operations priorities • Prioritized list of current and future programs (short-term and long-term importance; whether to maintain, expand, eliminate, decrease, or modify) • Prioritized list of short-term and long-term management/operations priorities to support programs	Small groups or large-group discussions	1:30–4:15 P.M. Including 15-minute break
Identification of issues that need further discussion by board and/or staff, and any additional information needed to help clarify priorities (such as client survey, etc.)	All	4:15–4:50 P.M.
Next steps, responsible personnel, time		
Evaluation of the day	What worked/didn't work/suggested changes	4:50–5:00 P.M.

Moderate Planning Process Workplan

Proposed Format	Who Involved	Possible Worksheets to Support Achieving Outcomes	Time Commitment
Meeting to assess organization's readiness; begin to identify issues to be addressed as part of the planning process and who to involve in the planning process May start to discuss what information is needed to help inform the planning process and how that information should be gathered; or, may wait until after planning retreat to see what information needs to be gathered	Executive director, board president or designated representative, and consultant[1]	Worksheet 1: Identify Planning Process Issues and Outcomes Worksheet 2: Set Up Your Planning Process for Success Worksheet 3: Develop a Plan for Gathering Information from Internal and External Stakeholders Worksheet 4: Design a Strategic Planning Process to Meet Your Organizational Needs	One or two meetings, two to three hours long (each)
Meeting to plan retreat	Executive director, board president, and/or chair of planning committee, consultant, and other board and staff as deemed necessary		One meeting, two to three hours long

[1] The organization may choose not to use an external consultant to facilitate the entire planning process, but instead may choose to have a consultant act as a neutral facilitator during some of the large-group meetings.

Moderate Planning Process Workplan *(Continued)*

Proposed Format	Who Involved	Possible Worksheets to Support Achieving Outcomes	Time Commitment
Board–staff planning retreat to discuss: • History of organization and/or state of the organization • Mission statement review or creation • Vision statement • Environmental assessment (SWOT) • Key issues, SWOT grid, and possible future program and management/operations priorities • Next steps, who is responsible, by when	If smaller organization, usually will include entire board and staff; if larger organization, usually entire board and staff representatives (management team). Line staff input to be gathered before retreat through either questionnaires or department meetings. Consultant to facilitate retreat. Some external stakeholders may also be invited to attend this meeting.	Worksheet 5: Create a Mission Statement Worksheet 6: Create a Vision Statement Worksheet 7: Articulate Your Organization's Values, Beliefs, and Guiding Principles Worksheet 8: Summarize Your Organization's History and Accomplishments Worksheet 9: Articulate Previous and Current Strategies Worksheet 10: Staff and Board Perceptions of Organization's SWOT SWOT Grid Analysis	Eight-hour retreat

(continues)

Moderate Planning Process Workplan *(Continued)*

Proposed Format	Who Involved	Possible Worksheets to Support Achieving Outcomes	Time Commitment
Meeting of planning committee to review notes from planning retreat and assess what additional information needs to be gathered. Information might include client satisfaction and needs surveys, Elements of an Effectively Managed Organization (EEMO™), staff assessment of programs and organization in relation to client needs and competitive position; program evaluation; interviews or surveys of key stakeholders.	Planning committee has discussion. May delegate responsibility for gathering information to individual members of the planning committee and/or staff.	Will depend on information that planning committee deems as needed to have informed discussions regarding future strategies and priorities. Possible worksheets may include: Worksheet 11: Evaluate Current Programs Worksheet 12: Summary of Data and Analysis of Possible Considerations for the Future Worksheet 13: Business Assessment Tools for Developing a Program Portfolio	Two to three meetings, two to three hours long (each)

Moderate Planning Process Workplan *(Continued)*

Proposed Format	Who Involved	Possible Worksheets to Support Achieving Outcomes	Time Commitment
Meetings of planning committee to assess previous current strategies, discuss issues, agree on criteria for prioritizing programs, and on long-term and short-term priorities Discussion by members of the planning committee as to what the final format for the strategic planning document may look like (e.g., whether a list of long-term and short-term priorities will suffice or whether the planning committee wants those priorities to be translated into formal goals and objectives language) Planning committee may identify that an additional half- or full-day board–staff planning retreat may be needed to complete discussion of key issues and setting priorities	Planning committee (with consultant if needed) has discussions. Some discussions may be delegated to appropriate groups (e.g., board of directors should discuss setting its long-term and short-term priorities; fund-raising staff and resource development may discuss funding strategies).	Worksheet 14: Summarize Your Future Program Portfolio Worksheet 15: Core Future Strategies Worksheet 16: Summary of Administrative, Financial, and Governance Priorities Worksheet 17: Long-Range Financial Projections	Will depend on number of issues that need to be discussed: usually two to five meetings, two to three hours long (each)

(continues)

379

Moderate Planning Process Workplan (Continued)

Proposed Format	Who Involved	Possible Worksheets and Templates to Support Achieving Outcomes	Time Commitment
Write formal goals and objectives for inclusion in strategic planning document (optional)	Those individuals designated by the planning committee to develop goals and objectives		
Meeting of planning committee to review strategic planning document; strategic planning document circulated to staff board	Planning committee		One to two meetings, two to three hours long (each)
Meeting of board of directors to approve strategic plan	Board of directors		Board meeting
Development of annual operating plan to implement strategic plan	Staff	Worksheet 18: Manage the Transition: The Changes Required for Success	Depends on size of organization
Evaluation of plans and the strategic planning process, celebration of the completion of the planning cycle	Planning committee	Worksheet 19: Evaluate the Strategic Planning Process	Two to three hour meeting
Monitor the strategic plan through the use of an annual planning retreat for the planning cycle	Planning committee coordinates and plans retreat	Worksheet 20: Monitor and Update the Strategic Plan	One-day retreat and time to plan retreat
Total Estimated Hours:			**50 – 70 hours**

Extensive Planning Process Workplan

	Suggested Strategic Planning Activities			
Phase 1	1.1. Identify reasons for planning			
	1.2. Set up your planning process for success			
Get Ready	1.3. Start discussions regarding how to involve internal and external stakeholders			
	1.4. Design a planning process to meet nonprofit organization's needs			
	1.5. Develop a "planning workplan" that articulates the outcome(s) of the planning process, strategic issues to address, roles, planning activities, and time frame			

Suggested Processes and Outcomes	Time Frame	Estimated Consultant Hours or Meetings
Consultant meet with Executive Director, with follow-up meetings with senior management and representatives of the board of directors (or strategic planning committee) to:		Series of meetings and discussions with executive director, representatives of the board, and senior management
• Identify reasons for planning, criteria for a successful planning process, and issues to be addressed as part of the planning process		
• Clarify consultant and nonprofit organization's board and staff's roles and responsibilities, processes to keep all board and staff informed of planning activities, products to be delivered, and time frame		
• Agree on what background information the consultant needs to be able to facilitate the process and what information needs to be gathered that will help inform strategic decisions (for example, should staff and/or board complete online surveys, etc.)		
• Decide on whether to use existing structures and/or establish a strategic planning committee to coordinate the planning work		
• Consultant revises initial workplan for review and approval by Executive Director and board		

Outcomes:
• **Agreement on who to involve in the planning process and what their involvement might be**
• **Agreement on a plan for planning (workplan)**
• **Articulation of initial strategic issues facing the organizations**

Estimated Consultant Hours for Phase 1:		**5–10 hours**

(continues)

Extensive Planning Process Workplan *(Continued)*

Phase 2	Suggested Strategic Planning Activities		
Articulate Mission, Vision, and Values	2.1. Write (or revisit) your mission statement		
	2.2. Draft a vision statement		
	2.3. Articulate/affirm your values, beliefs, and guiding principles		

Suggested Processes and Outcomes		Time Frame	Estimated Consultant Hours or Meetings
Discussion(s) of mission statement, vision of a preferred future and values, beliefs, and guiding principles			(Process to be agreed upon after Phase 1 discussions completed.) Discussions may take place at a retreat, special board and staff meetings, or strategic planning committee meetings.

Outcomes:
• **Agreed upon mission, vision, and values statements**

Estimated Consultant Hours for Phase 2:	5–15 hours

Extensive Planning Process Workplan *(Continued)*

	Suggested Strategic Planning Activities	Time Frame	Estimated Consultant Hours or Meetings
Phase 3	3.1. Summarize your organization's history and what has or has not been accomplished since last planning process		
	3.2. Articulate previous and current strategies		The number of meetings and hours will vary widely, depending on extent of data collection required and consultant role
Assess Your Situation	3.3. Collect perceptions of internal and external stakeholders regarding nonprofit organizations' strengths,		
	3.4. weaknesses, opportunities and threats (SWOT); collect empirical data to better understand the choices to be		
	3.5. made during the strategic planning process		
	3.6. Summarize findings from data gathered from internal and external sources, organization's strengths and weaknesses; trends in the environment that are or will impact organization; competitive advantage, needs in the community; start to make sense of data: emerging themes and priorities		

Suggested Processes and Outcomes			
(Organization's staff to assemble pertinent documents regarding agency's budget, service statistics, organizational charts, previous mission statements and planning documents, and other documents clarifying the organization's mandates, history, and operating trends. This information should be available to the consultant and members of the strategic planning committee.)			
Strategic planning committee to articulate previous and current strategies and discuss effectiveness of these strategies to date and relevance of strategies as we move forward			

(continues)

383

Extensive Planning Process Workplan (Continued)

Suggested Processes and Outcomes	Time Frame	Estimated Consultant Hours or Meetings
Extent of data collection from external and internal stakeholders, appropriate processes to use, and extent of consultant involvement to be decided upon after discussions with SP Committee. Consultant available for phone consultation, development and implementation of survey instruments, design of evaluation instruments, assistance in interviewing external and internal stakeholders, and facilitation of meetings. • Options: Staff and board fill out on line organizational assessment • Options: Board of directors to fill out an (on-line) board self assessment in preparation for their discussion of future board priorities (governance and support roles, membership, committees, expectations, etc.) • Options: External stakeholders' involvement may be through: surveys, interviews, focus groups, meetings, etc.		
Outcomes: • **Data to inform the setting of priorities in Phase 4**		
Estimated Consultant Hours for Phase 3:		20 – 60 hours

Extensive Planning Process Workplan *(Continued)*

	Suggested Strategic Planning Activities	Time Frame	Estimated Consultant Hours or Meetings
Phase 4 *Agree on Priorities*	4.1. Make sense of the data collected: review emerging themes, priority considerations derived from data collection		
	4.2. Business Planning—assess program portfolio and agree on competitive growth strategies		
	4.3. Develop a program portfolio that summarizes the proposed scope and scale of programs, resources required, and revenue potential. Do scenario planning if necessary.		
	4.4. Agree on core future strategies		
	4.5. Agree on administrative, financial, and governance priorities. Summarize the revenue potential and resources required to support organization's long-term vision.		

Suggested Processes and Outcomes			
Planning committee, ad hoc planning task forces, or other groups discuss and agree on strategies and overall program and administrative priorities Based on discussions, staff develops and presents to planning committee a suggested future program portfolio (scope and scale of future programs (including identification of resources needed to support the achievement of program objectives) and long term administrative priorities			The number of meetings and hours will vary widely, depending on extent of meetings required and degree of consensus regarding scenarios, core strategies and priorities

Outcomes:
- **Agreement on core future strategies and longer term program, governance, financial and administrative priorities**

Estimated Consultant Hours for Phase 4:	15–50 hours

(continues)

Extensive Planning Process Workplan *(Continued)*

	Suggested Strategic Planning Activities	Time Frame	Estimated Consultant Hours or Meetings
Phase 5 *Write the Plan*	5.1. Create goals and objectives. Components may include: introduction/executive summary; mission, vision, and values statement; core future strategies; program goals and objectives; financial, administrative, and governance goals and objectives.		
	5.2. Develop long-range financial projections		
	5.3. Write the strategic plan		
	5.4. Adopt the strategic plan		

Suggested Processes and Outcomes	Time Frame	Estimated Consultant Hours or Meetings
Designated drafts written of strategic plan, with assistance of consultant if necessary. Plan reviewed by strategic planning committee, circulated to appropriate stakeholders. Feedback incorporated into final draft. Final draft submitted to the board for final approval Executive summary of plan developed by executive director and/or designated writer and distributed to the community		The number of meetings and hours will vary widely, depending on the extent of consultant involvement in writing the plan.

Outcomes:
- **Approval of a Strategic Plan**
- **Executive Summary of the Plan for distribution to the public**

Estimated Consultant Hours for Phase 5:	5–30 hours

Extensive Planning Process Workplan *(Continued)*

Phase 6	Suggested Strategic Planning Activities		
Implement the Plan	6.1. Manage the transition period between the old and the new: assess the changes that need to happen (skills, systems and structures, and COTS culture) to support the strategic plan		
	6.2. Develop a detailed operation plan for upcoming year (first year's goals and objectives)		
		Time Frame	Estimated Consultant Hours or Meetings
Suggested Processes and Outcomes			
Staff discuss key changes in skills, systems and structures, and culture that need to happen sooner rather than later to support the strategic plan		TBD	The number of meetings and hours will vary widely, depending on the extent of consultant involvement in facilitation of annual operating plan
Executive Director and appropriate staff develop detailed annual operating plans to ensure the successful implementation of the strategic plan during the upcoming year			
Outcomes:			
• **Detailed operational plan and implementation timeline including goals and objectives, action steps, and implementation schedule**			
Estimated Consultant Hours for Phase 6:			**0 – 5 hours**

(continues)

Extensive Planning Process Workplan *(Continued)*

Phase 7	Planning Activities		
Evaluate and Monitor the Plan	7.1. Evaluate the strategic plan and the planning process		
	7.2. Monitor the strategic plan (at least once a year) and affirm/update/revise as needed. Develop next year's detailed implementation plan.		

Suggested Processes and Outcomes	Time Frame	Estimated Consultant Hours or Meetings
Strategic planning committee and consultant meet to • Evaluate completed strategic planning process; if necessary, identifying benchmarks, milestones, and key success factors • Discuss processes to monitor and evaluate implementation of plans	TBD	One meeting
Planning committee coordinates a yearly strategic planning meeting to assess and validate current strategies and ensure that the current strategic plan gives guidance to the development of upcoming annual operating plan. The planning committee may decide that the current strategic plan needs to be modified or significantly changed.	At least once a year	Consultant may or may not be involved
It may be time to start the strategic planning process again	Once every three to five years	

Outcomes:
• **An in-depth system to monitor and evaluate implementation of the plan(s) and achievement of success factors = best practices for future planning**
• **Processes in place to ensure that the plan(s) are modified as needed and that the Strategic Plan continues to provide guidance for the setting of current priorities for the following year**

Estimated Consultant Hours for Phase 7:	0 – 5 hours

Request for Proposal for Planning: Submitted by CompassPoint Nonprofit Services

Estimated Consultant Hours for Phase 1:	5–10 hours
Estimated Consultant Hours for Phase 2:	5–10 hours
Estimated Consultant Hours for Phase 3:	20–60 hours
Estimated Consultant Hours for Phase 4:	15–50 hours
Estimated Consultant Hours for Phase 5:	5–30 hours
Estimated Consultant Hours for Phase 6:	0–5 hours
Estimated Consultant Hours for Phase 7:	0–5 hours
TOTAL ESTIMATED CONSULTANT HOURS (50–170[1]):	
TOTAL ESTIMATED CONSULTANT COSTS @ $/hour[2]:	

[1] Consulting hours will vary widely and will depend on: amount of work done by staff or strategic planning committee versus using a consultant; extent of data that needs to be collected; the number of issues that need to be discussed; and degree of consensus regarding core strategies and priorities.

[2] Plus mileage and other travel-related expenses.

Elements of an Effectively Managed Organization (EEMO²™): An Assessment of Your Organizational Capacity

This assessment tool is designed to strengthen nonprofit organizations. A central assumption to this model is that when people leading organizations better understand how their organizations operate, they are better able to improve their organization's performance. The model provides a framework for collecting and organizing information to understand what's working, what needs to be improved, and where it will be useful to invest time and money in organizational capacity building.

Three key ideas are important to keep in mind about the approach of this model:

1. *The stance of the model is one of organization development versus clinical diagnosis.* In other words, the purpose of this project is to facilitate organizational planning, not to deliver an expert assessment of the organization's capacity.

2. *The model takes an explicitly asset-based approach.* We assume that each agency has extensive strengths, and this process should facilitate the organization's becoming stronger (as opposed to a focus on identifying and fixing flaws).

3. *The product of this assessment has two components: data and stakeholders.* The first product is data, which should help guide a board and staff

in making choices about how to best use organization resources. The second product is intangible and infinitely more valuable: an informed group of internal stakeholders who have committed to implement a realistic plan and share enthusiasm for how it may improve their collective ability to accomplish their particular mission for improving their community.

EEMO²™: A GUIDE TO ORGANIZATIONAL EFFECTIVENESS

Mission			
Administrative Capacity			
Planning	Human Resources and Leadership	Culture and Communication	Infrastructure: Technology and Facilities
Board Governance			
Finances			
Financial Capacity: Fund Development		**Financial Capacity: Financial Management**	

Elements of an Effectively Managed Organization: An Assessment of Your Organizational Capacity

For tracking purposes: (*Note:* No response will be attributed to any one individual.)

Position: ☐ Management (Managers and Directors) ☐ Program Staff ☐ Administrative/Support Staff

Name:

Mission

	Major Asset	Moderate Asset	Moderate Weakness	Major Weakness	Unknown
1. Core Programs: Consensus exists on the core program areas or core services the organization offers.	☐	☐	☐	☐	☐
2. Primary Constituencies: There is agreement on the primary constituencies the organization should be serving.	☐	☐	☐	☐	☐
3. Program Portfolio: Programs are chosen to support the mission of the organization and with respect to how they fit together (and are not just a collection of projects and activities) and how they meet needs in the community.	☐	☐	☐	☐	☐
4. Feedback: The organization has feedback mechanisms in place for regularly assessing constituencies' needs and satisfaction.	☐	☐	☐	☐	☐
5. Performance: The organization has a history of delivering successfully on program/service goals *and* of making changes or eliminating programs when they underperform.	☐	☐	☐	☐	☐

Elements of an Effectively Managed Organization *(Continued)*

	Major Asset	Moderate Asset	Moderate Weakness	Major Weakness	Unknown
6. Exciting: Programs/services elicit enthusiasm from staff and board as well as from supporters and clients and stakeholders. People feel that the programs/services are important, valued, high quality, and making an impact on constituents' lives.	☐	☐	☐	☐	☐
7. Reputation: The organization is respected by its peers in its field for being well run, delivering high-quality and innovative programming that meets the needs of constituencies.	☐	☐	☐	☐	☐
8. Alliances: The organization advances the organization's goals and expands its influence through participation in alliances and working collaboratively with other groups.	☐	☐	☐	☐	☐
9. Public Information: The organization's stakeholders and target populations are well informed about its work.	☐	☐	☐	☐	☐
10. Media Coverage: The organization receives the media coverage it needs to reach its target populations as well as potential and actual supporters.	☐	☐	☐	☐	☐

Comments/specific recommendations for mission: Questions 1 to 10

(continues)

Elements of an Effectively Managed Organization *(Continued)*

Administrative Capacity: Planning

	Major Asset	Moderate Asset	Moderate Weakness	Major Weakness	Unknown
11. **Vision:** A clear organizational vision exists and is widely supported by board and staff. The vision is inspiring and communicates the impact the organization wants to have in the world and what it will take to make that vision happen.	❑	❑	❑	❑	❑
12. **Purpose:** The organization's mission statement clearly articulates an agreed-on purpose—the ultimate result the organization is working to achieve. This purpose serves as a guidepost for organizational decisions.	❑	❑	❑	❑	❑
13. **Values:** Shared and explicit values and beliefs serve as the foundation on which the organization and its members do their work.	❑	❑	❑	❑	❑
14. **Strategic Plan:** A three- to five-year strategic plan that highlights core programs and organizational strategies is in place and guides the allocation of. resources.	❑	❑	❑	❑	❑
15. **Annual Plan:** Annual workplans exist for programs and administration; these workplans relate to the strategic plan.	❑	❑	❑	❑	❑

Elements of an Effectively Managed Organization (Continued)

	Major Asset	Moderate Asset	Moderate Weakness	Major Weakness	Unknown
16. Measures of Success/Impact: Programs have measurable goals relating to quantity, quality, and impact of work.	☐	☐	☐	☐	☐
17. Ongoing Planning and Evaluation: There is a commitment to ongoing planning and evaluation by the board and staff as an essential part of how the organization does its work. Plans are reviewed regularly and modified as needed to reflect trends in the environment, current and future client needs, and the organization's capacity to meet those needs.	☐	☐	☐	☐	☐

Comments/specific recommendations for administrative capacity—planning: Questions 11 to 17

Administrative Capacity: Human Resources and Leadership

	Major Asset	Moderate Asset	Moderate Weakness	Major Weakness	Unknown
18. Staffing: The organization attracts and retains staff members who have the appropriate experience and expertise to perform their duties well.	☐	☐	☐	☐	☐
19. Compensation: Benefits and paid compensation are competitive for the positions and relevant market(s)	☐	☐	☐	☐	☐

(continues)

Elements of an Effectively Managed Organization *(Continued)*

Administrative Capacity: Human Resources and Leadership

	Major Asset	Moderate Asset	Moderate Weakness	Major Weakness	Unknown
20. Policies and Procedures: Human Resources policies and procedures are appropriately documented, current with funding, regulatory, and legal requirements.	❏	❏	❏	❏	❏
21. Job Descriptions: Job descriptions are current (within a year), accurate, and provide an important reference point for assignment of responsibilities, compensation, and performance evaluation.	❏	❏	❏	❏	❏
22. Supervision and Professional Development: Employees receive appropriate supervision, annual performance reviews, needed training, and professional development opportunities.	❏	❏	❏	❏	❏
23. Workload: Workloads for all staff members are reasonable and manageable.	❏	❏	❏	❏	❏
24. Structure: A current, written organization chart exists and is used appropriately.	❏	❏	❏	❏	❏

Elements of an Effectively Managed Organization *(Continued)*

	Major Asset	Moderate Asset	Moderate Weakness	Major Weakness	Unknown
25. **Volunteer Management:** Responsibility for volunteer recruitment and management is clearly and appropriately assigned, and volunteers are integrated as an important part of the overall workforce of the organization.	❑	❑	❑	❑	❑
26. **Leadership:** Managerial leaders support shared values, attend to results, and lead by example where appropriate.	❑	❑	❑	❑	❑
27. **Support:** Managerial leaders take responsibility for creating an environment in which all personnel feel supported and motivated to produce quality results.	❑	❑	❑	❑	❑
28. **Shared Leadership:** Leadership is not overly dependent on one person but is a shared function among many people.	❑	❑	❑	❑	❑

Comments/specific recommendations for administrative capacity—human resources and leadership: Questions 18 to 28

(continues)

Elements of an Effectively Managed Organization *(Continued)*

Administrative Capacity: Culture and Communication

	Major Asset	Moderate Asset	Moderate Weakness	Major Weakness	Unknown
29. Culture: The organizational culture (e.g., patterns of norms, ways of interacting and relating) is in keeping with the work of the organization and is generally considered functional by staff, board, and volunteers.	❏	❏	❏	❏	❏
30. Decision Making: It is clear who makes what decisions and who has input into the decisions on all levels of the agency.	❏	❏	❏	❏	❏
31. Communication: Communication is clear, and the flow of information is adequate and efficient in the agency.	❏	❏	❏	❏	❏
32. Conflict: Conflicts are resolved constructively.	❏	❏	❏	❏	❏
33. Teamwork: There is a strong commitment among all employees to work effectively as a team. Team spirit within and among departments is encouraged and supported, and there is effective coordinated services among departments.	❏	❏	❏	❏	❏

Elements of an Effectively Managed Organization *(Continued)*

	Major Asset	Moderate Asset	Moderate Weakness	Major Weakness	Unknown
34. Meetings: Meetings in the agency are well-organized and well-rung, with the right people in attendance and at the appropriate frequency (neither too many, nor too few)	☐	☐	☐	☐	☐
35. Interdepartment Communications: People across the organization communicate well with one another.	☐	☐	☐	☐	☐

Comments/specific recommendations for administrative capacity—culture and communication: Questions 29 to 35

Administrative Capacity: Infrastructure—Technology and Facilities

	Major Asset	Moderate Asset	Moderate Weakness	Major Weakness	Unknown
36. Computer Hardware and Software: Staff members have enough computers and related software, printers, etc.	☐	☐	☐	☐	☐
37. Information Technology: Systems are networked; all staff members have e-mail access; an Internet/web presence exists.	☐	☐	☐	☐	☐
38. Use of Technology: Sufficient training and support exist to facilitate staff use of information technology.	☐	☐	☐	☐	☐

(continues)

Elements of an Effectively Managed Organization *(Continued)*

Administrative Capacity: Infrastructure—Technology and Facilities

	Major Asset	Moderate Asset	Moderate Weakness	Major Weakness	Unknown
39. Electronic Communications: The organization uses computers, e-mail, and electronic media to streamline communications.	☐	☐	☐	☐	☐
40. Web site: The Web site is consistent with the communications strategy of the organization; Web site is updated regularly and is accurate.	☐	☐	☐	☐	☐
41. Equipment: Equipment (e.g., copiers, fax machines, phone) is appropriate to meet the needs of the organization. Any special equipment (e.g., transportation, kitchen, recreation) is maintained and appropriate to uses.	☐	☐	☐	☐	☐
42. Facilities: Facilities are in good repair, current with all code/ADA etc. requirements, and used appropriately. There is sufficient office space to accommodate the needs of volunteer and paid staff members and constituencies/clients.	☐	☐	☐	☐	☐
43. IT/Facilities Management: Sufficient management resources are devoted to planning, managing, and trouble-shooting IT/facilities/equipment.	☐	☐	☐	☐	☐

Comments/specific recommendations for administrative capacity—technology and facilities: Questions 36 to 43

Elements of an Effectively Managed Organization (Continued)

Board Governance

	Major Asset	Moderate Asset	Moderate Weakness	Major Weakness	Unknown
44. Board/Staff Partnership: There is an effective working relationship between the board and the staff.	☐	☐	☐	☐	☐
45. Lines of Communication: There are clearly defined channels of communication between the board and the staff, and they are followed.	☐	☐	☐	☐	☐
46. Membership: The board has members who: • Are committed to the mission	☐	☐	☐	☐	☐
• Have the skills and experience the organization needs	☐	☐	☐	☐	☐
• Are able to represent those groups involved in the organization's work	☐	☐	☐	☐	☐

(continues)

Elements of an Effectively Managed Organization *(Continued)*

Board Governance

	Major Asset	Moderate Asset	Moderate Weakness	Major Weakness	Unknown
47. Effective Governance and Management Oversight: The board provides effective governance and delegates management to an executive director (or equivalent CEO), evaluates the performance of the executive director annually, and works collaboratively with the executive director.	☐	☐	☐	☐	☐
48. Support of the Staff: The board offers support and encouragement—and assistance when asked—to the staff.	☐	☐	☐	☐	☐

Comments/specific recommendations for board governance: Questions 44 to 48

General—Programs and Services

	Excellent	Good	Fair	Poor	Unknown
49. Overall, my rating of the organization's programs and services is:	☐	☐	☐	☐	☐

Why did you give the rating that you did? What changes would you recommend we make that would either maintain the quality of the programs and services or improve the quality?

Elements of an Effectively Managed Organization *(Continued)*

General—Administrative, Financial, Governance

	Highly Effective	Moderately Effective	Somewhat Effective	Not Effective	Unknown
50. Overall, my rating of the organization's administrative, financial, and governance capacity:	☐	☐	☐	☐	☐

Why did you give the rating that you did? What changes would you recommend we make that would either maintain the the effectiveness of administrative, financial or governance or improve their effectiveness?

(Note: The following financial capacity questions are only to be answered by management.)

Finances: Financial Management
The following questions are for managers and program directors only.

	Major Asset	Moderate Asset	Moderate Weakness	Major Weakness	Unknown
51. **Budgeting:** The organization has an effective budgeting process, including a program-centered approach to budgeting.	☐	☐	☐	☐	☐
52. **Monitoring:** Program managers are involved in the budgeting process, receive financial reports, and update projections on a regular basis.	☐	☐	☐	☐	☐

Comments/specific recommendations for finances—financial management: Questions 51 to 52

(continues)

Elements of an Effectively Managed Organization (Continued)

Finances: Fund Development

The following questions are for executive director and finance/development staff only.

	Major Asset	Moderate Asset	Moderate Weakness	Major Weakness	Unknown
53. **Resources:** There are sufficient resources to sustain the organization for the immediate future.	☐	☐	☐	☐	☐
54. **Diverse Funding:** Funding is attracted from multiple sources.	☐	☐	☐	☐	☐
55. **Long-Term Fundraising Plan:** The organization has a realistic fund development plan for long-term financial stability.	☐	☐	☐	☐	☐
56. **Annual Fundraising Plan:** Staff and board members have agreed to a written fundraising plan based on the annual plan. The fundraising plan has specific goals and its own budget.	☐	☐	☐	☐	☐
57. **Performance:** Fund development is consistently achieved close to target levels.	☐	☐	☐	☐	☐

(continues)

Elements of an Effectively Managed Organization *(Continued)*

	Major Asset	Moderate Asset	Moderate Weakness	Major Weakness	Unknown
58. Roles and Responsibilities: Staff and board resource development roles and responsibilities are clear; people have the necessary fundraising skills; and distribution of work is effective in getting the work of fund development accomplished.	☐	☐	☐	☐	☐
59. Tracking of Donations: The organization has effective record keeping to track and acknowledge donations and meet grantors' reporting requirements.	☐	☐	☐	☐	☐

Comments/specific recommendations for finances—fund development: Questions 53 to 59

Finances: Financial Management
The following questions are for executive director and finance/development staff only.

	Major Asset	Moderate Asset	Moderate Weakness	Major Weakness	Unknown
60. Financial Reporting: There are effective financial reporting and monitoring systems in place to: • Track expenses on a program as well as funder basis.	☐	☐	☐	☐	☐
• Ensure that revenue and expenses are monitored.	☐	☐	☐	☐	☐

(continues)

Elements of an Effectively Managed Organization *(Continued)*

Finances: Financial Management
The following questions are for executive director and finance/development staff only.

	Major Asset	Moderate Asset	Moderate Weakness	Major Weakness	Unknown
• Ensure that timely and accurate financial reports are generated.	☐	☐	☐	☐	☐
• Assess whether financial performance ratios reflect a degree of financial stability.	☐	☐	☐	☐	☐
• Ensure that the board has timely and accurate financial reports needed to provide fiscal oversight.	☐	☐	☐	☐	☐
• Comply with all federal, state, and local regulations, including annual reporting requirements and payment of withheld taxes.	☐	☐	☐	☐	☐
61. **Compliance:** The annual audit is completed in a timely manner; the form 990 and other required annual information returns are filed by the deadline. Reports to funders are filed on a timely basis.	☐	☐	☐	☐	☐

Elements of an Effectively Managed Organization *(Continued)*

	Major Asset	Moderate Asset	Moderate Weakness	Major Weakness	Unknown
62. Asset protection: There is a clear separation of financial staff's duties, and an up-to-date system of internal control exists.	☐	☐	☐	☐	☐
63. Accounting: Paperwork is filed on a timely basis; filing systems are adequate; information is secured, computerized systems are adequate, and there is sufficient accounting staff to meet accounting needs.	☐	☐	☐	☐	☐

Comments/specific recommendations for finances—financial management: Questions 60 to 63

Self-Assessment of
Board of Directors*

Please rate your assessment of the board of directors' performance in each category as:

4 = Outstanding   3 = Good   2 = Fair   1 = Poor   DNK = Do Not Know

Evaluation of how the board as a whole fullfills its *governance* roles and responsibilities	OUTSTANDING	GOOD	FAIR	POOR	DO NOT KNOW
Mission: The board understands the mission and purpose of the organization.	4	3	2	1	DNK
Legal: The board ensures compliance with federal, state, and local regulations and fulfillment of contractual obligations, including payment of payroll taxes and filing of required reports.	4	3	2	1	DNK
Financial: The board safeguards assets from misuse, waste, and embezzlement through financial oversight and making sure that effective internal controls are in place.	4	3	2	1	DNK

*Source: "Boardroom Dancing: How to Lead and When to Follow," a seminar by Jude Kaye, and J. Masaoka, *The Best of the Board Café* (St. Paul, MN: Amherst H. Wilder Foundation, 2003).

Evaluation of how the board as a whole fullfills its *governance* roles and responsibilities (Continued)	OUTSTANDING	GOOD	FAIR	POOR	DO NOT KNOW
CEO: The board monitors and evaluates the performance of the CEO on a regular basis and delegates the day-to-day management to the CEO.	4	3	2	1	DNK
Planning: The board participates with staff in determining program and administrative strategies and overall long-term priorities.	4	3	2	1	DNK
Programs: The board approves an annual operating plan, monitors implementation, and makes sure there are program evaluations to measure impact.	4	3	2	1	DNK
Efficiency and Impact: The board ensures a realistic budget that maximizes use of resources.	4	3	2	1	DNK
Financial Viability: The board makes sure that the organization has an overall fundraising strategy to support the effective delivery of services and monitors the implementation of the funding plan.	4	3	2	1	DNK
Policies: The board approves personnel and other policies and reviews them periodically to ensure they are up to date and relevant.	4	3	2	1	DNK
Evaluation: The board regularly assesses whether the organization is achieving its purpose (effectiveness), at what cost (efficiency), and is meeting the needs of the community.	4	3	2	1	DNK

Overall, how well do you think the board does in fulfilling its governance responsibilities?

❑ Outstanding   ❑ Good   ❑ Fair   ❑ Poor

What recommendations and/or comments do you have regarding any of your ratings in terms of board governance?

4 = Outstanding   3 = Good   2 = Fair   1 = Poor   DNK = Do Not Know

Evaluation regarding board composition and processes in place that support *board effectiveness* (Continued)	OUTSTANDING	GOOD	FAIR	POOR	DO NOT KNOW
Board members clearly understand their board responsibilities and fulfill them.	4	3	2	1	DNK
The board has a clear policy on the responsibilities of board members in fundraising.	4	3	2	1	DNK
The board currently contains an appropriate range of expertise and diversity to make it an effective governing body.	4	3	2	1	DNK
The board ensures effective governance through evaluation of the board itself, committees, and its leadership, and ensures the board's own continuity.	4	3	2	1	DNK
The board actively recruits, orients, and trains new board members, and removes those members who are not fulfilling their agreed-on responsibilities.	4	3	2	1	DNK
The board encourages and supports individuals to treat fellow board members and staff with trust, respect, and understanding.	4	3	2	1	DNK
Board and committee meetings are interesting, well run, and effective.	4	3	2	1	DNK
The board has the necessary effective board leadership—an individual and/or group of individuals who are willing and able to help the board fulfill its governance and support functions.	4	3	2	1	DNK

Overall, how well do you think the board is doing in terms of clarity of roles, board composition, evaluation of self, leadership, and encouraging meeting and decision-making processes that ensure that the board's work gets done?

❏ Outstanding   ❏ Good   ❏ Fair   ❏ Poor

What recommendations and/or comments do you have regarding any of your ratings in terms of board processes and structures?

4 = Outstanding   3 = Good   2 = Fair   1 = Poor   DNK = Do Not Know

Evaluation of the fulfillment of *your support responsibilities*	OUTSTANDING	GOOD	FAIR	POOR	DO NOT KNOW
Fundraising: I participate with staff in raising adequate financial and other resources.	4	3	2	1	DNK
Public Relations: I act as an ambassador to the community on behalf of the organization and its clients.	4	3	2	1	DNK
Volunteerism: As needed, I volunteer to assist staff and/or recruit new volunteers.	4	3	2	1	DNK
Advises staff in areas of expertise: I act as a sounding board for the executive director and other executive staff.	4	3	2	1	DNK
Credibility: I lend my name and personal reputation to the organization to use in brochures, grant proposals, and other marketing materials.	4	3	2	1	DNK
I understand and fulfill my governance and support responsibilities as a member of the board.	4	3	2	1	DNK
I am knowledgeable about the organization's mission, programs, and services.	4	3	2	1	DNK
I come prepared to board and committee meetings and follow through on commitments.	4	3	2	1	DNK

How well do you think you do in fulfilling your support responsibilities (e.g., fundraising, public relations, volunteerism, advising as needed, adding credibility, understanding roles, knowledgeable about programs and services, and following through on commitments)?

❏ Outstanding   ❏ Good   ❏ Fair   ❏ Poor

How well do you think your colleagues do in fulfilling their support responsibilities (e.g., fundraising, public relations, volunteerism, advising as needed, adding credibility, understanding roles, knowledgeable about programs and services, and following through on commitments)?

❏ Outstanding   ❏ Good   ❏ Fair   ❏ Poor

What recommendations and/or comments do you have regarding any of your ratings in terms of either your or your board colleagues' fulfillment of support responsibilities?

Sample Techniques Used in Client Needs Assessment and Program Evaluation

Formal program evaluation is a highly developed field with an extensive body of literature. Evaluation of major programs such as Head Start can cost millions of dollars and take place over many years. Although program evaluation is important to agencies in the strategic planning process, a full discussion of program evaluation is beyond the scope of this workbook. Because program evaluation often involves tracking clients over time, an agency that does not have an existing program evaluation process will likely be unable to conduct a significant evaluation during the relatively short period during which the strategic plan is developed. Here is a sampling of techniques used in client needs assessment and program evaluations.

WRITTEN SURVEY OF CLIENTS RELATED TO CLIENT SATISFACTION

One of the questions asked in a written survey of parents of middle school students who participated in a program for at-risk students was:

Would you recommend this program to other parents?

❑ Yes

❑ No

❑ Not sure

Two of the questions asked in a written survey of participants in a CPR class, conducted at the conclusion of the class, were:

How would you rate your confidence in your ability to deal with an emergency first-aid situation?

	Not at all confident			Very confident	
Before the class?	1	2	3	4	5
After the class?	1	2	3	4	5

Was this class fun?

WRITTEN SURVEY OF CLIENTS RELATED TO OUTCOMES

The following question was asked on a written survey mailed to clients six months after they had completed a four-session job-seeking course:

Please indicate your job status at the time you took the course and today:

My job status:	Time of the course	Now
Employed full-time	❑	❑
Employed part-time but wanting full-time or more work	❑	❑
Employed part-time and satisfied with part-time	❑	❑
Unemployed	❑	❑
Full-time student	❑	❑
Part-time student	❑	❑
Other	❑	❑

TELEPHONE SURVEY OF CLIENTS

Three months after attending a new-dads workshop, participants were telephoned and asked the following, among other questions:

Looking back on the workshop, what was the most valuable thing you got out of it? Would you recommend the workshop to other new fathers?

COLLECTION OF OBJECTIVE DATA

As part of an evaluation of an elementary school garden project, the change in science grades and CTBS scores of students participating in the program were compared with changes in grades and scores of students who did not participate in the program.

After Neighborhood Recycling Week activities, the total weight of recycled materials brought to the recycling center each week was compared with the total weight received before Recycling Week.

EXAMPLE OF COMBINING OBJECTIVE DATA AND TELEPHONE SURVEY

After 120,000 booklets on senior services were distributed in a local community, telephone interviews were conducted with a random sample of the households that had received booklets. One of the questions asked was:

Have you recently received a booklet on services to seniors available in our neighborhood? [If not: Is it possible that someone else in your household received the booklet and you weren't aware of it?]

At the same time, calls to the Senior Central Information Line were tracked before and after distribution of the booklet. The program found that although only a minority of phone respondents remembered having received the booklet, calls to the Information Line took a dramatic jump upward in the two weeks following the booklet distribution.

FOCUS GROUP

In a focus group, approximately 5 to 12 individuals are brought together to discuss aspects of the program. In an evaluation of an awards program made to unsung community heroes, past recipients of the award were brought together for a luncheon at which questions were posed to the group by an outside facilitator. One of the questions asked was:

Looking back on receiving the award, which aspects of the award had the greatest impact on you? For example, was it the cash award? The awards ceremony? Articles in the newspaper about the award? Other aspects?

A focus group for a program training new board members of arts organizations was held one evening. Among the questions asked were:

Of the speakers you heard in the program, which ones do you remember? What sticks in your mind about any one of them or what they said?

Did you like having a light dinner available at the beginning of the sessions? Some people have said they would have preferred having the sessions earlier and shorter, whereas others have said they found the dinner a great opportunity to meet others. What are your reactions?

INTERVIEWS WITH COMPETITORS AND POTENTIAL COLLABORATORS

An AIDS organization serving Asians/Pacific Islanders with HIV conducted interviews with selected leaders from both other AIDS organizations and from Asian/Pacific Islander community organizations. Two of the interview questions for those from other AIDS organizations were:

When Asian or Pacific Islander clients come to your agency for AIDS services, do you ever refer them to the AAA agency? Under what circumstances, and why? Why not?

If there were just one thing you could change about the AAA agency, what would it be?

In an interview with the head of a Filipino neighborhood association, the following question was posed:

Are members of your association generally aware of the AAA agency's services? When AIDS comes up, is the AAA agency mentioned? What is said about the AAA agency? What other agencies are mentioned and what is said about them?

TESTS

Post-test. In a post-test, participants in a learning program are given a test at the end of the program to evaluate whether they have learned the new knowledge or skill. In an empowerment program for high school girls, participants learned how to change car tires. At the end of the program, each girl had to change a tire by herself, observed by the instructor and two other participants.

Pre- and post-test. The same test is given to participants before and after the learning program. A workshop that trains hospice volunteers asked the following question in a written test given both before the workshop and at the conclusion of the workshop:

Name three precautions that should be taken by hospice volunteers related to touching patients:

1.

2.

3.

Observation

Open-ended observation. In an evaluation of an infant care training program for mothers, staff members go to the homes of children whose mothers had participated in the program and observed home life, including physical environment, interaction between mother and child, safety, and other issues.

Focused observation. In a focused evaluation done during the second year of the infant safety program, staff members visited homes with checklists, including the following:

• Is there a working smoke detector present in the home?

• Did you observe electric outlet covers in place? Did you observe any electric outlets at child height without outlet covers?

• Was there a pillow present in the infant's sleeping area?

Conducting Focus Groups*

Focus groups can be a key part of the information-gathering phase of strategic planning. By gathering the ideas, thoughts, and perspectives of individuals who represent each of your stakeholders, you achieve many benefits:

- The ideas, perspectives, and wisdom of those who are key to your future success are gained.
- You have many different concepts, or takes, on the future and future needs to add to those of the management, staff, and board.
- The summary report, which includes many of the comments of those interviewed, gives the board members and staff an incredible amount of information about your stakeholders, what they value, what needs they see, and what ideas they have for your future. It is a great learning document and helps your core group get to hear the stakeholders' perspective and vision (i.e., how they see your future role in the community). Having this information at hand, read, and discussed before creating the vision statement or priorities enables the strategic planning group to see options and possible futures and choose those that are a good match for the needs of your local community.

Focus groups allow people to add to the thoughts of others, interacting in a way that gives you a lot of insight and ideas. This approach takes more time and logistics, but it is often the format of choice for the best and most interesting information yield.

---

*The material in this appendix was developed by Jan Cohen. We thank her for allowing us to include it in this workbook.

Suggestions for Facilitators of Focus Groups

Focus Group Planning Advice

- An experienced moderator or facilitator, who can manage the group so everyone participates, is crucial to success.

- Focus groups should be 60 to 90 minutes in length, but never exceed 90 minutes in length; five to seven questions, with follow-up questions, is adequate to obtain the information needed and not impose on the participants' time.

- Aim for at least 8 but not more than 14 people in each group; 10 to 12 is ideal. Expect fewer people to attend than say they will come. This varies greatly from population to population, but everyone who commits seldom shows up. Therefore, invite 10 to 20 percent more people than you actually need to each group. However, have enough chairs available in case everyone shows up.

- Plan to conduct at least two sessions with people from each targeted stakeholder group. (For example, if you are doing research for needs for day care in a San Francisco neighborhood, you might schedule three parent groups, in English, for parents between ages 25 to 35; two groups in Spanish for parents between ages 25 to 35; two groups of teen parents; two groups of parents who are over 35; possibly two groups of parents of children with special needs; and two groups of employer representatives.)

- Include people who have used the service/product/attended the program and liked it, as well as those for whom it didn't work (they were not satisfied/it didn't meet their needs/interests) and those who never came/never tried it but are a part of the targeted group. You can mix dissatisfied/satisfied/never users in one group. As a general rule, don't combine teens and adults in one group.

- To increase the focus group participation rate, you might offer participants an incentive, such as lunch or a cash payment. You can also schedule the session at a time when these people might already be together for some other purpose (e.g., meeting, luncheon, picking up kids).

- When working with groups for whom English is not their first language, consider utilizing a native speaker to facilitate, rather than using an interpreter, if possible. Have a discussion with this facilitator, who is fluent in this language and culturally competent, before the session to plan how you are going to work together. Give that person the questions in advance so they can be translated correctly into the appropriate language.

- If there will be a recorder, have a discussion in advance about whether they will be taking notes or recording on flip charts. Give that person the questions in advance or at least at the beginning of the session.

- If you are going to facilitate and record on flip charts simultaneously, utilize a backup note taker or tape recorder. (If you tape the session, you can only do this with written permission of participants.) Board members or other volunteers are encouraged to be note takers. It gives them a chance to listen to the customers directly, while being too busy writing to comment or respond to them.

- Always debrief the session with the note taker and cross-check/ consolidate notes and flip charts to be sure all comments from all participants are included.

Drafting the Questions

- Keep questions simple. Use informal/casual language and enthusiasm. Don't use jargon, abbreviations/acronyms, or other insider language. Choose words the participants might use.

- Use open-ended questions to which participants can respond without any pressure toward specific answers or direction.

- Focus on unmet wants and needs rather than an evaluation of what currently exists. You are not looking for customer feedback on staff or the current quality of services from this organization.

- Avoid asking "why," but ask them to say more, to elaborate.

  Examples:

  ○ "How might an organization help you in dealing with your immigration problems? Exactly how would that work to best meet your needs?"

  ○ "What would you use of the children's health services that are currently offered?" Tell me about what would make it better for you? What hours should it be open, what programs or other features would you like, if they were offered?"

- "If you were in charge of this program, what changes would you make so that more people would sign up (or "attend," "choose this")?" "How would that work?" or "So you would offer XXX. And what other changes would you make or new things would you add?"

- Be cautious about giving examples, so that you aren't leading participants in any way. Participants, in trying to please you, will be inclined to say positive things about current strategies and go down the path of any hints you give.

Convening the Focus Group Session

1. The executive director should welcome the group, thank them for coming, explain why this format was chosen, and explain why they were selected to be invited to this group. He or she should also say a bit about the nonprofit organization, this strategic planning process, and why their input is needed (their immense value to the planning process). This part should take no more than six to eight minutes. Then he or she can introduce the facilitator and note taker.

   OR

   Introduce yourself and your note taker. Welcome the group. Thank them for coming. Say a bit about the nonprofit, this strategic planning process, and why the participants' input is needed (their immense value to the planning process). Explain your relationship to the process, including the fact that you are not on the staff or the board).

2. Ensure that they understand that your role as facilitator is to gently steer the discussion so that the organization obtains the benefit of their experience and opinions about what would be desirable for themselves and others similar to them ("your friends").

3. Remind the participants of the objective of the focus group:
   - To understand service users/program attendees/audiences and what they might want or need that would work better for them than what is available
   - To benefit from informed analyses of trends combined with their individual thoughts and ideas about wants/needs/services

4. Ask participants to respond to some previously prepared questions that are key to this planning process. Let them know that this is brainstorming and all ideas are welcome. "Don't screen or be shy about what might really work for you or your friends (or clients)."

5. Reiterate the task at hand, which is to think about their experiences and those others have told them about, then to imagine how services or programs "might really work, if we could make any changes you want, to meet current and future needs."

6. Invite participants to briefly introduce themselves.

7. Promise anonymity of all comments, both in summary discussions with staff and board and in all written reports (i.e., no one comment will be attributed to an individual). Ask for their agreement to keep the discussion confidential as well.

8. Assure them that there will be time for their general comments and questions. Mention that it is really critical to the planning process that we cover all of the prepared questions first. Ask that they respect this agenda, so that the strategic planning team can gather and utilize as many ideas and as much input as possible.

9. Ask the participants to be sure to speak one at a time, so that the notes from the group will be comprehensive and clear. "We don't want to miss any ideas, because you never know which idea will be the seed of an important service or change to our programs."

10. Thank people for their ideas as you go on to each next question.

11. Don't let one or two people dominate the group (see next page on difficult behaviors). Your goal is to capture everone's thoughts and ideas. Remind them of the importance of gathering everyone's opinion. "We need and encourage everyone to speak." Tell people that you may not call on those who have had a chance to say something in response to a question, until others have had an opportunity to share their suggestions. Then enforce this rule.

12. Record their actual language (i.e., exact expressions used) on flip charts and recheck to be sure you got it right (or have the entire session recorded and transcribed afterward).

Concluding the Focus Group Session

1. Thank the participants for investing their valuable time and thoughtfulness in the process. Express the fact that the organization really

appreciates the time, energy, thought, and great ideas they shared today. "You are really helping this organization to hear what the community needs."

2. If you notice some concerns, strong feelings, or passion in the participants, consider acknowledging that this session has brought up a lot of emotional feelings in addition to ideas for future services and programs. Thank them again for their energy and assure them that the staff can get back to them about some of their feelings or concerns. Then be sure before these individuals leave that you get their names and phone numbers. Make sure that this information gets to the executive director within 24 hours, so that participants can be contacted with whatever interventions are appropriate.

3. Assure them that their comments and ideas will be taken into consideration in designing the future services and products and programs of this organization.

4. Remind them and reassure them that all comments from all focus groups go into one consolidated report. All identifying information will be deleted and all comments made anonymous before being presented to the staff and board.

5. Share an overview of the planning process timeline and milestones. Let them know when, or if, they will hear from the organization again and in what form (e.g., "A summary report will be sent to you" or "You will be invited to a presentation of the priorities for future services when the plan is written and approved"). If all they will receive is a thank-you letter, don't lead them on to expect more than this.

TIPS ON HOW TO DEAL WITH CHALLENGING BEHAVIORS

Lead-Ins (or Outs) for Groups in Which a Person Is Dominating the Conversation or Rambling

-   I appreciate the fact that you are so thorough in responding to my question, but now I need to ask you (or others) about . . .

-   You are certainly giving me a lot of information about . . . Thanks, but now let's switch to . . .

- I appreciate your thoughts on that issue, but I really want to get your opinion on some other questions, and I only have a few more minutes.

- I apologize if it seems abrupt, but now I'd like to shift our attention to . . .

- Tell me about . . . (Go on to the next question. Yes, you have interrupted the person!)

- In a group: Stand behind the person and ask if others have had similar experiences.

- You certainly have given me a lot of information on . . . and I appreciate your detail, but now let's deal with an entirely different topic. Or in a group: Now let's give the others a chance to comment on their experience, or give their ideas, etc.

- I need to shift our attention from . . . to the next question. Give me a specific example of . . . (or one of your next questions).

Note: Do not encourage or allow whiners or negative persons to ramble. They frustrate you and everyone else and do not usually give positive input. However, if you can turn their whining into real program/service suggestions from them or others in the group, you may get some very good ideas. Utilize these suggestions, plus other leading statements or questions, to quickly move these people to ideas for changes in services or rotate the questions to other speakers.

Lead-Ins for Groups Where People Need to Be Encouraged to Participate

- At the beginning, as part of the introduction, let the group know the following:
  - We need and encourage everyone to participate.
  - Every opinion is important.
  - You don't have to agree. It's okay to disagree, but we really need your thoughts.

- Use round-robin techniques to go around the room and get everyone's opinion on a question (but don't use this technique on the first question).

- Smile, look at the person, and casually ask things like: What do you think would be really helpful? What might work better for you? If it was up to you, how would you provide (or offer or design) this service? Or ask similar questions to bring them out. However, don't walk toward the person as you ask these questions because it is too intimidating.

- Always nod or thank people for each suggestion, reminding them periodically about how helpful they are being (and smile while looking all around the group so people know you mean it).

- Ask follow-up questions, but don't interrogate or put people on the spot. Make the question casual with wording such as, "How do you think it might work better for you and your friends with similar needs or others who use the service or attend this program?"

Lead-Ins to Deal with Whiners and Negative Comments and Turn Them Around

- Acknowledge that this is an issue for this person.
- This is the place where we identify issues but not the place where we get the answers. We will be sure to have people get back to you.

Techniques and Tools for Managing Group Process: A Toolbox of Meeting Process Tools and Techniques*

Because so much of the work of strategic planning takes place in meetings, here are some meeting process tools and techniques to help you have more effective meetings.[1]

SETTING UP MEETINGS FOR SUCCESS

Creating Effective Agendas

Agendas for all meetings should be prepared and distributed to all participants ahead of time. Agendas should include the following information (see Exhibit G.1):

- Date and time frame of meeting
- Location of meeting
- Outcome(s) of meeting
- List of meeting attendees

---

*This is by no means a complete list of all the meeting process tools and techniques you could use. For additional help in running meetings, the following three books are recommended: Michael Doyle and Davis Straus, *How to Make Meetings Work* (New York: Jove Books, 1983); Roger M. Schwarz, *The Skilled Facilitator—New and Revised* (San Francisco: Jossey-Bass, 2002); and Sam Kaner, *Facilitator's Guide to Participatory Decision-Making* (Philadelphia: New Society Publishers, 1996).

- List of materials people should bring to the meeting
- Detailed proposed agenda

Meeting Agreements

To ensure successful meetings, it is a good idea to get the group to agree on basic meeting agreements (ground rules) as to how to work together. These meeting agreements might include the following guidelines:

- Listen as an ally.
- Meetings will start and end on time.
- No side conversations will be held.
- Focus on issues, not personalities.
- Be specific and use examples.
- Share all relevant information.
- Use short, succinct statements.
- Keep to the point, and keep the discussion focused.
- Focus on interests, not positions.
- No interruptions.
- Okay to disagree constructively.
- All members should participate fully.
- Seek first to understand, then to be understood.
- Work to create decisions you can support.
- The past has a vote, but it doesn't have veto power.

Clarify Roles and Responsibilities for the Meeting

Make sure there is clarity about who is going to facilitate the meetings, who needs to be present at the meetings, and how information is going to be recorded (minutes). Clarify in advance who makes decisions and how decisions are to be made; those involved in the planning process should know in advance whether they have the power to make a decision or whether they are being asked for their input. Decide whether it is most effective for the president of the board, chair of the planning committee, or executive director to run the meeting, or whether it is appropriate and useful to bring in an outside facilitator.

EXHIBIT G.1	EXAMPLE OF DETAILED PROPOSED AGENDA		

Agenda Topic	Time Allocated	Process to Be Used	Personnel Responsible
History profile	3:00–3:30 P.M.	Presentation	Executive director
Previous strategies	3:30–4:00 P.M.	Brainstorm list Discuss prior and current effectiveness	All
External stakeholder involvement	4:00–4:45 P.M.	Brainstorm list of who to involve in the planning process Discuss what questions they should be asked, and how to best gather that information	All
Next steps, personnel responsible, and by when	4:45–5:00 P.M.	List and agree	All
Evaluation of meeting		What worked Changes for next meeting	All

GENERATING IDEAS: BRAINSTORMING

Brainstorming is a commonly used meeting process. The outcome of brainstorming is to come up with as many ideas as possible within the time allowed. Guidelines for brainstorming include the following:

- During brainstorming, all ideas are okay.
- There should be no discussion of ideas until the brainstorming is complete.
- Build on others' ideas.
- Creativity is encouraged.

EXHIBIT G.2   FLIP CHART

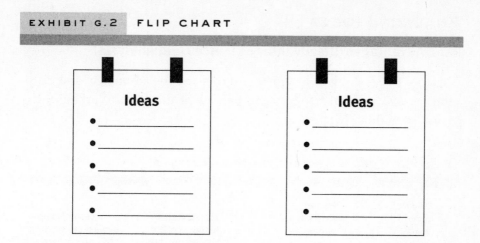

Consider using the round-robin technique as a way of encouraging everyone to speak rather than anyone calling out an idea when they think of it: Go around in a circle and have everyone make one comment on the topic at hand; people have the option of passing. At the end of the round robin, go back to those who have passed and ask if they have anything to add. People who have offered ideas can add additional ideas only after the round robin is completed. It is best to record ideas on a flip chart (see Exhibit G.2) so they can be seen and remembered by everyone on the team.

ORGANIZING IDEAS: SORT BY CATEGORY

After all ideas have been generated, it is sometimes useful to group them into larger categories. The actual process of grouping is usually best done by an individual or small group and then presented back to the larger group for changes and approval. For example, after a group has brainstormed a list of strengths and weaknesses, the meeting leader might suggest that, during the break, the group should sort the ideas into the following categories: program service delivery; program evaluation; staffing and benefits; board (governance); communications and decision making; fund-raising; image/public relations; organizational structure and information systems; other. (*Note:* Sticky notes are a useful tool. Put each idea onto a sticky note and then sort the notes into the groupings).

ANALYZING IDEAS

Rank Advantages/Disadvantages (Force Field Analysis)

This tool (see Exhibit G.3) allows you to assess the advantages and disadvantages of a particular suggestion, or look at the forces working for or against something happening.

EXHIBIT G.3	FORCE FIELD ANALYSIS

Why we should merge +	Why we should not merge −	Forces working for our starting this new program	Forces working against our starting this new program
		⟶	⟵
		⟶	⟵
		⟶	⟵

Evaluate Using Criteria

A criteria grid (see Exhibit G.4) can be used to help analyze an idea based on an agreed-on set of criteria. To use the criteria grid, list and agree on criteria for a successful solution. Then the group evaluates alternative solutions against the criteria. The facilitator might say, "Let's agree on the three major success criteria that will meet our information needs. Then we can check equipment options against the criteria."

PRIORITIZING IDEAS

Assigning an A, B, or C Priority

Use the same process suggested by time-management experts. List all ideas and then record whether the idea is an A, B, or C priority. (A = highest priority/most important; B = moderate priority; C = lowest priority/least important). The colored stick-on dots sold in most stationery stores are very helpful: Give everyone some red, blue, and green

EXHIBIT G.4   CRITERIA GRID

Criteria

		1	2	3
Alternatives	A			
	B			
	C			

dots. The red dots represent an A priority (most important); blue dots represent a B priority (something to consider, but not the highest priority); and green dots represent a C priority (it's a nice idea, but probably not all that important in relation to A and B). To make sure that not everything gets considered an A priority, you might give people an equal number of red, blue, and green dots, the total of which adds up to the number of ideas.

Rank Order Technique (Sometimes Known as N/3)

This is a useful tool for narrowing down a large list of ideas. For example, you have just brainstormed a list of 30 different services you are either currently offering or would like to consider offering. How do you quickly conduct a straw poll with a large group to find out which of the services are most important? A quick way to find out which services the group thinks are important is to take the total number of items on your list (N = number of ideas) and divide them by three. Give everyone that number of votes.

For example, with a list of fifteen items, divide 15 by 3, which equals 5. Each person votes for five of his or her highest-priority items. The facilitator would say, "Let's see which of these items have the highest priority for you. There are fifteen different services you could offer, but you will probably not be able to do them all. Let's brainstorm a list of the criteria we should use to choose our top third, and then I will ask each of you to use that list of criteria to select your top five. Okay, so how many selected service A? How many for service B? and so on. Now, let's see which alternatives got the highest votes."

Multivoting or Weighted Voting

Multivoting is a similar tool to N/3, and like N/3, it is used to narrow down lists of ideas generated through brainstorming. Unlike N/3, where individuals are given one vote for each idea, in multivoting individuals are able to assign weights or different values to their votes. For example:

- Each individual has ten total votes, which may be distributed any way he or she chooses on the particular list of ideas being evaluated.

- No particular idea can receive more than four votes from an individual. In other words, one might choose to assign four votes to Choice A, four votes to Choice B, two votes for Choice C, or any other combination as long as he or she does not exceed four on any single choice.

- The ideas being voted are written on flip chart paper. Individuals can then write their vote next to the issue they have chosen (or, each individual can be given ten stick-on dots that he or she could place besides the list of ideas).

- The total number of votes are tallied (see Exhibit G.5). It is best to narrow the list to the top five to eight choices, depending on the size of the list.

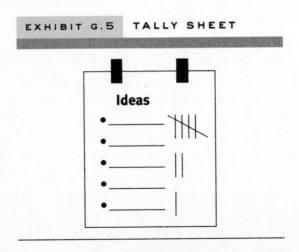

EXHIBIT G.5   TALLY SHEET

Keeping the Meeting Focused: Use of the "Bin" or "Parking Lot"

The *bin* (also known as the *parking lot*) is a way of capturing ideas or issues that arise in a meeting but don't fit into the agenda or the part of the planning process on which the team is working. Rather than discussing these ideas and losing valuable time, or losing the idea by not discussing it at all, the planning committee can create a bin. This is merely a flip chart sheet on which the idea or issue is listed. The sheet is affixed to the wall in subsequent meetings, and issues may be discussed when appropriate or identified as future agenda items. Before the end of this process, all issues listed on the bin should be resolved.

Tips on Using Task Forces

If task forces are assigned to do some of the planning work, it is essential that the planning committee stay engaged to provide necessary guidance to the subgroups and ensure that all of the pieces fit together. The planning committee should provide sufficient guidance to the task force upfront to set up the committee for success. Before the ad hoc committees start their work, clarify membership and roles of committee members. The primary requirement for membership is knowledge about the topic and/or interest in the topic and a willingness to become knowledgeable. Should an ad hoc task force be composed of only board or staff members or a partnership of both board and staff members? Staff members are often the most up-to-date and knowledgeable about a topic; board members may not be as well informed, but they are responsible for keeping the larger picture in mind—what is best for the community and helps the organization achieve its mission while remaining financially viable. As such, the task force's membership might be representatives from both board and staff. In addition, certain task forces might benefit from having nonboard or nonstaff members—interested external stakeholders whose knowledge of the topic would add depth and wisdom to the conversation.

Make sure that each task force is given a mandate as to what it is supposed to accomplish: Generally speaking, most task forces are asked to develop specific recommendation(s) about the topic at hand. These recommendations would then be brought back to a larger group (e.g., an all-staff or all-board retreat) or to a coordinating body such as the strategic planning committee. Rather than presenting one option, some task forces might be asked to discuss and present a few options for consideration, with supporting analysis for the various choices.

For example, a task force might be given the mandate: How should our agency respond to the unmet needs of housing for people with disabilities?

In this example, the task force would be given a series of questions to answer or data to gather (if that data has not already been collected in Phase 3):

- What statistics are available regarding the number of homeless individuals or individuals with substandard housing that is not accessible?
- Who in the county currently provides housing services?
- What type of services do they provide?
- Are there other organizations also facing this issue?
- What legal constraints do we have regarding the provision of housing?
- For any proposals: What are the costs? What are the risks? What are the advantages of moving in this direction? What are the disadvantages?

Regardless of the type of task force, each task force should have (1) a chair whose responsibility it is to call the meetings, facilitate discussions, and make sure that notes are kept and progress is made toward accomplishing the mandate; (2) clear time lines—by what date should they have completed their work? and (3) clarity regarding its decision-making authority—ad hoc planning committee task forces are advisory and not final decision makers.

SAMPLE OF A MEMO CLARIFYING A TASK FORCE MANDATE

Strategic Plan Consumer Demographics Task Force

Goal   Develop recommendations in response to this mandate: Are our consumer demographics changing and, if so, how do we respond to the new consumer base (i.e., best meet the needs of our consumers)?

Task Force Membership   Two board members and three staff members. Committee should consider expanding membership to include interested external stakeholders whose knowledge of the topic would add depth and wisdom to the discussion.

Process   Begin by selecting a task force chair. This person will be responsible for setting up team meetings, facilitating team meetings including setting meeting agendas, and making sure that notes are kept and progress is made toward accomplishing the mandate. Follow the time line as described following in the development of the task force's recommendations.

Time Line

- Hold first task force meeting before December 12, 2003.

- Review mandate; discuss questions and research activities; identify task force member(s) who will be responsible for gathering data needed for analysis in order to develop recommendations for the strategic plan.

- Complete research/data-gathering activities, along with task force meetings to develop recommendations, by January 9, 2004. Submit recommendations to executive director for review and clarification, if necessary, by January 9–16, 2004.

- Task force recommendations submitted to the board of directors at January 24, 2004 daylong strategic planning retreat for review, discussion, and approval.

Questions to Be Answered/Data to Be Gathered by the Task Force

- Have the consumer demographics changed during the last five years?

- If the consumer demographics have changed, why? Is the reason internal (i.e., the nature of our programs or change in programs?) Is the reason external? (i.e., other agencies are narrowing the scope of whom they provide services to)

- If the demographics have changed, what do staff members need to meet the needs of our consumers?

- Do we want to do targeted outreach to specific populations to change the existing demographics?

Outcomes

Based on the answers to these questions and research, develop specific recommendations, with supporting analysis, on how we could best respond to unmet housing needs over the next three to five years. The task force may suggest one option or more than one option. For any of the recommendations, answer the following questions:

- What are the costs?
- What are the risks?
- What are the advantages of moving in this direction?
- What are the disadvantages?

Sample Possible Recommendation

Our review of five years of consumer demographics shows that there has been a 40 percent increase in the number of consumers with mental health disabilities, partly because mental health agencies in our area have narrowed eligibility for their services to individuals and our eligibility criteria is much broader. To better serve this population, service staff needs training. Cost should average $200 per staff person and should include time off to attend trainings off-site as needed. The advantage is that staff will be better equipped, and more comfortable, when handing the complex issues that are more often associated with persons who have mental disabilities. The disadvantage is that there is a possibility that by staff being better trained to assist this target population, we would continue to see an increase in services to this group.

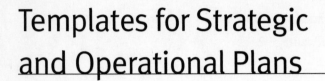

Templates for Strategic and Operational Plans

Strategic Plan Formats Strategy with List of Priorities

Strategy:

Background/Commentary:

Long-Term Priorities:

1.

2.

3.

4.

5.

Strategic Plan Formats Goal with Long-Range and Short-Range Objectives

Goal:

Background/Commentary:

What do we want to have accomplished in the next two to five years?	Intermediate milestones	What do we want to accomplish this upcoming year?	Measures of success, feedback, and evaluation mechanisms	Who is responsible?	By when?

Annual Operating Plan Format Strategic Plan Goal with Short-Range Objectives and Implementation Plan

Strategic plan goal:

Strategic plan objective (if applicable):

Annual operating plan objective:

Benchmark(s) and method of measuring success:

Action steps	Personnel responsible	Time frame or by when	Status as of (date)

Feedback mechanisms:

Financial resources required:

External Stakeholders: Process Recommendations and Suggested Questions

Whether interviewing external stakeholders, first identify whether the reason to talk with them is primarily to assess your situation or to build relationships. If the reason is primarily information gathering, a consultant might be utilized to gather that information. If the reason is primarily to build a relationship, the interviewer should be a board or staff member.

INTERVIEWING AN EXTERNAL STAKEHOLDER

- Call the individual, introduce yourself, and explain that the organization is engaged in a strategic planning process and that the interviewee's input into this process would be invaluable. List the questions that you would like him or her to answer.

- Remember, you want to limit the number of questions that you ask because most busy people have limited time. You need to estimate how much time it will take to complete the set of questions; be upfront about the amount of time you are expecting the interview to take. The amount of time needed should range from 20 to 45 minutes. Under rare circumstances, the time might extend to an hour or more.

  The estimated time frame depends on the type and number of questions to be asked, and the time needed for the answers. The actual time frame might be more or less than your estimate, but be respectful of the interviewee's schedule—the interview shouldn't take more than 45 minutes, and you should use that time wisely. Ask the person for a convenient date/time to speak with him or her on the phone (you might offer to meet in person with them, if appropriate).

- Make sure you indicate that the input of several individuals or organizations is being sought during the strategic planning process, and that while all of the input will be seriously listened to, differing input and limited resources may mean that not all ideas will be put into the plan.

- If he or she wishes for confidentiality (i.e., no specific comment would be specifically attributed), then offer that confidentiality if it is possible to do so, but be clear that feedback will be included in the overall feedback you and others are getting from other individuals (unless you have come up with some other agreement with the interviewee). After you interview the individual, type up your notes.

- *Follow-up:* Send the people you interview a note thanking them for their participation, and make sure that you close the loop on their participation by sending them either a copy of the strategic plan or an executive summary of the plan once the planning process is completed.

Suggested Format for Writing a Stakeholder Interview

- Name of person interviewed (if confidential, only identify type of stakeholder, such as "major donor")

- Name of interviewer

- Date of interview

- Key points made by person being interviewed

- Interviewer conclusions: Aha! moments, such as suggested strategies or priorities; biggest surprise; most important information gleamed from the interview

- Any other comments/observations

- Optional: Attach detailed notes

Suggested Questions

Following are suggested questions for gathering specific information from all external stakeholders.

Assess an Organization's Situation: Strengths, Weaknesses, Opportunities, and Threats

- What do you think are the organization's strengths and weaknesses?
- What trends do you think are happening in the city, state, and nation that might have a positive or negative impact on the organization? What are the opportunities or threats facing the organization? And how might the organization respond to those trends.
- What do you think are the major obstacles to our organization's success?

Assess Stakeholder Perception of the Delivery of Services in Terms of Quality and Competitive Position

- What do you [or your organization] expect from our organization—what is the criteria you use to judge our performance? How well do we perform against those criteria?
- What do you think are the best ways our organization can help our constituencies? Given the myriad of the programs and projects that we currently offer (provide list if appropriate), are there any that you think we should primarily focus our resources (or are there specific projects and programs that you think we should be emphasizing over the next three years that you think would make a significant impact in our ability to achieve our mission)?
- Who are other groups that are doing similar work? What distinguishes our organization from the competition?
- What are the service gaps that you think might exist for our clients, and what role should we be filling in meeting those gaps? Are there additional or increased programs or services that you think we should be offering if resources were available?
- What do you think our organization should be doing more or less of?
- Who else should we be talking to who could inform our strategic planning process?

Assess Collaboration and Partnerships

- How can our organization best partner or work with you?
- How well do you think our current partnership is going? Are there ways we can increase our work together—or make it work better? How might we work together to accomplish our overlapping missions?
- Are there groups (national, regional, and local) we should be aligning ourselves with to help accomplish our purpose?

Understand How Your Organization Might Best Leverage Your Resources and Garner Additional Support

- How could we better utilize our members and/or the public to become true advocates for our organization?
- Do you have any ideas about how we might increase our visibility and/or improve our image throughout our geographic location?
- How can we get our name out in the community so more people will avail themselves of our services?
- How good do you think we are at positioning ourselves in the political arena? Are there things we should be doing to be able to work with administrations from both political parties? How can we more effectively work with government officials and legislators? Are there some key allies we should be working more closely with?

Following are suggested questions for gathering information from specific types of external stakeholders

Major Donors

- Why did you first get involved with our organization?
- What are the particular projects and programs that are of the most interest to you? (Name or show list of all projects if they are not familiar with all that the organization does.)
- Are there some other projects and programs that you would be interested in having our organization support if resources were available?
- How would you prioritize our possible efforts to raise discretionary endowment funds versus using resources to raise funds for specific

projects? (Depending on the relationship you have, you may or may not ask this question if you are considering starting an endowment fund.)

- What ideas do you have about how we might increase our membership and/or fundraising efforts?
- How do you best like to be communicated with? How might we best keep you informed of our organization's progress?

Foundations

- How do you think our organization is doing? How do you see the organization fitting in the overall service delivery system and what do you think makes our organization unique?
- What are the prospects for funding from your organization? Are there other funders who might be interested in supporting our work? (Ask for names.)
- What do you think are most important issues facing our organization today?
- Who else should we be talking to who could inform our strategic planning process?

Media

- What major issues and challenges are affecting the constituencies served by our organization?
- How would you like us to keep you informed about what is happening in the field?
- Do you have any ideas about how we might increase our visibility? How can we raise our image and name?

Groups that Do Similar Work

Note: Much of this information can be found on the Internet, in IRS Form 990, and in annual reports.

- What services do you offer?
- How are you funded?

- How many clients do you serve?
- How do you measure success?
- How are you structured?
- What are the main challenges you experience in delivering services?
- Where do you see our organization fitting in within the matrix of service providers?

Selected References

Barry, Bryan W. *Strategic Planning Workbook for Nonprofit Organizations*. St. Paul, MN: Amherst H. Wilder Foundation, 1986.

Bean, William C. *Strategic Planning that Makes Things Happen*. Amherst, MA: HRD Press, 1993.

Below, Patrick J., George L. Morrisey, and Betty L. Acomb. *The Executive Guide to Strategic Planning*. San Francisco: Jossey-Bass, 1987.

Bielefeld, Wolfgang. "Funding uncertainty and nonprofit strategies in the 1980s." *Nonprofit Management and Leadership* 2, no. 4. San Francisco: Jossey-Bass (Summer 1992).

Bryson, John M. *Strategic Planning for Public and Nonprofit Organizations: A Guide to Strengthening and Sustaining Organizational Achievement*. Rev. ed. San Francisco: Jossey-Bass, 1993.

Doyle, Michael and David Straus. *How to Make Meetings Work*. New York: Jove Books, 1983.

Drucker, Peter F. *Managing the Nonprofit Organization: Principles and Practices*. New York: HarperCollins, 1990.

Hax, Arnold C. and Nicholas S. Majluf. *Strategic Management: An Integrative Perspective*. Englewood Cliffs, NJ: Prentice Hall, 1984.

Kotler, Philip and Alan Andreasen. *Strategic Marketing for Nonprofit Organizations*. 4th ed. Englewood Cliffs, NJ: Prentice Hall, 1991.

Kearns, Kevin P. "Comparative advantage to damage control: clarifying strategic issues using SWOT analysis." *Nonprofit Management and Leadership* 3, no. 1. San Francisco: Jossey-Bass (Fall).

McNutt, Paul and Robert W. Backoff. *Strategic Management of Public and Third Sector Organizations*. San Francisco: Jossey-Bass, 1992.

Mintzberg, Henry. *The Rise and Fall of Strategic Planning*. New York: Free Press, 1994.

Nanus, B. *Visionary Leadership: Creating a Compelling Sense of Direction for Your Organization.* San Francisco: Jossey-Bass, 1992.

Osborne, David and Ted Gaebler. *Reinventing Government: How the Entreprenuerial Spirit Is Transforming the Public Sector.* Reading, MA: Addison-Wesley, 1992.

Peters, Thomas J. and Robert H. Waterman Jr. *In Search of Excellence: Lessons from America's Best-Run Companies.* New York: HarperCollins, 1982.

Porter, Michael E. *Competitive Strategy: Techniques for Analyzing Industries and Competitors.* New York: Free Press. 1980.

Schwartz, Peter. *The Art of the Long View.* New York: Doubleday, 1991.

Steiner, George A. *Strategic Planning: What Every Manager Must Know.* New York: Free Press, 1979.

Tregoe, Benjamin B. and John W. Zimmerman. *Top Management Strategy: What It Is and How to Make It Work.* New York: Simon & Schuster, 1980.

United Way of America. *Strategic Management and United Way.* Alexandria, VA: United Way Strategic Planning Division, 1988.

Index

About the CD-ROM

System Requirements

- A computer with a processor running at 120 Mhz or faster
- At least 32 MB of total RAM installed on your computer; for best performance, we recommend at least 64 MB
- A CD-ROM drive

NOTE: Many popular word processing programs are capable of reading Microsoft Word files. However, users should be aware that a slight amount of formatting might be lost when using a program other than Microsoft Word.

Using the CD with Windows

To install the items from the CD to your hard drive, follow these steps:

1. Insert the CD into your computer's CD-ROM drive.
2. The CD-ROM interface will appear. The interface provides a simple point-and-click way to explore the contents of the CD.

If the opening screen of the CD-ROM does not appear automatically, follow these steps to access the CD:

1. Click the Start button on the left end of the taskbar and then choose Run from the menu that pops up.
2. In the dialog box that appears, type d:\setup.exe. (If your CD-ROM drive is not drive d, fill in the appropriate letter in place of d.) This brings up the CD Interface described in the preceding set of steps.

Applications

The following applications are on the CD:

Adobe Reader is a freeware application for viewing files in the Adobe Portable Document format.

Microsoft Word Viewer is a freeware viewer that allows you to view, but not edit, most Microsoft Word files. Certain features of Microsoft Word documents may not display as expected from within Word Viewer.

Excel Viewer is a freeware viewer that allows you to view, but not edit, most Microsoft Excel spreadsheets. Certain features of Microsoft Excel documents may not work as expected from within Excel Viewer.

Microsoft PowerPoint Viewer is a freeware viewer that allows you to view, but not edit, Microsoft PowerPoint files. Certain features of Microsoft PowerPoint presentations may not work as expected from within PowerPoint Viewer.

OpenOffice.org is a free multi-platform office productivity suite. It is similar to Microsoft Office or Lotus SmartSuite, but OpenOffice.org is absolutely free. It includes word processing, spreadsheet, presentation, and drawing applications that enable you to create professional documents, newsletters, reports, and presentations. It supports most file formats of other office software. You should be able to edit and view any files created with other office solutions.

NOTE: Shareware programs are fully functional, trial versions of copyrighted programs. If you like particular programs, register with their authors for a nominal fee and receive licenses, enhanced versions, and technical support. Freeware programs are copyrighted games, applications, and utilities that are free for personal use. Unlike shareware, these programs do not require a fee or provide technical support. GNU software is governed by its own license, which is included inside the folder of the GNU product. See the GNU license for more details. Trial, demo, or evaluation versions are usually limited either by time or functionality (such as being unable to save projects). Some trial versions are very sensitive to system date changes. If you alter your computer's date, the programs will "time out" and no longer be functional.

Customer Care

If you have trouble with the CD-ROM, please call the Wiley Product Technical Support phone number at (800) 762-2974. Outside the United States, call 1(317) 572-3994. You can also contact Wiley Product Technical Support at *http://www. wiley.com/techsupport*. John Wiley & Sons will provide technical support only for installation and other general quality control items. For technical support on the applications themselves, consult the program's vendor or author.

To place additional orders or to request information about other Wiley products, please call (877) 762-2974.